# FOUR PLAYS OF IBSEN

TRANSLATED
FROM
THE
NORWEGIAN
BY
R. V. FORSLUND

CHILTON
BOOK
COMPANY
*Philadelphia*
*New York*
*London*

# FOUR
# PLAYS
# OF
# IBSEN

# CONTENTS

# TRANSLATOR'S NOTE

These translations have come about as the end products of stage productions. My first intent was to translate them for the living stage; for them to be interpreted by directors, spoken by actors and only secondarily for them to be put in libraries and reading rooms.

At this time, I do not presume to add to the already numerous volumes of theses and biographies that concern themselves with Ibsen the social reformer, the crusader for the emancipation of woman, etc., but will deal with Ibsen the dramatist, his language structure and how his plays translate into the American idiom.

I do believe wholeheartedly in an American idiom with its own characteristics; an idiom that is, in my opinion, far more compatible with Norwegian than is the British idiom.

Surely this is not a new thought, but one the truth of which I experienced firsthand. An off-Broadway production of my translation of "Little Eyolf" was unanimously well-received by the New York critics. On the strength of this, Johan Fillingor, a Norwegian director, took the translation for a production in London at the Royal Academy. At the first reading it was clear to me that the American idiom did not, in all cases, fit the English actor and it was necessary for me to make extensive changes into the British idiom. Only in this way was it possible to re-capture the rhythm and inflection of Ibsen's language, the naturalism of his dialogue and the inner life of the play itself. The actors were comfortable with the language and were thereby able to identify themselves more closely to their characters and to the play as a whole. The end results were an understanding of and an acceptance by the audience, and, in general, good Ibsen!

It is interesting to note here, that what had happened was the reversal of that which is so often experienced by American actors performing British translations.

There is a sameness within the Ibsen language structure that gives the plays an inner rhythm and harmony, and which must be maintained in translation. We find in the "Master Builder" such a uniformity of tone that three very different people, the doctor, Ragnar and Solness, speak in much the same manner.

Within this over-all language structure, let me point out Gina and Hjalmar ("The Wild Duck") whose linguistic habits are "variations within the theme" and illustrate how subtle Ibsen's art is.

Gina is a plain, uneducated woman whose speech and grammar is that of the backstairs and servants' quarters. When she tries to cover her shortcomings or when she is under stress, as she is in front of Gregers, her former employer's son, some of her words emerge as malaprops or mispronunciations.

Hjalmar is extremely sensitive to this particular abuse of language, his fault being just the opposite of Gina's.

Ibsen has brilliantly juxtaposed them in the play. At one point Hjalmar corrects her, saying:

"I believe I've told you before that this weapon is called a pistol."

She had called it a "pifstle." Hjalmar is a garrulous, self-deluded man with a misplaced ego who considers himself not only a man of science but also a man of letters. We know that he re-cited poetry in his youth and that he perpetually made notes in preparation for the writing of his autobiography that would never, of course, be written. Having this passion and facility for ornate language he bursts into flowery, shallow declamations at any given opportunity. A few examples:

"Yes! I shall rescue that ship-wrecked old man! He was already overboard when the storm broke."

"I was totally happy each time I came back to this simple house and she would run to greet me with her sweet, squinting eyes."

"I am a man constantly attacked by armies of sorrows."

His pseudo-philosophizing, his self-indulgence in rhetoric reaches an embarrassing culmination at the death of his daughter, Hedvig, when he bursts into an over-pious eulogy. He uses the personal pronoun of the second person singular, which is considerably more rare in Norwegian speech than in American English.

"Oh thou up there—if thou art there—why hast thou done this unto me?"

If I have done my work properly, at no time should the language draw attention to itself. It is merely a means to an end, a medium through which the author's thought and intent reach us. Ibsen's people do not say all things in a beautiful and perfect manner. The words flow in a totally naturalistic way, sometimes with incomplete sentences and poor grammar. There is a generous smattering of dashes and exclamation points, and the dialogue is orchestrated with ejaculated utterances, often taking the place of words altogether. This is Ibsen's language, the language of naturalism that at no time approaches the arch and formal language of the Victorian era in which he lived and worked. The early translators ignored this fact or perhaps they did not fully understand Ibsen's free style, his stream of con sciousness speech, his deliberate economy of vocabulary. He was too far ahead of his time. Time and again the translators missed the immediacy and flow of the dialogue and, in truth, its inherent realism.

Where is this realism to be found then? In Ibsen the man? Will anecdotes or quotations from various correspondences or criticisms that fill the bookshelves with conflicting opinions give a definitive answer? They may bring to light some parallel truths, some glimpses of his personality and life patterns, but should these be of primary interest to the translator who deals with the word? No. Ibsen himself was reluctant to discuss his plays but insisted they speak for themselves, and I agree.

As Ibsen the artist filters through the fifth manuscript of the play, it is Ibsen the author, not Ibsen the man who is speaking. I hear more clearly another voice, the one I shall listen to—Ibsen the dramatist—for I am constantly reminded that an audience comes to the theater to see living people, to see a vital Ibsen play. And that's the thing.

June '68                                                    RVF

# WHEN
# WE
# DEAD
# AWAKEN

A DRAMATIC EPILOGUE IN THREE ACTS

1899

## CHARACTERS

PROFESSOR ARNOLD RUBEK   *a sculptor*

MRS. MAJA RUBEK   *his wife*

PROPRIETOR   *the proprietor of the health resort*

ULFHEIM   *the owner of a country estate*

MRS. IRENE VON SATOW   *a traveling lady*

NURSE   *her traveling companion*

LARS   *Ulfheim's servant*

GUESTS OF THE BATH AND MOUNTAIN LODGE

CHILDREN

WAITERS

The entire play takes place in Norway sometime around 1899. ACT ONE takes place at a health resort beside the sea, where special health baths are featured. ACT TWO takes place on the grounds of a mountain lodge halfway up the mountain. ACT THREE is higher up on the mountaintop.

# ACT I

A seaside bath resort in Norway. The stage area is a pleasant park-
like place with walks, fountains, old trees, and bushes. Scattered
around are several small tables with chairs and occasional summer
garden furniture. UPSTAGE, the background is a typical view of the
Norwegian Sea. Fingers of land stretch out into the quiet sea and
several islands dot the distance. At STAGE RIGHT a portion of the
main building can be seen. At STAGE LEFT there is a small pavilion
covered with ivy and wild vines. Outside the pavilion is a small table
and two chairs.

AS THE CURTAIN RISES it is a quiet, calm, sun-warmed summer morning. PROFESSOR RUBEK and MAJA RUBEK are seated at a table, having
just finished lunch. They are drinking champagne and Seltzer water,
and each is reading his own newspaper. PROFESSOR RUBEK is a distinguished middle-aged gentleman. He is dressed in summer attire
except for a black velvet jacket. MRS. RUBEK is rather youthful, and
she has a happy, lively face. Her eyes are full of mocking mischie-
vousness with just a suggestion of tiredness about them. She is wearing an elegant traveling dress.

MAJA (Sits for a moment, waits for RUBEK to speak, then drops
the newspaper, sighs): Oh no, no.
RUBEK (Looking up from the newspaper): Well, Maja? What's
the matter now?
MAJA: Just listen—to the silence!
RUBEK (Smiles patronizingly): You can hear it?
MAJA: What?
RUBEK: Silence.
MAJA: Yes. Yes, I really can.

RUBEK: Perhaps you're right, *mein kind*, one *can* hear silence.

MAJA: God knows I can when it's so positively overpowering as it is here. So—

RUBEK: Here at the Baths?

MAJA: No, not just at the Baths. I mean everywhere here at home. Down in the village there is plenty of noise, but all the sounds this far north seem to have something dead about them.

RUBEK (*With a searching look*): Then you're not particularly happy now that you're home again, Maja?

MAJA: Are you?

RUBEK (*Avoiding her*): Me?

MAJA: Yes. You've been away so much longer than I have. Are you particularly happy now that we're home again?

RUBEK: No, to be honest. No. Not entirely—

MAJA (*Lively*): There! You see—I sensed it all the time!

RUBEK: Perhaps I've stayed away too long this time. I've been so completely detached from all this—all this—this domestic home life.

MAJA (*Excited. Pulling her chair closer to him*): So! Now you see for yourself! I told you it would be better for us to travel again—away from here as soon as possible.

RUBEK (*A bit annoyed*): Yes, yes, yes, and you know very well we intend to do just that, my dear Maja.

MAJA: Why not leave at once? Think how cozy and comfortable we could be down there in our lovely new house—

RUBEK (*Smiles patronizingly*): Shouldn't you say "home," Mrs. Professor Rubek?

MAJA (*Curtly*): I prefer house. Let us leave it at that.

RUBEK (*Pauses. His eyes dwell on her.*): Deep down you are a strange little person, Maja.

MAJA: Am I?

RUBEK: Yes, I think so.

MAJA: Why? Just because I can't stand being idle up here in this . . .

RUBEK: And which one of us made our coming up here such a matter of life or death?

MAJA: I'll admit it—I did.

RUBEK: Well, it certainly wasn't I.

MAJA: Good Lord! Who could have possibly dreamed that everything would be so terribly changed? In such a short time, too! Imagine—it's not more than four years since I went away.

RUBEK: As a married woman, yes—

MAJA: Married? What has that to do with it?

RUBEK: —and became Frau Professor and got yourself a splendid home— Oh, I beg your pardon—I should have said an aristocratic manor house and a villa on Lake Taunitzer, which has since become the most fashionable spot. Yes, very splendid and impressive, all of it, Maja.

MAJA (Offhandedly): Yes—yes—and there's room enough for us not to get in each other's way. We've never had a shortage of room.

RUBEK: You've been living in a more elegant and spacious environment in general, Maja. You now move in a fashionable society in more gracious surroundings than you were used to at home.

MAJA (Looking at him): Ah! Then you think I have changed?

RUBEK (Looking at her): You have, Maja.

MAJA: Just me, and not the people here?

RUBEK: Oh yes, perhaps they've changed a little. I admit I find them less friendly, even unsympathetic.

MAJA: Well, good. I'm glad you agree with me on that at least.

RUBEK (Changing the subject): Do you know what kind of mood these people and their lives put me in?

MAJA: No. Tell me.

RUBEK: Well, when I look around, it makes me remember the night we spent on the train coming up here—

MAJA: Silly! You were sitting up sound asleep all the time!

RUBEK: Perhaps not. The silence. . . . It became so quiet at all the train stations. I heard the silence then, as you do now, Maja.

MAJA: As I do? Oh. Hmm.

RUBEK (Continuing): —that silence. That's how I knew we had

finally passed the border. How I knew we were home, at last. At every little station the train pulled to a stop and rested—rested. And then the silence took over. It was so peaceful. There was no traffic, no—

MAJA: Why did they stop, then, when there was no one there?

RUBEK: I don't know. No passengers came in, no passengers went out. But the train held still for a long—an endless—time. And at each station I saw two switchmen walking up and down the platform. One always held a lantern in his hand. I heard them speak to each other in muffled, toneless sounds—sound without meaning. And the sounds went into the silence, into the night.

MAJA: Yes, you're right, there were always two men walking back and forth—talking.

RUBEK: Talking about nothing! (*Changing to a livelier tone*) But just wait until tomorrow! Our great, luxurious steamship will come into the harbor, and we'll go aboard at last and sail up the coast—northward! Far, far north. Right on to the Arctic Sea!

MAJA: Yes. But then you won't get to see anything of the country, nor of the people—and that is what you wanted.

RUBEK (*Curtly and snappishly*): I've already seen more than enough.

MAJA: Do you think a sea voyage will be good for you?

RUBEK: It's a change.

MAJA: Yes, yes that's true. Well, as long as it will be the right thing for you. . . .

RUBEK: For me? Ha! There's not a thing in the world wrong with me!

MAJA (*Rises and goes over to him*): Oh but there is, Rubek. I'm sure you must feel it yourself.

RUBEK: My dearest Maja, I can't imagine what you mean.

MAJA (*Behind him, bending over his chair*): You don't honestly mean that, do you? Oh no. I think you know quite well what is wrong with you, Rubek. You've begun to wander. You find no rest or peace—no contentment anywhere—either at home

6

nor abroad. And just lately, my dear, you've become very unsociable.

RUBEK (*A bit sarcastically*): Really, Maja, you've noticed all that?

MAJA: No one knowing you could help but notice. It's also very sad to me that you've lost all interest in your work.

RUBEK: I've lost that, too?

MAJA: Remember how you used to work from morning to night without one sign of fatigue?

RUBEK (*Darkly*): Used to . . . ah, yes.

MAJA: But ever since you finished that big group . . . that one with all the figures—

RUBEK (*Nodding thoughtfully*): My major work. "The Day of Reawakening."

MAJA: Oh yes—the one that traveled all over the world and made you so famous!

RUBEK: Yes. Perhaps *that* was the disaster, Maja.

MAJA: How do you mean that?

RUBEK: Once I had created my masterpiece . . . (*Throwing out his hands passionately*) . . . because "The Day of Reawakening" is a masterpiece! Or or least in the beginning it was. No, it still is, and it will always, always, always be!

MAJA (*Looking at him in wonder*): Of course, my dear Rubek— all the world knows that.

RUBEK (*Curtly, with rebuff*): All the world knows nothing! Understands nothing!

MAJA: Well, at least they sense something.

RUBEK: What they think they sense is something that was never even there. Something I never had in mind. Oh yes, and for that "something" they go into ecstasies. (*Growling to himself*) It's not worth the pain any more to continue wearing myself out for the mob and the masses—or for "all the world"!

MAJA: Then you think it's better, I mean more worthy of you, to go around doing nothing but portrait busts every now and then?

7

RUBEK (*With a sly smile*): They are not just "portrait busts," my dear Maja.

MAJA: What on earth do you mean? Of course they are! You know very well that for the last two or three years, or whenever you got that big group ready and out of the house—

RUBEK: I assure you—they are not *just* portrait busts!

MAJA: Oh Rubek. What are they, then?

RUBEK: They capture a striking likeness on the surface . . . that, my dear, is true. But underneath, there is something hidden—something lurking inside, behind, under, around those portrait busts. A secret something that no one can see.

MAJA: So?

RUBEK (*Conclusively*): Only I can see it. And it gives me such great pleasure. People stand around in amazement and gape at the "striking likeness," as they say. (*Lowering his voice*) But deep down, somewhere there lurks the respected honest horse faces, the stubborn donkey muzzles with their lop-ears, the low-browed hound skulls with bloated swine snouts, the dull, brutal ox faces. Sometimes they—

MAJA (*Indifferently*): Ah yes, all the dear, domestic animals.

RUBEK: Exactly! Just our dear, domestic animals, Maja. All the animals which man in his attempt to civilize himself has deprecated in his own image and which—in return—have deprecated man.
(*He empties his champagne glass and giggles to himself.*)
And it is for these insidious "works of art" that our excellent socialites flock to me, pay me in advance—and in handsome round figures, too! They pay almost their weight in gold, as the saying goes.

MAJA (*Filling up his glass*): Shame, Rubek! Come. Drink and be happy!

RUBEK (*He strokes his forehead several times and leans back in his chair.*): I am happy, Maja. Really happy—well, in a way. (*After a short silence*) There is a certain amount of happiness in being independent in all things—don't you think so,

Maja? In possessing all the things that one could possibly desire. All the worldly goods.

MAJA: Oh, those things are all right, I guess. (*Looking at him*) But you promised me something else once—do you remember? That day when we agreed on that . . . that difficult point?

RUBEK (*Nods and helps her*): On getting married? It wasn't easy for you to make the decision, was it, Maja?

MAJA (*Remaining unruffled*): —And we agreed that I would travel with you and live abroad forever and be content. But can you remember what you promised me that day?

RUBEK (*Shaking his head*): I must admit I don't. What was it?

MAJA: You promised to take me up on a high mountain and show me all the splendor of the world.

RUBEK (*Startled*): Oh, did I promise that to you, too?

MAJA (*Looking at him*): Me too? Who else?

RUBEK (*Indifferently*): No, no, no, I only meant that if I promised to show you all—

MAJA: All the splendor of the world? Yes, that's what you promised me. And then you said all that splendor would be mine and yours.

RUBEK: That was one of those expressions I used to use.

MAJA: Just an expression?

RUBEK: Yes, something left over from my school days. The kind of thing I used to say to get the neighborhood children to play with me in the mountains and the forests.

MAJA: Then you only wanted me to play with, too?

RUBEK (*Passing it off as a jest*): Well, it's been a pleasant game, hasn't it, Maja?

MAJA (*Coldly*): I do not travel with you just to play games!

RUBEK: That could be.

MAJA: And then you never took me up to any mountain, never showed me—

RUBEK (*Irritated*): All the splendor of the world? No, I haven't. But let me tell you this, little Maja. You are not a creature for mountain climbing.

MAJA: You thought I was once.

RUBEK: No, never.

MAJA (*With control*): You made me believe you thought so!

RUBEK: That was four or five years ago— (*He stretches himself in his chair.*) four or five years—that is a long, long time, Maja.

MAJA (*Bitterly*): Has it seemed that long to you, Rubek?

RUBEK: Only now it begins to. Only now and then.

MAJA (*Going back to her chair*): Well, I shall not hold you in chains a moment longer. (*She sits and begins to read her newspaper. There is a silence.*)

RUBEK (*Looking at her teasingly*): Is Mrs. Professor Rubek offended?

MAJA (*Coldly, without looking up*): No. Not in the least.
(*Guests of the Baths, mostly ladies walking singly and in small groups, begin to cross the park. They travel from the RIGHT and exit LEFT. Waiters carry refreshments from the hotel behind the pavilion. The PROPRIETOR of the Baths enters. He is elegantly dressed in formal morning clothes, complete with gloves, and carries a walking cane. He sees the RUBEKS and walks over to them. He bows and removes his hat.*)

PROPRIETOR: A most respectful good morning to you, Mrs. Rubek—and to you, Professor Rubek.

RUBEK: Good morning, good morning.

PROPRIETOR (*To MAJA*): Might I inquire if you slept well?

MAJA: Oh yes, fine, thank you. Just splendidly. But then I always sleep like a log.

PROPRIETOR: That indeed is a compliment. The first night in a strange place can often be rather awkward. And you, Professor Rubek?

RUBEK: My night's rest is often poor. Especially of late.

PROPRIETOR (*Sounding concerned*): Oh, I am sorry to hear that. But a few weeks' rest here at the Baths will no doubt improve all that.

RUBEK (*Looking up*): Tell me, do any of your patients have the habit of bathing in the middle of the night?

PROPRIETOR (*Surprised*): At night? No, Professor, not that I know of.

RUBEK: You're certain?

PROPRIETOR: Oh yes. I don't know of any guest here who is so ill that a night bath should be necessary.

RUBEK: Well, then, is there a guest who would take a walk here in the park at night?

PROPRIETOR (*Smiles and shakes his head*): No, Professor Rubek, I am afraid that would be quite against the rules.

MAJA (*Irritated*): Good heavens, Rubek! It's only what I told you this morning. You were simply dreaming!

RUBEK: Oh? So that's what I was doing, eh? Thank you, Maja. (*To the* PROPRIETOR) I happened to get up during the night, unable to sleep. I wanted to check on the weather—

PROPRIETOR (*Intently*): Oh yes, of course. And so?

RUBEK: When I looked out of my window, I happened to catch out of the corner of my eye a luminous figure in amongst the trees.

MAJA (*Smiling at the* PROPRIETOR): And then the Professor goes on to imagine that the figure was dressed in a bathing costume. . . .

RUBEK: . . . or something similar, I said. I couldn't see too clearly, but what it was I saw was something white.

PROPRIETOR: That seems most peculiar. Was it a gentleman or was it a lady?

RUBEK: I'm almost certain that it was a lady. I also saw a dark figure following behind—like a shadow.

PROPRIETOR (*Startled*): A shadow? Rather like someone in black, perhaps?

RUBEK: Yes, it could have been that—as far as I could make out.

PROPRIETOR (*Suddenly understanding*): And this shadow—the black—following just behind the white figure . . . ?

RUBEK: Yes. Following at a short distance.

PROPRIETOR: Aha! Then I can no doubt give you an explanation, my dear Professor!

RUBEK: Well—what was it, then?

MAJA (*Simultaneously*):  Hasn't the Professor just been dreaming all of this?

PROPRIETOR (*Suddenly whispering, he indicates the* UPSTAGE RIGHT *area.*):  Quiet, please, if you don't mind, madame. Do you see her? Please don't speak loudly right now.

(*A slim lady enters in the background. She is dressed in a cream-colored cashmere gown and is followed by a* NURSE *in black. They move forward, crossing the park area to the small pavilion. The* TRAVELING LADY's *face is pale and tired and, like a mask, the very lines seem to have stiffened. Her eyelids are sunken, and it is as if the eyes were unable to see. Her dress hangs down to her feet, and the folds of the skirt cling to her legs. Over her head, neck, breast, and shoulders and across her arms she wears a large shawl of white crepe. She keeps her arms crossed over her breast. She steps with stiff and measured strides and her entire body seems immovable. The* NURSE *also moves in this manner, with an added air of servitude. She follows close behind the* LADY *and her dark brown, piercing eyes never leave her. Waiters with napkins on their arms come out of the hotel and watch the strangers with curiosity, who, taking no notice of them, enter into the pavilion.*)

RUBEK (*Rises involuntarily and stares at the closed pavilion*):  Who was that woman?

PROPRIETOR:  She is a traveling lady who has rented our little summer pavilion.

RUBEK:  Is she a foreigner?

PROPRIETOR:  Apparently. In any case, they both arrived here from abroad about a week ago. They have never been guests at our Baths before.

RUBEK (*Looking firmly at him*):  It was she! She I saw in the park last night!

PROPRIETOR:  Yes, it most probably was. That is exactly whom I thought of immediately.

RUBEK:  What is the lady's name?

PROPRIETOR:  She is registered as Madame de Satow with companion. That's all we know.

RUBEK (*Thinking it over*):  Satow? Satow?

MAJA (*Smiling mockingly*): Do you happen to know the name, Rubek? Do you?

RUBEK (*Shaking his head*): No, not at all. Not as far as I remember. Satow? It sounds Russian or Slavic. (*To the* PROPRIETOR) What language does she speak?

PROPRIETOR: When the ladies speak to each other it is in a language I can't quite figure out, but otherwise she speaks a very good Norwegian.

RUBEK (*Blurting out*): Norwegian? Are you positive?

PROPRIETOR: Yes, I am rather positive.

RUBEK (*Nodding at him eagerly*): Then you've heard her speak?

PROPRIETOR: Oh yes, I have spoken to her myself on one or two occasions. Only a few words, however. She's not very talkative. But—

RUBEK: But was it in Norwegian?

PROPRIETOR: Pure and good Norwegian. Except—I must admit —she has a slight north-country accent.

RUBEK (*Stares straight ahead and whispers as if to himself*): Even that!

(*There is an offstage noise of shouting and dogs barking, at some distance away. The* PROPRIETOR'*s attention is drawn away for the moment.*)

MAJA (*A little upset and hurt*): Perhaps the lady modeled for you once, Rubek? You'll remember her, perhaps—if you think hard enough.

RUBEK: Maja!

MAJA (*With a wry smile*): Well, in your younger days, Rubek. But then he had so many—countless models—long ago, of course—

RUBEK (*In the same tone*): Oh no, little Mrs. Maja, you are wrong there. In those days I actually had only one. I only needed one model for all I created.

PROPRIETOR: Well now, I'm frightfully sorry to say it, but you must excuse me, please. I think there is something to which I must attend immediately. Mrs. Rubek . . . Professor.

(*The noise of shouting and dogs barking increases, as if coming closer.*)

PROPRIETOR (*To* RUBEK, *in a whisper*): I see someone it is rather embarrassing for me to meet in the presence of ladies—you understand.

RUBEK (*Looking in the direction of the noise*): Who? That hunter there?

PROPRIETOR: It is a certain Mr. Ulfheim from—

RUBEK: Ulfheim! The big estate owner?

PROPRIETOR: Yes. That's the very one. The "bear killer," as they call him.

RUBEK: Yes, yes, Ulfheim. I know him.

PROPRIETOR: Well—who doesn't!

RUBEK: I know him very slightly. Is he a patient of yours at last?

PROPRIETOR: Strangely enough, not yet. He just stops here once a year on his way up north to the bear country. Now please, you must excuse me for the time being.

(*He makes his way toward the hotel. A large, gruff, commanding voice is heard.*)

ULFHEIM (*Offstage*): Hold on there! Damn it, you—stop a minute! Why in hell's name do you always scurry away from me?

PROPRIETOR (*Stopping*): I beg your pardon—I do not scurry, Mr. Ulfheim.

(ULFHEIM *enters, followed by a servant,* LARS, *with a pack of hunting dogs.* ULFHEIM *is dressed in a hunting suit, a three-quarter-length jacket with large patch pockets, a felt hat with a feather in it, and high boots. His hair and beard are ungroomed and matted. He is slim, sinewy, and tall and speaks with a loud voice. He is of uncertain age, but we know he is no longer young.*)

ULFHEIM (*Pounces on the* PROPRIETOR): Is this the way you receive your guests, eh? You run around here with your tail between your legs as if the devil were biting at your heels!

PROPRIETOR (*Calmly, without answering him*): Did Mr. Ulfheim have the pleasure of arriving on the steamship?

ULFHEIM (*Growling*): I haven't had the pleasure of even smelling a steamship! Don't you know I sail my own cutter? (*He stands with his hands on his hips and calls to his servant.*) Take good care of your relatives, Lars! See to it that they are underfed. Keep 'em damn well ravenous. Fresh meat bones, but not too much meat on 'em. Do you hear? And raw, too! Still streaming with blood and reeking—be sure, now! And get something in your own belly. (*He kicks at him.* LARS *avoids the blow.*) Now then, get the hell out of here! (*The servant* LARS *exits in a hurry with the dogs.*)

PROPRIETOR: Would Mr. Ulfheim like to wait in the dining room for the time being?

ULFHEIM: What? Sit in there with all those half-dead flies and people? A thousand times no, my kind Proprietor!

PROPRIETOR: Well yes, yes, as you please, Mr. Ulfheim.

ULFHEIM: Here, now! Make that kitchen maid of yours get my provisions together. Plenty of food, now, and ample on the aquavit! And you can tell her that if she doesn't please me, either Lars or myself will personally come back and get the devil to—

PROPRIETOR (*Interrupting*): Oh yes—yes, yes, we already know that, Mr. Ulfheim. We are quite used to your ways around here. (*Turning to the* RUBEKS) Shall I give the waiter any order for you, Professor? Or for you, Mrs. Rubek? Anything?

RUBEK: No thank you. Nothing for me.

MAJA: Nor me, thank you.

(*The* PROPRIETOR *goes into the hotel.* ULFHEIM *looks at* RUBEK *and* MAJA *for a while in silence, then tips his hat.*)

ULFHEIM: Death and damnation! I believe the country bumpkin himself has strayed into gentle society!

RUBEK (*Looking up*): What do you mean by that, my good sir?

ULFHEIM (*Speaking more politely*): If I am not mistaken, I believe that I am in the presence of the sculptor of no small means—Rubek himself!

RUBEK (*Nodding*): Yes. We have met socially several times, the last autumn I was here at home.

ULFHEIM: Ah, but that was many years ago, and at the time, my good man, your name was not so well known as it is now. Rubek! Why—in those days even a grubby bear hunter dared to step near you.

RUBEK (*Smiling*): I still don't bite!

MAJA (*Insisting on recognition, says haughtily*): Are you really a bear hunter?

ULFHEIM: Bears mostly, madame. But any kind of wild game that comes my way will do. (*He sits down at the next table, close to the hotel.*) Eagles, owls, women, elks, and reindeer . . . so long as they're fresh and juicy and rich with warm blood. (*He drinks from his pocket flask.*)

MAJA (*Watching him intently*): But it is the bear that you prefer?

ULFHEIM: Bears, yes. I like them best. Because in a tight spot— I get the chance to use the knife! (*Smiling a little*) We both like to work in hard materials, madame, your husband and I. He struggles against his blocks of marble, and I tear against the tense, quivering sinews of the bear. In the end we both conquer our material. Subdue and conquer! And so—we are created lord and master! You can be damn sure we don't give up before our battle is won. Not before that moment of final mastery—no matter how difficult the raw material may be!

RUBEK (*In deep thought*): Strange—there is some truth in your words.

ULFHEIM: You're damn right there is! Marble is dead and determined not to let your hammer—with all its magnificent power—bring it to life. Exactly like my stubborn bears when I force them out of their lairs.

MAJA: And you're on your way right now to hunt in the forest?

ULFHEIM: Far up into the high mountains I go. I'll just bet you've never been up on that high mountain, have you, madame?

MAJA: No, never.

ULFHEIM: Well, death and damnation! You'll have to come up this summer. Come with me—you're welcome, both of you. You and the Professor.

MAJA: Thank you, but Rubek plans a sea voyage this summer.

RUBEK: Up north along the coast and through the fiords.

ULFHEIM (*Spitting*): What in hell's name are you going to do in those Godforsaken gutters? Ha! Imagine the Rubeks socializing, as they say, in the ditch water! Ha! Ha! I should say the dish water.

MAJA: Did you hear that, Rubek?

ULFHEIM: No. Come with me instead—up to the high mountains. Up so high that at last everything is clean and free. Free from any trace of human contamination. Ah—you cannot imagine what that means to me. But for such a little Mrs. as yourself—

(*He is stopped by the entrance of the* NURSE, *who comes out of the pavilion and crosses into the hotel.* ULFHEIM *follows her with his eyes.*)

ULFHEIM: Damnation, look at that thing! Did you see that black vulture? Who's getting buried?

RUBEK: I didn't know anyone here had—

ULFHEIM: Well, there's someone lying around here, hidden in some nook or cranny just about ready to give up the ghost. These creeping old dilapidated fossils—sick and rickety— should all be accommodating enough to get themselves buried. And the sooner the better!

MAJA: Have you ever been ill, Mr. Ulfheim?

ULFHEIM: Never. If I had, I wouldn't be sitting here! But God knows some of my best friends have been sick, poor devils.

MAJA: Really? Well, what did you do for them?

ULFHEIM: Shot them, of course.

RUBEK (*Looking at him*): Shot them?

MAJA (*Pushing back her chair*): You mean you killed them?

ULFHEIM (*Nodding*): I never miss my mark, madame.

MAJA: How could you possibly force yourself to kill someone?

ULFHEIM: I'm not talking about human beings—

MAJA: You said your best friends!

ULFHEIM: Best friends? Damn it, woman, I mean my dogs!

MAJA: Your dogs are your best friends, Mr. Ulfheim?

ULFHEIM: I have no one closer! My honest, trusty, and loyal-to-the-death hunting companions. When one of them gets sick or feeble—so PLAFF! And with that my dear one is dispatched to the happy hunting ground.

(*The* NURSE *comes out of the hotel with a tray on which there is milk and bread. She places it on the table outside the pavilion, then goes into the pavilion.*)

ULFHEIM (*Smiling spitefully*): Look at that. Trash. They call that food fit for human consumption? Watered-down milk and soft doughy bread! You should see my comrades at feeding time. Would you like to see them?

MAJA (*Smiles at* RUBEK *and rises*): Oh yes. I would like that.

ULFHEIM (*Rising*): There! There's the lady after my own heart, madame! Come with me, then, and you shall see how they devour big hunks of bloody meat bones in one gulp. How they cough them up and gulp them down again. It is a real treat to see! So come now and I'll show you . . . and at the same time we'll talk about our mountain trip. Come!

(*He waves her on as he exits. She follows after him. Almost at the same moment, the* TRAVELING LADY *appears from the pavilion and sits at her table. She is about to drink the milk when she stops and looks at* RUBEK *with a stare—inexpressive and vacant.* RUBEK *remains seated at his own table and returns the empty stare—solemnly and profoundly. Finally he rises, crosses to her, and speaks to her in a low voice.*)

RUBEK: I recognize you so easily, Irene.

IRENE (*Puts down her glass and speaks in a toneless voice*): You didn't have to guess, did you, Arnold?

RUBEK (*Without answering*): And you recognize me too, I see.

IRENE: With you it is a different thing.

RUBEK: Why different with me?

IRENE: Oh, you are still alive.

RUBEK (*Not understanding*): Alive?

IRENE (*After a short silence*): Who is she? The one who sat with you at the table?

RUBEK (*Reluctantly*): She? Oh, she is my . . . my wife.

IRENE (*Nodding slowly*): Ah, yes. That is good, Arnold. Then she does not concern me.

RUBEK (*Uncertainly*): I do not understand that.

IRENE: She is one who came to you after my lifetime.

RUBEK (*Looking sternly at her*): After your lifetime? What do you mean by that, Irene?

IRENE (*Without answering*): And the child? Is it still well? Our child was immortalized and continues to live after me—celebrated and honored.

RUBEK (*Smiling with far-off recollection*): "Our child"? Yes, we called it that then.

IRENE: Yes, then—during life.

RUBEK (*Trying to assume a cheerful tone*): Yes, Irene, "our child" has become world-famous. No doubt you've read about it?

IRENE (*Nodding*): And made his father famous, too. That was your dream.

RUBEK (*With quiet emotion*): And it is to you I owe everything—everything, Irene. Thank you for that.

IRENE (*Sits for a while, lost in thought*): I only wish I had done the right thing at that time, Arnold.

RUBEK: Well, what was that?

IRENE: I wish I had put our child to death. Killed it.

RUBEK: Killed it? Irene, you don't know what you're saying.

IRENE (*Whispering*): Yes. *Killed* it. Before I went away from you. I should have crushed it, crushed it into dust.

RUBEK (*Shaking his head with reproach*): You couldn't have done that, Irene. You wouldn't have had the heart.

IRENE: No. At that time I didn't have that kind of heart. But since—I have murdered it again and again, in the daylight and in the dark. I have killed it in hate—in revenge and in anguish.

RUBEK (*Walks over to her table and asks slowly*): Irene, tell me now, at last, after all these years—why did you leave me? Without a trace—never to be found?

IRENE (*Shaking her head slowly*): Oh Arnold, why ask me that now? Now that I'm already on the other side?

RUBEK: Was there someone else?

IRENE: The one there *was* had no further use of my love—no further use of my life, either.

RUBEK (*Changing the subject*): Let us not speak of what used to be.

IRENE: No. No, let us not speak of things beyond the grave— that is, beyond the grave for me.

RUBEK: Where have you traveled, Irene? It was as if you had been wiped off the face of the earth. I searched endlessly for you.

IRENE: I receded into the shadows while the child stood there in the light, transfigured.

RUBEK: Have you traveled far around the world?

IRENE: Yes. Traveled in many kingdoms, in many countries.

RUBEK (*Looking sympathetically at her*): And what have you found for yourself to do?

IRENE (*With a dark, compassionate look*): Oh? Hmm, let me think. Yes, now I remember. I had been standing on the revolving stages in music halls. Standing naked like a statue in the "art pantomimes." And so I labored and so harvested . . . bushels of money! I was not used to *that*! Because you never had any money. Also, I was always with men . . . many men. Men whom I could drive mad with passion, whose minds I could twist to my will. *That* I was not used to, either, with you, Arnold. You were more on your guard.

RUBEK: You married, didn't you?

IRENE: Yes, I married one of them.

RUBEK: Who is your husband?

IRENE: He was a South American. A distinguished diplomat. (*She stares in front of her with a frozen smile.*) I twisted his mind until he became mad—quite mad. Incurably insane. While it was happening it was all so ludicrous. Even now, I could laugh inside when I think of it—if there were anything inside me.

RUBEK: Where is he now?

IRENE: Oh, in a churchyard somewhere or other. With a high, stately monument over him and a lead bullet rattling around in his skull.

RUBEK: Did he kill himself?

IRENE: Yes. He preferred to do *that* for himself.

RUBEK: Don't you mourn for him, Irene?

IRENE (*Bewildered*): For whom should I mourn?

RUBEK: Why, for him—for Satow, of course.

IRENE: Oh. His name wasn't Satow.

RUBEK: No?

IRENE: Satow is the name of my second husband. He's Russian.

RUBEK: And where is he now?

IRENE: Far away in the Ural Mountains, among all his gold mines.

RUBEK: Then he's alive?

IRENE (*Shrugging her shoulders*): Alive? Alive? Actually, I have killed him.

RUBEK (*Shaken*): Killed . . . ?

IRENE: Yes. With a fine, sharp dagger I have with me always in my bed.

RUBEK (*With an outburst*): I do not believe you, Irene!

IRENE (*With a gentle smile*): It's just as well you don't, Arnold.

RUBEK (*Looking at her with compassion*): Have you never had a child?

IRENE: Yes, I have had many children.

RUBEK: And where are they now?

IRENE: I killed them.

RUBEK (*Severely*): Now you're lying again.

IRENE: I have killed them, I tell you. I murdered them without mercy. As soon as they came into the world—and long, long before that. One after the other.

RUBEK (*Heavily and solemnly*): There is a hidden meaning in everything you say.

IRENE: What can I do? Every word I speak is whispered in my ear.

RUBEK: And yet I believe that I'm the only one who can sense the meaning.

IRENE: You *should* be the only one.

RUBEK (*Rests his hands on the table and looks deeply at her*): There is a little string inside you that has snapped, and it has shattered you into pieces.

IRENE (*Calmly*): That always happens at the death of a young warm-blooded woman.

RUBEK: Oh Irene, stop it! Stop these delusions. You are living —living!

IRENE (*Rising slowly, trembling*): I was dead for many years. They came and tied my arms behind my back. They lowered me down—down into a chamber with iron bars in front of a trap door. The walls were thick and padded so that no one above—on earth—could hear the shrieks from my grave. But now I am beginning to stand up—halfway—to rise from the dead. (*She sits down again.*)

RUBEK (*After a pause*): And you accuse me?

IRENE: Yes.

RUBEK: *I* am guilty of what you call your death?

IRENE: Yes. Guilty for my having to die. (*Changing to an indifferent tone*) Why don't you sit down, Arnold?

RUBEK: May I?

IRENE: Yes, and you needn't be afraid of freezing. I haven't turned to ice yet.

RUBEK (*Moves the chair and sits at her table*): There. Now we're sitting just as we used to, once upon a time.

IRENE: A little distance from each other, too, as once upon a time.

RUBEK (*Moving closer*): It had to be like that, then.

IRENE: Did it?

RUBEK: There had to be a distance between us.

IRENE: It had to be? Yes. I suppose it had to be, Arnold.

RUBEK (*Continuing*): Do you remember your answer when I asked if you would follow me out into the distance—far, far out?

IRENE: Oh yes. I raised three fingers into the air and I swore that I would follow you to the ends of the world and the end of our lives. That I would serve you in all things. Yes.

RUBEK: As a model for all my creations . . .

IRENE: . . . in free nakedness. Abandoned and—

RUBEK (*Moved*): And you did serve me, Irene. So cheerfully, so recklessly!

IRENE: With all my youthful, throbbing blood I served you!

RUBEK (*Nodding with gratitude*): That you can say without a single regret.

IRENE (*Shaking her clenched fist at him*): I fell down at your feet and served you, Arnold! But you—you—

RUBEK: I never did you any wrong, Irene, never.

IRENE: Yes you did! You committed a crime against the innermost part of my being!

RUBEK (*Starts*): I—?

IRENE: Yes! I completely exposed myself with no inhibitions to your inspection. (*Softly*) And not one single time did you touch me . . .

RUBEK: Irene, didn't you know? Didn't you know how many times I was totally spellbound by your beauty?

IRENE (*Continuing undisturbed*): . . . and yet, I always sensed that if you *had* touched me, I would have killed you instantly. I always carried a sharp needle with me then. I had it hidden in my hair. (*She strokes her forehead meditatively.*) Yes, but . . . no . . . and yet, and yet, you could—

RUBEK (*Emphatically*): I was an artist, Irene.

IRENE (*Looking at him squarely, darkly*): Yes, just that. That's just it!

RUBEK: First and foremost I was an artist. I used to get so ill—absolutely ill—with an insatiable desire to create. I had to give it life. I had to create my life's work! (*Lost in memory*) It shall be called "The Day of Reawakening." It shall be created in the image of a young woman who has just awakened from her sleep of death. . . .

IRENE: Our child—yes.

RUBEK (*Continuing*): She shall be the world's purest, most glorious woman. She who awakens, awakens from the dead. And then I found you. I could use you for all of her. And how you followed me—so joyously, so willingly! You gave up family, home, everything and followed my work.

IRENE: To follow you meant that I awakened from the innocence of my childhood.

RUBEK: That was the reason I needed to use you. You and no

one else! You had become a sacred creation to me. You could only be touched with the thoughts of a worshipper. I was still young then, Irene, and filled with superstition. Oh, I believed so deeply that if I dared touch you or desire you my mind would be profaned and I would never finish the work. I still believe there is some truth in that.

IRENE (*Nodding with a touch of scorn*): First the work of art is born—then the work of man!

RUBEK: Judge me if you wish, but remember I was overwhelmed —dominated by the enormity of my work. I was sick with the urge to create, and in gratifying that urge I was ecstatically happy.

IRENE: And so you mastered your task, Arnold.

RUBEK: Thanks and praise to you! For I have only you to thank for the ultimate achievement. I had to create the purest woman, as I saw her in the moment of her reawakening. Not astonished by anything new or unknown or unexpected, but simply filled with sacred happiness as she discovers herself unchanged. She—the woman of the earth on a higher, freer, more joyous realm after her long dreamless sleep of death. (*Continuing, slowly*) And so I created her. In your image I created her, Irene.

IRENE (*Putting her hands flat on the table, she leans back in her chair.*): And so you were finished—with me.

RUBEK (*Reproachfully*): Irene!

IRENE: You no longer needed me.

RUBEK: How can you say that!

IRENE: You began to look around for other ideals.

RUBEK: I found no one. No one after you. . . .

IRENE: No other models?

RUBEK: You were never a model to me! You were the very source of all my expression.

IRENE (*Quiet for a moment*): And what poetry have you composed since—in marble, I mean—since that day I left you?

RUBEK: I composed no poems. After that day I frittered my life away in sculpturing.

IRENE: And the woman you live with?

RUBEK (*Interrupting vehemently*): Don't speak about her now! It tears my heart!

IRENE: Where are you planning to travel with her?

RUBEK (*Suddenly tired*): Oh—I must go on a boring, lonesome boat trip that will take us slowly up the northern coast.

IRENE (*Looks at him with an almost hidden smile and whispers*): Go instead to the mountains. High up into the highest mountains . . . as high up as you can . . . and then higher, higher! Always higher, Arnold.

RUBEK (*Tense and expectant*): Do you want to go up there?

IRENE: Do you have the courage to meet me once more?

RUBEK (*Struggling with himself, uncertain*): If we could . . . if only—

IRENE: Why can't we do what we wish at last? (*She looks at him and whispers pleadingly.*) Come, Arnold. Oh, please come . . . up to me! (MAJA *enters from around the corner of the hotel. She is bubbling and radiant with happiness. She hurries over to the table where she was seated with* RUBEK.)

MAJA (*Still at the corner, without looking about*): Rubek, you may say what you want, but Rubek—oh. (*She sees* IRENE.) Oh, I beg your pardon. You have already made an acquaintance, I notice.

RUBEK (*Curtly*): Renewed an acquaintance. (*Standing*) What is it you want of me?

MAJA: Merely to tell you this. You may do as you want, but I'm not going with you on that loathesome steamship!

RUBEK: Why not?

MAJA: Because I want to go up into the forest and the mountains. That is what I want! (*Ingratiatingly*) Now you must give me your permission, Rubek—you must—please. Oh please, I promise to be so good, so very good afterwards.

RUBEK: Who's put you up to this?

MAJA: He has. That hideous bear killer. Oh—you have no idea how many wonderful things he has told me about the mountains and the life up there! All his stories are so nasty and hideous, and so sickening, too! At least, most of them are.

I'm almost certain they're all lies. But it's fascinating and quite irresistible just the same. Oh please let me go with him! Just to see if those terrifying stories are true. Please? Oh *may* I go, Rubek?

RUBEK: As far as I'm concerned, you may—you may go into the mountains as far and for as long as you wish. I might be traveling that way myself.

MAJA (*Quickly*): No! No, no, you don't have to do that. Not for my sake.

RUBEK: The mountains are my choice, too. My mind's made up.

MAJA: Oh, thank you! Thank you. May I go tell that bear killer right away?

RUBEK: Just tell the bear killer whatever you like.

MAJA: Oh thank you, thank you, thank you! (*She tries to squeeze his hand, but he withdraws.*) Oh dear, how sweet and kind you are today, Rubek!

(MAJA *runs into the hotel. At the same moment, the door to the pavilion slowly and silently begins to open, as if someone behind it were spying. It is the* NURSE, *who is listening, unnoticed by the others.*)

RUBEK (*With resolution*): Then it is destined we shall meet up there!

IRENE (*Rising slowly*): Yes we shall meet, to be sure. I have searched for you so long.

RUBEK: When did you begin searching for me, Irene?

IRENE (*Flavored with bitterness*): From the moment it occurred to me that I had given you something I could never replace, Arnold. Something so precious that one should never part with it.

RUBEK (*Bowing his head*): That is bitter, and true. You gave me three—four years of your youth.

IRENE: Oh, I gave you more. Much more! Wasteful as I was then.

RUBEK: Yes, you were wasteful, Irene. You gave me all your naked beauty . . .

IRENE: . . . to behold—

RUBEK: . . . and to immortalize.

IRENE: Yes, for your own glorification. And the child's.

RUBEK: For you too, Irene.

IRENE: But the most precious gift you have forgotten.

RUBEK: The most precious? What gift was that?

IRENE: My living soul. I gave it to you, and it was so young! I stood there naked, yes, but I was completely empty inside. Without a soul. (*She stares at him fixedly.*) It was because of that that I died, Arnold.

(*The* NURSE *opens the door completely and steps aside while* IRENE *passes through. The* NURSE *follows her and closes the door.* RUBEK *stands and looks after them.*)

RUBEK (*In a whisper*): Irene!

CURTAIN

# ACT II

*A health lodge halfway up the mountain. The treeless landscape stretches endlessly toward a long mountain lake. Beyond the lake rises an immense range of mountain peaks with bluish snow in the crevasses.* DOWNSTAGE LEFT *a brook falls down a steep mountain wall and flows evenly over the smooth stretch of landscape, disappearing off* RIGHT. *Dwarf trees, plants, heather, and stones follow the path of the brook.* DOWNSTAGE RIGHT *is a small slope covered lightly with heather. On top of the slope there is a small stone bench.*

AS THE CURTAIN RISES, *it is a late summer afternoon near sunset. In the distance children can be heard singing, dancing, and playing. At times they are seen. Some are dressed in everyday clothes, others in peasant costumes. Their happy laughter is heard throughout the scene.*

PROFESSOR RUBEK *is seated on the bench with a blanket over his shoulders. He watches the children at play.*

MAJA *enters. She shades her eyes to look at the view. She wears a flat tourist cap, a short skirt (calf-length and hiked-up) and high laced walking boots of stout leather. She carries an alpine stick.*

❧

MAJA (*Seeing* RUBEK, *she calls to him in the manner of a mountaineer.*): Halloa! (*She walks to him. Uses her stick to jump across the brook*) Oh! How I've been running around looking for you, Rubek!

RUBEK (*Nodding indifferently*): Did you come from the lodge?

MAJA: Yes. I was looking all over for you among those half-dead flies. (*There is an embarrassed silence.*)

RUBEK: I noticed you were not at dinner.

MAJA: No, we had our dinner under the open sky, we two.

RUBEK: "We two?" And just who is the other half of "we two"?

MAJA: That hideous bear killer, of course.

RUBEK: Of course.

MAJA: Tomorrow morning early we are going off again.

RUBEK: After bears?

MAJA: Yes. Off to kill Papa Bear himself.

RUBEK: Have you found any tracks?

MAJA (*Haughtily*): Oh, there are no bears here on these naked mountains—you know that!

RUBEK: Where, then?

MAJA: Deep down. Deep down in the mountain crevasses where the forest is so thick that it's utterly impossible for regular city people to get through.

RUBEK: And the two of you are going down there tomorrow?

MAJA (*Throwing herself down in the heather*): Yes. That's what we've decided. Or maybe we shall leave this evening. If you have no objections, of course.

RUBEK: Me? Far from it—

MAJA (*Quickly*): Lars is coming with us, of course—and all the dogs.

RUBEK: I haven't made the slightest inquiry about Mr. Lars or his dogs. Won't you please sit down here—correctly, on the bench?

MAJA (*Sleepily*): No thank you. I am resting here so nicely in the soft heather.

RUBEK: I can see that you're very tired.

MAJA (*Yawning*): I almost think that I am beginning to be just that.

RUBEK: But that usually comes afterwards—when all the excitement is over.

MAJA (*In a sleepy voice*): Yes. I'll lie here and close my eyes. (*There is a pause. Then with sudden impatience*) Oh Rubek, how can you stand it? Just sitting—listening to nothing? Nothing but those children screaming and playing their silly games.

RUBEK: There is such harmony in their movements. It's almost music. Every once in a while in the middle of all their clumsiness I see it. So I enjoy sitting here watching for those few isolated moments. It pleases me.

MAJA (*Smiling a bit spitefully*): Oh yes. You are always first and foremost the artist!

RUBEK: And I want very much to remain one!

MAJA (*Turning on her side with her back to* RUBEK): There is not a trace of the artist in him.

RUBEK (*Attentive*): Who? Who has no trace of the artist in him?

MAJA (*Sleepily*): He. The other one, of course.

RUBEK: Mr. Bear Hunter, you mean?

MAJA: Yes. Not a trace of the artist in him, not a trace.

RUBEK (*Smiling*): You know, I believe you are completely right about that.

MAJA (*Flaring up vehemently, without moving*): Ooh—and he's so ugly! (*She tears at a tuft of heather and throws it away.*) So ugly—so ugly—

RUBEK: And that is why you're so eager to trust yourself with him in the wilderness?

MAJA (*Flopping over on her stomach, she faces him directly.*): You're ugly too, Rubek!

RUBEK: Have you just discovered that?

MAJA: No. I've seen it for a long time.

RUBEK (*Shrugging his shoulders*): One gets older. One gets older, Mrs. Maja.

MAJA: That's not exactly what I mean, Rubek. Your eyes have begun to have a tired look. It's a weariness, as if you've given up. I notice it whenever you are gracious enough to glance at me.

RUBEK: Since when have you noticed that?

MAJA: Little by little this ugly look has come into your eyes. It's almost as if you were nursing an evil plot against me.

RUBEK (*Friendly but solemn*): Oh? Come and sit here beside me, Maja. We must talk to each other.

MAJA (*Rising halfway up*): May I sit on your lap, as I used to?

RUBEK: No—of course not! They can see us from the lodge. You may sit here beside me on the bench.

MAJA: No thank you! In that case I would much rather stay exactly where I am. (*She rolls over on her back.*) I can hear you very well from here. (*Looks questioningly at him*) Well, what was it you wanted to talk about?

RUBEK (*Beginning slowly*): Why do you think I agreed to make this trip with you this summer?

MAJA: Well, among other things, you insisted that it would be so good for me. But now—

RUBEK: But now?

MAJA: Well, now I don't believe for a moment it was because of that.

RUBEK: What do you believe?

MAJA: I believe it was all because of that pale lady.

RUBEK: Mrs. Von Satow?

MAJA: Yes. That woman who was constantly hanging on our heels. And last night she showed up here at the lodge, too.

RUBEK: But how in the world was I—?

MAJA: Well, you used to know her so well—intimately—before you knew me.

RUBEK: And forgot her, too—long before I met you.

MAJA (*Sitting straight up*): Can you forget so easily, Rubek?

RUBEK (*Curtly*): Yes, I can. It is extremely easy . . . (*Adding harshly*) . . . when I want to .

MAJA: Even a woman who has modeled for you?

RUBEK (*Dismissing her*): When I can use her no longer—yes!

MAJA: A woman who has completely undressed herself before you?

RUBEK: That means nothing to an artist! (*Changing his tone*) And how, if I may ask, was I supposed to know she was even in the country?

MAJA: Oh, you could have seen her name in the newspaper on one of those lists of travelers.

RUBEK: Yes, I could have. But you forget I didn't have the slightest idea what her name was. I had never heard of any Mrs. Von Satow.

MAJA (*With pretended fatigue*): Good God! Then there was some other reason that made you absolutely have to come up here!

RUBEK (*Serious*): Yes, Maja, there was some other reason. Something completely different, and that's what we have to talk about now—once and for all.

MAJA (*In a fit of suppressed laughter*): Oh good heavens—how solemn you look!

RUBEK (*Suspiciously, scrutinizing her*): Yes, perhaps a little more solemn than is necessary.

MAJA: What do you mean?

RUBEK: Perhaps that's a good thing for both of us.

MAJA: You're beginning to make me curious, Rubek.

RUBEK: Just curious? Aren't you just a bit disturbed?

MAJA (*Shaking her head*): No. Not a bit.

RUBEK: Good. Now listen to me, Maja. Do you remember down at the Baths you said I seemed to be getting nervous?

MAJA: Well, that's true.

RUBEK: Do you think you know why?

MAJA: Goodness, how could I know? (*Quickly*) Perhaps you're nervous because you've grown weary of constantly being with me.

RUBEK: Constantly? Say, rather, eternally.

MAJA: Well, living together every day, then. We have been together, the two of us lonely people, for some four or five years down there—hardly out of each other's sight for an hour. The two of us quite alone.

RUBEK (*Intensely*): Well?

MAJA (*A little oppressed*): And you're not a particularly social person, Rubek. You always prefer to go off by yourself, thinking your own thoughts and keeping them to yourself. I could never talk to you about the things that really concerned you —your art—and such. I— (*With an impatient gesture*) My God! I wouldn't care to, either!

RUBEK: Well, well, well. That's why we always sat by the fireplace and talked about your interests.

MAJA: Well, good Lord—I had nothing else to talk to you about!

RUBEK: Perhaps it was just small talk, but it helped pass the time for both of us.

MAJA: You're right—time passed. Time is passing you right by, Rubek. Ah! I suppose that's really the reason why you're so . . . restless, so—

RUBEK (*Nodding vehemently*): —so without any will! (*Twists on the bench, nervously*) Oh, no! I cannot hold on to this wretched life much longer.

MAJA (*Rises and looks at him for a moment*): If you want to get rid of me, you've only to say so.

RUBEK: What kind of talk is that? Get rid of you?

MAJA: If you really want to get rid of me, Rubek, please say so. I shall leave immediately.

RUBEK (*Smiling almost imperceptibly*): Is that supposed to be a threat, Maja?

MAJA: I know very well that my leaving you couldn't possibly be a threat.

RUBEK: How right you are! (*After a pause*) It is impossible for you and me to go on living together like this.

MAJA: And so?

RUBEK: That's just it! There is no "and so," Maja. We can no longer be together in our loneliness, but that doesn't necessarily mean that we must separate.

MAJA (*Smiling scornfully*): Just separate a little, you mean?

RUBEK (*Shaking his head*): That's not necessary either.

MAJA: Well then, come out with it! What do you intend to do with me?

RUBEK (*A bit unsurely*): What I feel now—so vitally, so painfully—is that I need to have someone around me who is truly close to me.

MAJA (*Interrupting him anxiously*): And I'm not that, Rubek?

RUBEK (*Rejecting her*): No, Maja. Not in the ultimate sense. I must have a relationship with someone who will fulfill in me all those things I lack. I need someone who will complete me and be in harmony with all my endeavors.

MAJA (*Slowly*): Well, it's true—in such difficult matters I could be of no help to you.

RUBEK: And I'd appreciate it very much, Maja, if you didn't try.

MAJA (*With an outburst*): By God! And I've no desire to, either.

RUBEK: I'm well aware of that. It wasn't my intention when I bound myself in marriage to you to find that kind of life companion.

MAJA (*Studying him*): I can see that you're thinking of someone else.

RUBEK: Can you? I've never noticed before that you were a mind reader. Can you actually read my thoughts? Can you?

MAJA: Yes, I can. I know you so well, Rubek, so well.

RUBEK: Well then, perhaps you can tell me who I am thinking of?

MAJA: Yes, I certainly could.

RUBEK: Well? Won't you be so kind as to tell me, then?

MAJA: You're thinking of that . . . that model you used once. (*With a sudden outburst*) Do you know that the people down at the lodge think she's mad?

RUBEK: Really? And what do the people down at the lodge think about you and the bear killer?

MAJA: That has nothing to do with this! It was the pale lady you were thinking about, wasn't it?

RUBEK (*Calmly*): Yes—exactly of her. When I could no longer use her and she deserted me—traveled away, alone—when she disappeared without any reason—

MAJA: You took me on as a sort of makeshift wife, I suppose?

RUBEK (*Unfeelingly*): Yes. To be honest, you were something like that, little Maja. I had gone around alone, brooding, for a year—or a year and a half. I had put the last touch, the very final touch, upon my work "The Day of Reawakening," and it went out into the world and brought me back fame—and all other kinds of glory, too. (*Warmly*) But I could not love my own creation any more. People's flowers and incense nauseated me. Their praise discouraged me so that all I wanted was to run away and hide in the deepest forest. Since you're a mind reader, do you know what happened to me then?

MAJA (*Offhandedly*): Well, I know what you did. You made portrait busts of wealthy ladies and gentlemen.

RUBEK (*Nodding*): By special appointment. Yes. And I threw those animal faces in behind the masks gratis! Understand? (*Smiling*) But that wasn't exactly what I was thinking of.

MAJA: What was it, then?

RUBEK (*Seriously*): Well, suddenly all this talk about the artist's vocation and the artist's mission—and that sort of thing— struck me as being so hollow. There was no core of truth to it.

MAJA: What could you possibly have wanted instead?

RUBEK: Life, Maja.

MAJA: Life?

RUBEK: Yes. Wouldn't life in the sunshine and beauty be something especially valuable? So much more so than eking out one's last days in a raw, damp hole, dragging one's dead-tired body into the perpetual struggle against masses of clay and blocks of stone.

MAJA (*With a small sigh*): Well yes, it always seemed that way to me.

RUBEK: And then I became wealthy enough to live in luxury and in the idle, quivering sunshine. I could afford to build not only a beautiful villa on the lake, but an exquisite town house as well—and everything that goes with them.

MAJA (*Using his tone*): And so, of course, you could afford to treat yourself to a wife like me. You even allowed me to play among your worldly goods.

RUBEK (*Jesting in order to change the subject*): Didn't I promise to take you with me up to the highest mountain and show you all the splendor of the world?

MAJA (*With a gentle expression*): And haven't you? Here we are in the mountains, Rubek. But you haven't shown me the splendor of the world yet.

RUBEK (*Smiling irritatedly*): How difficult you are to please, Maja! So absolutely impossible to please. (*Suddenly flaring up*) But do you know what makes me more desperate than anything? Can you guess?

MAJA (*Quietly, defiant*): No doubt the fact that you've bound yourself to me for life.

RUBEK: I wouldn't have put it so heartlessly.

MAJA: But your meaning would have been just as heartless.

RUBEK: No, no, no—that is not the whole truth, Maja. You simply have no concept of what the artist's nature is.

MAJA: Good God! I haven't the slightest idea of what my own nature is!

RUBEK (*Continuing undisturbed*): I live so intensely, Maja. We artists all do. I feel I've lived a whole life in the few years we've known each other. And now I realize there's no happiness for me in idle enjoyment. Life is just not meant that way for me—and my kind. I must keep laboring, creating one work after another until my last breath. (*Forcing himself to continue*) That is why I can't continue any longer this way with you, Maja. Not with you alone.

MAJA (*Calmly*): In plain language, wouldn't that mean you're bored with me?

RUBEK (*Blurting out*): Yes, that's exactly what it means! I'm bored. Desperately bored and tired. I've gone limp in this life with you. There, now you have it! (*Controlling himself*) I know these are ugly, hard words I'm saying. I know that very well. But you've nothing to be guilty of, Maja. I willingly admit that. I'm the one who has changed. I have undergone an inner transformation. (*Half to himself*) A reawakening of my true life.

MAJA (*Folding her hands involuntarily*): Then why in the world can't we part?

RUBEK (*Amazed*): Would you be willing?

MAJA: Yes. Well, if there's no other way out then—

RUBEK: But there is another way—there is another way out.

MAJA (*Shaking her index finger at him*): Now you're thinking of the pale lady again!

RUBEK: Yes. To be quite honest, I never stop thinking of her now that I've met her again. Let me tell you a secret, Maja.

MAJA: Yes.

RUBEK (*Indicating his chest*): In here, you see, in here—I have a little tiny safe. And in this miniature safe of mine I used to store all my artistic visions. Then one day she went away without a trace and the lock snapped shut. She always had the key, and she took it with her. And you, little Maja, when you came along? You had no key. That is why all the contents lie unused in there—and the years pass by and I have no way to get at my treasures.

MAJA (*Making light*): Then get her to unlock it for you!

RUBEK (*Not understanding*): Maja?

MAJA: Well, she's here at the lodge now. I suppose it's because of the safe that she's come.

RUBEK: I haven't said a single word about it to her!

MAJA (*With feigned innocence*): Oh dear Rubek, why do you make all this fuss over some insignificant little—

RUBEK: It seems insignificant to you, does it, Maja?

MAJA: Yes, it certainly does. As far as I'm concerned, you may attach yourself to whomever you wish. (*Nodding to him*) I shall always be able to find a place for myself!

RUBEK: What do you mean?

MAJA (*Evasively unconcerned*): Well, I could always move into the villa if necessary. But no—no, that won't do. It seems to me that with that huge house of ours in town, there must be enough room for three people.

RUBEK (*Not certain*): And you think that would be possible for long?

MAJA (*In a light tone*): Good Lord—if it doesn't work out, it doesn't! It's nothing to waste words over.

RUBEK: And what do we do, Maja, if it doesn't work out?

MAJA (*Not troubled*): Well, we'll simply stay out of each other's way. Completely. I will always manage to find a new place in the world for myself. Something free. Free! Oh so free! No use to be distressed over that, Professor Rubek! (*Suddenly pointing to the right*) Look there! There she is!

RUBEK (*Turning around*): Where?

MAJA: Out there. Striding along—looking like a marble statue! She's coming this way.

RUBEK (*Stands, looks about, and shades his eyes*): Isn't she the living image of my "Reawakening"? (*To himself*) And once I believed I could replace her and move her into the shadows. Remodel her. Oh, I must have been mad!

MAJA: Now what does all that mean, Rubek?

RUBEK (*Avoiding her*): Oh nothing, nothing. Nothing that you could ever understand.

(IRENE *enters from* UPSTAGE RIGHT. *The* CHILDREN *who are playing have caught sight of her and run to meet her. They surround her. Some are shy and timid, others friendly and confident. She speaks to them in low tones and motions for them to go down to the lodge and that she will rest beside the brook. The* CHILDREN *run out to the* LEFT, *jumping over the brook.* IRENE *goes up to the wall of rock and baths her hands in the falling water.*)

MAJA (*In a low voice*): Go speak to her, Rubek, in private.

(*Starts to leave*)

RUBEK: Where will you go in the meantime?

MAJA (*Meaningfully*): From now on I must go my own way. (*She leaves him, jumps over the brook with the help of her stick. Stops beside* IRENE) Professor Rubek is up there. He has been waiting for you, madame.

IRENE: What does he want?

MAJA: He says that he wants you to help him open a safe. It snapped shut years ago, he says.

IRENE: And I can help him?

MAJA: He seems to think you're the only one who can.

IRENE: Then I must try.

MAJA: Yes, you really must try, madame. (*She exits, walks toward the lodge*)

(*After a short pause* RUBEK *comes over to* IRENE. *The brook is between them. There is another short pause.*)

IRENE: She —she said you had been waiting for me.

RUBEK: I have been waiting for you year after year after year— without knowing it.

IRENE: I could not come to you, Arnold. I had lain down and had a long, dream-filled sleep.

RUBEK: But now you are awakened, Irene!

IRENE (*Shaking her head*): I am still heavy with the deep, deep sleep.

RUBEK: The light of this dawn shall brighten both of us. You shall see!

IRENE: Don't believe that!

RUBEK (*Urgently*): I do believe it. I know it . . . now that I've found you again.

IRENE: Reawakened!

RUBEK: Transfigured!

IRENE: No, only reawakened, Arnold, not transfigured.

RUBEK (*He crosses to her, balancing himself on the stepping-stones under the waterfall in order to get to her.*): Irene, where have you been all day?

IRENE (*Pointing*): Far, far over there—deep in the wastelands.

RUBEK (*Diverting her attention*): You don't have your friend with you today.

IRENE (*Smiling*): Her eyes are upon me, nevertheless.

RUBEK: How is that possible?

IRENE (*Glancing around*): I can assure you it is. She never loses sight of me, no matter where I am. (*Suddenly whispering*) One beautiful sunny morning I shall kill her.

RUBEK: You want to do that?

IRENE: Yes, desperately. I only wait for the chance.

RUBEK: Why? Why, Irene?

IRENE: She practices black magic! (*Mysteriously, as if in secret*) Just imagine, Arnold, she has formed herself into my shadow.

RUBEK (*Trying to calm her*): Well, well, we must all have shadows—

IRENE (*With an outburst*): I am my own shadow! Can you understand that?

RUBEK (*Sadly*): Yes, yes, Irene. I understand. I understand.

IRENE: I am my own shadow.

(RUBEK *sits down on the stone beside the brook.* IRENE *stands in back of him, leaning on the rock wall. There is a short pause.*)

IRENE: Why do you sit there and turn your eyes away from me?

RUBEK (*Slowly shaking his head*): I don't dare . . . I don't dare look at you.

IRENE: Why not, Arnold? Why don't you dare look at me any more?

RUBEK: You have a shadow that brings you pain, and I have a heavy conscience.

IRENE (*With a sudden happy cry of relief*): Ahhh! At last!

RUBEK (*Standing up*): Irene—what is it?

IRENE (*Motioning him off*): Still! Keep still! (*She draws in a long breath, as though relieved of a heavy burden*) Oh! There—they have let go of me for a while. We can sit down now and talk to each other just as we used to before—when I was alive.

RUBEK: Oh, if we only could talk as we did then.

IRENE: Sit down there where you sat before, and I shall sit beside you.
(*He sits. She sits on another stone close to him. There is a short silence.*)

IRENE: Now I have come back to you, Arnold, from a country far, far away.

RUBEK: Yes, at last! After an infinitely long journey.

IRENE: —Returned home to my lord and master.

RUBEK: To our—to our place, Irene.

IRENE: Have you waited every single day for me?

RUBEK: How could I dare wait—

IRENE: No, I suppose you couldn't—because you didn't understand.

RUBEK: Was there someone else? Is that why you disappeared so suddenly?

IRENE: Couldn't it have been because there was you, Arnold?

RUBEK: I don't understand you.

IRENE: When I had served you with my soul and my body and the statue stood by itself, finished—our child, as you called it—it was then that I laid at your feet my most precious sacrifice. I erased myself for all time.

RUBEK (*Bowing his head*): And left my life a waste.

IRENE (*Suddenly inflamed*): That was exactly what I wanted. Never, never again should you create anything after you had made our only child!

RUBEK: It was jealousy, then?

IRENE (*Coldly*): No. Something closer to hate.

RUBEK: Hate? You hated me?

IRENE (*Again vehemently*): Yes, you! I hated the artist who so completely, without grief, without any kind of concern, took a young human being and tore the soul out of its warm-blooded body because it was needed for a work of art!

RUBEK: How can you say that? You used to glow with desire as you posed. You had an almost holy passion to be with me in the midst of my work. Each morning it brought us together as if for an act of devotion.

IRENE (*Coldly as before*): I will tell you one thing, Arnold.

RUBEK: Yes?

IRENE: I never loved your art before I met you—nor after.

RUBEK: But the artist, Irene?

IRENE: The artist I hated!

RUBEK: The artist in me, too?

IRENE: Most of all in you. When I undressed completely and stood there before you—then I hated you, Arnold.

RUBEK (*Vehemently*): No, you couldn't have. It isn't true!

IRENE: I hated you because you stood there so unfeelingly—

RUBEK (*Laughing*): Unfeelingly? Did you think that?

IRENE: At any rate, so intolerably self-controlled! And then you were so thoroughly an artist—only an artist and not a man. (*Changing to a warm, intimately concerned voice*) But that statue in the wet, living clay—Oh how I loved it! Each day I watched it grow and finally emerge as a human being, alive and vital—easing its way out of the raw, shapeless mass, full of soul. It was our creation. I knew that it had come to life because of me, too. Our child—mine and yours.

RUBEK (*Sadly*): It was that in spirit and in truth.

IRENE: So you see, Arnold, it is for our child's sake that I have made this long pilgrimage.

RUBEK (*Suddenly alert*): For the marble statue?

IRENE: Call it what you wish. I call it our child.

RUBEK (*Uneasily*): You want to see it finished? In the marble? But you always felt marble was so cold. (*Eagerly*) Perhaps you don't realize, Irene, but it's in a great museum, far out in the world somewhere.

IRENE: Yes, I have heard it told as a legend.

RUBEK: Museums were always detestable to you. You always called them mausoleums.

IRENE: They are. But I will make a pilgrimage to that marble mausoleum—that place where my soul and my child's soul lie buried.

RUBEK (*Alarmed*): No! You must never see that statue again, Irene. Do you hear me? Please promise me. Never, never see it!

IRENE: Do you think it would make me die again if I did?

RUBEK (*Clenching his fists*): Oh, I don't know what I think! How could I have ever imagined that you'd dedicate your life so completely to that statue? You disappeared before it was even finished.

IRENE: It *was* finished. That's why I could go away from you and leave you to yourself.

RUBEK (*Sits with his elbows on his knees, rests his head in his hands, and covers his eyes*): It was not then what it became later.

IRENE (*Quietly and quickly she takes a small object from her bosom. She half-unsheathes a knife with a sharp, narrow blade, whispering hoarsely.*): Arnold, have you done something evil to our child?

RUBEK (*Avoiding her*): Evil? It's not so easy for me to decide what you could call it.

IRENE (*Breathlessly*): What have you done—tell me!

RUBEK: I shall tell you if you will sit down calmly and listen.

IRENE (*Hiding the knife*): I shall listen as calmly as a mother can when she—

RUBEK (*Interrupting*): And you mustn't look at me when I speak.

IRENE: No. I mustn't look at you. (*She sits behind him on a rock.*) I shall sit here and be your shadow. Now tell me.

RUBEK (*Takes his hands from his eyes and stares ahead*): When I found you, I knew at once how I could use you for my life's work—

IRENE: "The Day of Reawakening." You called it that—I called it our child.

RUBEK: I was so young then, and innocent. I thought that the resurrection had to be told as the most beautiful thing, and the most beautiful way of telling it was as a young, untouched woman without any earthly experiences—one who awakens to the light and glory, detached from anything that is ugly or impure.

IRENE (*Quickly*): Yes! That is how I stand there now in our work?

RUBEK (*Evasively*): Well . . . not exactly like that, Irene.

IRENE (*Rising, intently*): No? I am not standing there as I always stood for you?

RUBEK (*Without answering*): In the years that followed I became more wise to the world, Irene. My conception of the reawakening became more complex. That small, round pedestal where your figure stood so erect and lonely was no longer large enough for all the things I wanted to add to the composition.

IRENE (*Reaching for the knife*): What did you add to it? Tell me!

RUBEK: Everything I saw in the world around me I included in that composition. I was *compelled* to include all of them, Irene. I could not help myself. I widened the pedestal until it became spacious—huge! On it I placed the curving earth —round and bursting from within with life—and out of a crevice in the solid crust there came swarms of men and women with their hidden animal faces. All the men and women as I knew them from life!

IRENE (*Breathless with suspense*): And in the midst of this swarming crowd stands the young woman who knows the joy of birth? I still stand like that, don't I, Arnold?

RUBEK (*Avoiding her*): Not exactly in the middle. Unfortunately, I had to move that statue back a little to achieve the overall effect—you understand. Otherwise it would have dominated the entire work.

IRENE: But is my face still transfigured with the light of that joy?

RUBEK: Yes it is, Irene . . . in a way. I had to subdue it a little as my conception changed and made new demands.

IRENE (*Rising noiselessly*): And this composition expresses life as you see it now, Arnold?

RUBEK: Yes. Yes, I suppose it does.

IRENE: And in it you have pushed me away and subdued my light. I stand as a background figure now in a group? (*She draws the knife.*)

RUBEK: Not a background figure—nor foreground either, Irene. But in a finer sense, let us say, a figure who stands on the safe middle ground. Or something like that.

IRENE (*Whispering hoarsely*): You have just pronounced your own doom! (*She is ready to strike.*)

RUBEK (*Turns and looks at her*): Doom?

IRENE (*Quickly hides the knife and speaks as though choked in pain*): My whole soul—you and I and our child—we, we all lived in that solitary figure.

RUBEK (*Eagerly tears off his hat and dries his perspiring brow*): Perhaps, but now listen to where I have placed myself in this group. In the foreground beside a spring—exactly like that one—sits a man so guilt-ridden that he cannot free himself from the crust of the earth, and so he sits there twisting his fingers in the whirling water to cleanse them. He is eternally tortured by the thought that he will never, never succeed. I call him "Regret for a Misused Life." Never in all eternity will he be free to reawaken, to ever know a new life. He must remain forever in his own hell.

IRENE (*Brittle and cold*): Poet!

RUBEK: Why poet?

IRENE: Because you are soft and stupid and wallowing in self-indulgence, forgiving yourself for everything you did and thought! You have killed my soul and so you model yourself in remorse and self-accusation, posed in repentance. . . . (*Smiling*) And with that you think you have bought atonement!

RUBEK (*Defiantly*): I am an artist, Irene. I am not ashamed of the human frailties that perhaps are a part of me. For I am first and foremost, and never will be anything but, an artist.

IRENE (*Looks at him with evil in her smile. Says softly and gently)*: You are a poet, Arnold. *(Softly stroking his hair)* My big, beloved aging child. Can't you see that?

RUBEK *(Displeased)*: Why do you insist upon calling me a poet?

IRENE *(With malice in her eyes)*: Because there is something apologetic in that word, my friend. Something that suggests a foregiveness of all sins and spreads a cloak over all frailties. *(Suddenly changing her tone)* But I was a human being, then. And I, too, had a life to live and a human destiny to fulfill. And see! I left it all, untouched! I sacrificed it all in order to humble myself and serve you. Oh, that was my suicide—the mortal sin against myself . . . *(Half whispering)* . . . a sin that I can never expiate—never.

*(She sits beside him on the bench and watches him closely without his noticing. Absent-mindedly she picks some mountain roses off the bushes.)*

IRENE *(With apparent self-control)*: I should have borne children into this world, many children, real babies—not the kind that are hidden away in mausoleums. That was my vocation. I should never have served you, poet!

RUBEK *(Lost in soulful recollection)*: Those were beautiful days, Irene—miraculously beautiful—now when I think back on them.

IRENE *(Looking at him, gently)*: Can you remember what you said when you were finished? Finished with me and our child? *(Nodding to him)* Can you remember that one word, Arnold?

RUBEK: Did I say one word that you still remember?

IRENE: Yes, you did. Can't you remember it?

RUBEK *(Shaking his head)*: No, quite honestly I can't. Not for the moment, at least.

IRENE: You took both my hands and held them warmly. I stood there in breathless anticipation. Then you said, "And now, Irene, let me thank you from the bottom of my heart. This," you said, "has been a blessed episode for me."

RUBEK *(Doubtfully)*: Did I say "episode"? That isn't a word I often use.

IRENE: You said "episode."

RUBEK (*Attempting cheerfulness*): Well now, when you come right down to it, it *was* an episode.

IRENE: With that word, I left you.

RUBEK: You take everything so painfully to heart, Irene.

IRENE (*Stroking her forehead*): That might be true. Let us shake off all the painful things that strike too deep. (*She plucks the petals of a rose and sprinkles them into the brook.*) Look there, Arnold! Our little birds are swimming.

RUBEK: What kind of birds are they?

IRENE: Can't you see? They're flamingos. They're rose-red.

RUBEK: Flamingos don't swim; they just wade in the water.

IRENE: Then they're not flamingos. They're plain sea gulls.

RUBEK: They could be sea gulls with red heads. Yes. (*He picks wide green leaves from the bushes and throws them into the brook.*) Now I send my ships out after them.

IRENE: There mustn't be any men on board who kill birds!

RUBEK: No. No men to capture them. (*Smiling at her*) Can you remember that summer on Lake Taunitzer when we sat like this outside that little farmhouse . . .

IRENE: . . . Saturday evening when we had finished our work for the week.

RUBEK: . . . and went out on the train and stayed there all through Sunday—

IRENE (*With a sudden gleam in her eyes*): Was that an episode, Arnold?

RUBEK (*As if not hearing*): You used to let your birds swim in the brook then, too. They were water lilies which you—

IRENE: They were white swans!

RUBEK: I mean swans, of course. I remember one day I fastened a large, downy leaf to one of the swans.

IRENE: —And so it became Lohengrin's boat with a swan pulling it!

RUBEK: How happy you were with that game, Irene.

IRENE: We played it over and over again.

RUBEK: Every single Saturday all summer long.

IRENE: And you said I was the swan that guided your boat.

RUBEK: Did I say that? Well, I probably did. (*Becoming ab-*

*sorbed in the game*) Look! Look how the sea gulls are swimming downstream.

IRENE (*Laughing*): And all your ships have run ashore.

RUBEK (*Throws in more leaves. Follows them intensely*): I have more ships—ships in reserve, Irene! (*Throws in more leaves and watches them. After a pause*) Irene, I bought that little farmhouse at Lake Taunitzer.

IRENE: Did you? How often you said you would, if you could only afford it.

RUBEK: I've been able to afford it many times over since then. So, I bought it.

IRENE (*Stealing a glance at him*): Do you live there now—in our old house?

RUBEK: No, I had it torn down long ago. I built myself a large, comfortable villa on the same land with a park around it. And there we—I usually spend my summers.

IRENE (*Controlling herself*): So you and—and the other—live there now?

RUBEK (*Somewhat defiantly*): Yes. When my wife and I are not traveling, as we are this year.

IRENE (*Looking far ahead of her*): Beautiful ... so beautiful was life at Lake Taunitzer.

RUBEK (*In retrospect*): All the same, Irene—

IRENE: All the same—? Yes. We had all of life and its beauty, and we let it slip through our fingers.

RUBEK: And now it is too late even for regret.

IRENE (*There is a pause. She sits quietly. Points at the landscape*): Oh look, Arnold! The sun is setting behind the mountain peaks. Just look how red it shines. It makes all the heather glow with red—and all the slopes.

RUBEK: It has been a long time since I've seen a sunset in the mountains.

IRENE: Or a sunrise?

RUBEK: I don't believe I ever saw the sun rise.

IRENE (*Smiling, lost in recollection*): I saw a miraculously beautiful sunrise once.

RUBEK: Did you? Where was it?

IRENE: High, high up on the breath-taking mountaintop. You lured me up there on a promise to show me all the splendor of the world if I only— (*She stops short.*)

RUBEK: If you only—what?

IRENE: If I did what you told me to do. Oh how eagerly I followed you up into the heights! I fell on my knees and worshipped you and served you. (*She sits in silence and then says softly*) Then I saw the sunrise.

RUBEK: Wouldn't you like to come and live with us down there in the villa?

IRENE (*With a scornful smile*): Together with you and the other one?

RUBEK (*Urgently*): Together with me—just as in our creative days. You could unlock all the things within me that have snapped shut. Would you like that, Irene?

IRENE (*Shaking her head*): I no longer have that key, Arnold.

RUBEK: Yes, you have. No one but you has ever had it. Help me. Help me to live my life over again.

IRENE (*Immovably, as before*): Impossible—empty dreams. Idle, dead dreams, our life together—there can be no reawakening for us—

RUBEK: Let's make believe, then. (*He throws more leaves into the brook.*)

IRENE: Yes—playing, playing, now and always, then and now; playing.
(*They sit and throw leaves and petals into the brook and watch them as they sail away.* UPSTAGE LEFT *on the slope,* MAJA *and* ULFHEIM *enter in hunting outfits.* LARS *follows after with the dogs.* MAJA *and* ULFHEIM *stop and look around.* LARS *continues walking and exits* RIGHT.)

RUBEK: Ah! There goes little Maja and her bear hunter.

IRENE: Your woman, yes.

RUBEK: Or his.

MAJA (*Seeing the two figures by the stream, shouts to them*): Good night, Professor! Dream of me. I'm going out now for some adventure!

RUBEK (*Standing up, shouts*): What adventure do you seek?

MAJA (*Coming closer*): Life! Life must come before everything else!

RUBEK: Ah! Now you want that, too—eh, little Maja?

MAJA: Yes! Yes indeed! I've made up a song about it. It goes like this— (*She sings, joyfully*)

> I am free! I am free! I am free!
> I am free as a bird. I am free!

(*Speaking*) Yes—I think at last I've finally awakened to life. At last!

RUBEK: Well, it sounds as if you have.

MAJA: Oh how wonderful it feels to be awakened!

RUBEK: Good night, little Maja . . . and good luck with your—

ULFHEIM: Quiet, for God's sake! You don't wish a hunter good luck! Can't you tell we're out to shoot?

RUBEK: What will you bring back from the hunt, Maja?

MAJA: You are going to get some bird of prey, Rubek. You can make a sculpture of it. I'll just wound it in the wing.

RUBEK (*Laughs mockingly and bitterly*): Yes. Just wounding things without knowing it. That's been your way for a long time, Maja.

MAJA (*Throwing her head back*): Oh, just let me take care of myself from now on. And . . . (*She nods, smiles mischievously*) . . . farewell! You have a quiet, peaceful summer night high up on the mountain yourself!

RUBEK (*Jokingly*): Thank you. And may all the devil's bad luck go with you and your hunting!

ULFHEIM (*Bellowing with laughter*): There! There's the blessing as it should be!

MAJA (*Laughing*): Thank you, thank you, Professor! (*They leave over the slope and out* RIGHT. *There is a short pause.*)

RUBEK: A summer night, high, high up on the mountain—yes, that would have been life.

IRENE (*Suddenly, with a wild expression*): Would you want a summer night high up on the mountain with me?

RUBEK (*Stretching out his arms*): Yes! Yes! Come!

IRENE: My beloved lord and master!

RUBEK: Oh Irene!

IRENE (*Smiles. Fumbles with the knife at her bosom*): It will be only an episode. (*Whispering quickly*) Hush! Don't look around, Arnold.

RUBEK (*Whispering*): What is it?

IRENE: That face is staring at me.

RUBEK (*Turning involuntarily*): Where? (*With a shock*) Ah! (*The* NURSE's *head is halfway visible in the bushes on the slope* LEFT. *Her eyes are immovably fixed on* IRENE.)

IRENE: So we must part. No, stay seated. Please hear me. (*She rises, leans over him, and whispers.*) You must not follow me now. Till we meet again tonight—high, high up on the mountain.

RUBEK: You will be there, Irene?

IRENE: I will be there. Wait for me.

RUBEK (*Repeating dreamily*): A summer night with you, high, high up on the mountain. With you—with you— (*Their eyes meet.*) Oh Irene, that could have been life! And we have wasted it all, we two.

IRENE: Ah! The first time we see all these irredeemable moments is when—

RUBEK: When?

IRENE: When we dead awaken.

RUBEK: Yes. But what do we really see?

IRENE: Only . . . that we have never lived. (*She starts to exit.*) (*The* NURSE *steps aside.* IRENE *passes and goes out. The* NURSE *follows her.* RUBEK *remains seated, very still beside the brook.* MAJA *is heard singing triumphantly, higher in the mountains.*)

MAJA (*Singing* OFFSTAGE):
> I am free! I am free! I am free!
> I am free as a bird. I am free!

**CURTAIN**

# ACT III

*A wild spot high up in the mountains. There is a sheer precipice in the background, and in the distance the snow-clad peaks rise to such heights that the tops are lost in the drifting mists. At* STAGE LEFT *on a stone formation is an old, tumble-down hut.*

AS THE CURTAIN RISES, *dawn is breaking but the sun has not yet risen. The wind is whistling around the crags.* MAJA *enters, flushed and irritated.* ULFHEIM *follows her, half-angry, half-smiling. He holds her by the arm.*

MAJA (*Trying to free herself*): Let me go! Let me go, I said!

ULFHEIM: Come, come now—next thing I know you'll be biting me! You're as bad-tempered as a pack of wolves!

MAJA (*Striking his hand*): Let me go! I tell you, take your hands off me! Now behave yourself!

ULFHEIM: No—I'll be damned if I will!

MAJA: Then I refuse to go one more step with you! Do you hear? Not one single step!

ULFHEIM: And just how do you expect to get away from me up here?

MAJA: I'll jump over that edge if I have to!

ULFHEIM: Ahh! You'll smash yourself into little pieces of dog's food! So deliciously bloody! (*He laughs and then lets her go.*) You're very welcome, my lady friend, to jump over the edge right now if you so desire. It's a damned dizzy, fascinating drop!

MAJA (*Straightens her skirt and looks at him with anger*): Well, you're a fine gentleman to go hunting with!

ULFHEIM: You mean—to go sporting with!

MAJA: Oh—so this is what you call sport?

ULFHEIM: Yes, I take the privilege of calling it that. It's the sport I like best!

MAJA: Well! Of all the— (*After a short pause*) Why did you let the dogs loose up there?

ULFHEIM (*Blinks his eyes, laughs*): So they could do a little hunting on their own. You can understand that, can't you?

MAJA: You know that isn't true! It wasn't for the dogs' sake that you let them go.

ULFHEIM (*Still smiling*): No? Well, then, why did I do it? You tell me, my fine little lady.

MAJA: You wanted to get rid of Lars! You sent him to run after them and bring them all back here, you said. Oh that was really nice of you! And in the meantime—oh!

ULFHEIM: And in the meantime?

MAJA: Never mind!

ULFHEIM: Lars won't find them. You can depend on that. He'll stay away until the time is up.

MAJA (*Looking at him angrily*): Yes—I'm certain that he'll do just that!

ULFHEIM (*Grabbing her arm*): Ah, yes. Lars knows my habits in this sport!

MAJA: Do you know what you look like, Mr. Ulfheim?

ULFHEIM: I should imagine I look most like myself!

MAJA: Yes. You're right—exactly! You are the living image of a satyr.

ULFHEIM: A satyr?

MAJA: Yes, precisely. A hairy old satyr.

ULFHEIM: Isn't that some kind of monster? Something the trolls call a wood-devil?

MAJA: Yes, and that's just what you are with your goat's beard and legs. A ram! Yes, and satyrs have horns, too!

ULFHEIM: Aha! So they have horns, too?

MAJA: Yes, a pair of nasty, disgusting little horns right here. (*She points to her forehead.*) Just like yours.

ULFHEIM: Can you see my poor little horns already?

MAJA: Yes—I can see them very clearly.

ULFHEIM (*Taking the dogs' leashes out of his pocket*): Well then, I'd better tie you up.

MAJA: Have you gone insane? You want to tie me up?

ULFHEIM: If I'm the devil, let me act like one! So that's it—you can see my horns, eh?

MAJA (*Pacifying him*): There, there, there. You just behave yourself, Mr. Ulfheim. (*Changing the subject*) Tell me, where is your hunting castle that you spoke so high and mighty about? You said it was around here someplace.

ULFHEIM (*Pointing with a flourish to the hut*): Here. You have it in front of your very eyes.

MAJA (*Staring at him*): That old pigsty there?

ULFHEIM (*Smiling smugly*): It has housed more than one king's daughter, let me tell you!

MAJA: Was it there that the evil prince came to the king's daughter disguised as a brown bear as you told me?

ULFHEIM: Yes, Mrs. Hunting Companion. That is the very place. (*With an inviting gesture*) If you would care to do us the honor of stepping in, so—

MAJA: I wouldn't set foot one inch in there!

ULFHEIM: The right couple could doze away a summer night very pleasantly in there—wile away a whole summer, if it should come to that!

MAJA (*Impatiently*): Thank you. But one needs quite an appetite to enjoy that kind of thing—! But now, I'm very bored with both you and this hunting trip. I want to go down to the lodge now, before the people start waking up.

ULFHEIM: And just how are you planning to get back from here in that amount of time?

MAJA: That will be your problem. After all, there must be some way.

ULFHEIM (*Pointing to the precipice*): God knows there is! Straight down there.

MAJA (*Worried*): Well, there—you see—you will help me. With just a little effort you could—

ULFHEIM: But just you try it! I dare you.

MAJA (*Doubtfully*): You don't think I'd dare?

ULFHEIM: Never in this world, if I didn't help you!

MAJA (*Uneasily*): Well, come help me, then. What else do I have you here for?

ULFHEIM: Do you want me to carry you piggy-back?

MAJA: Oh rubbish!

ULFHEIM: Shall I carry you in my arms?

MAJA: Don't start that nonsense again!

ULFHEIM (*Suppressing anger*): I did it once. Once I took a young girl, a child—I carried her in my arms. I lifted her out of the slop of the streets and carried her in my arms. No, on my hands—outstretched—I carried her. My only desire was to carry her like that through life, so that her little feet would never feel the stones. Her shoes were so thin and worn when I found her.

MAJA: And so you did pick her up and carry her on your hands?

ULFHEIM: Yes. I lifted her up out of the filth and carried her as high and carefully as I could. (*With a growl*) And what was my thanks for that?

MAJA: Well—what?

ULFHEIM: Horns! She gave me those horns, the ones you saw so plainly. Ha! Isn't that a juicy little story, Mrs. Bear Murderer?

MAJA: Oh yes. It's amusing enough—yes. But I know another little story that's even more amusing.

ULFHEIM: How does that one go?

MAJA: Like this. There was once a child—a foolish child—and she lived with her mother and her father in very poor surroundings. Then one day there came the high and mighty lord of the manor. He came right into her shabby world. He was great and famous, and he took the little girl in his arms, just as you did, and traveled far, far away with her.

ULFHEIM: Was she so eager to be where he was?

MAJA: Oh yes! But then I told you, she was a very foolish little child.

ULFHEIM: He must have been especially handsome—

MAJA: Oh no, he wasn't! He wasn't unusually handsome at all. But he deceived her all the same. He didn't keep his promise. You see, he had promised her that he would take her up to the highest mountain where there was light and sunshine beyond all measure.

ULFHEIM: Ah! So he was a mountain climber, then?

MAJA: Yes, in a way he was.

ULFHEIM: And so he took this child right up there with him?

MAJA (Tossing her head): Yes, he took her, all right! He lured her into a cold, clammy cage where there was never any sun nor fresh air—it seemed to her—but only walls of gilt, with huge petrified human ghosts lined up against them.

ULFHEIM: I'll be damned if she didn't pay the piper! Served her right!

MAJA: Yes. But don't you think it's a rather funny story just the same?

ULFHEIM (Studying her for a while): Listen to me, my good hunting companion.

MAJA: What is it you want now?

ULFHEIM: Couldn't we patch up our ragged lives?

MAJA: Has Mr. Ulfheim taken a fancy for remnants and does he want to become a tailor of leftovers?

ULFHEIM: Yes, he has. Couldn't the two of us try to piece together all the rags and tatters and make some kind of human existence out of all of them?

MAJA: And when those poor tatters are worn out—what happens?

ULFHEIM (Throwing his arms open): Then we will stand there, free and exposed, the way we truly are!

MAJA (Suddenly laughing): Yes! You with your goat's legs! Yes!

ULFHEIM: And you without two stitches holding together long enough to cover your little—

MAJA: Let's go!

ULFHEIM: Wait! Where are you going, little bird?

MAJA: Down to the lodge, of course.

ULFHEIM: And after that?

MAJA: We bid each other a polite farewell and "thanks for the pleasure of your company."

ULFHEIM: Do you think we'll be able to do that?

MAJA: Oh yes. After all, you didn't tie me up.

ULFHEIM: I have a castle to offer you.

MAJA (*Pointing to the hut*): The mate to that one?

ULFHEIM: It hasn't fallen apart yet.

MAJA: And all the splendor of the world, too, I suppose?

ULFHEIM: A castle, I tell you . . .

MAJA: Thank you very much, but I've had enough of castles.

ULFHEIM: . . . with splendid hunting grounds for miles around.

MAJA: Are there also great works of art in your castle?

ULFHEIM (*Slowly*): There are no art works, but—

MAJA: Well that's a blessing!

ULFHEIM: Will you go with me as far and as long as I demand?

MAJA: There is a tame bird of prey keeping watch over me.

ULFHEIM (*Wildly*): We will shoot a bullet in its wing, Maja.

MAJA (*Looks at him for a moment, then speaks to him resolutely*): Ah! So come, then. Carry me down into the depths!

ULFHEIM (*Putting his arm around her waist*): It's high time, too! The mist is already over us.

MAJA: Is the way down dreadfully dangerous?

ULFHEIM: This mountain mist is more dangerous.

(MAJA *tears herself loose from him and walks over to the precipice and looks down. She draws back quickly.* ULFHEIM *walks over to her and laughs.*)

ULFHEIM: Ha! Does it make you dizzy?

MAJA (*Faintly*): Yes, that too! But look over there—the two of them, climbing up!

ULFHEIM (*Looking over the precipice*): It's only your bird of prey and his strange lady.

MAJA: We must get down without their seeing us. Can we?

ULFHEIM: Impossible! The path is too narrow. Besides, it's the only way down.

MAJA (*Steeling herself*): Well then, let's defy them—meet them head on!

ULFHEIM: Spoken like a true bear killer!

(RUBEK *and* IRENE *appear in the distance. Over his shoulders is his blanket. She has a fur cape thrown loosely over her dress, and a swan's-down hood over her head.*)

RUBEK: Hello there, Maja! So we two meet again?

MAJA (*Pretending to be self-assured*): At your service. Won't you please come up?

RUBEK (*Comes to the top, turns, and helps* IRENE. *Coldly, to* MAJA): So you've been on the mountain all night as we have?

MAJA: Yes. I've been hunting. You gave me permission, you know.

ULFHEIM (*Pointing down the precipice*): Did you come up that path?

RUBEK: You saw us, didn't you?

ULFHEIM: Us? Ah! The lady too?

RUBEK: Of course. That goes without saying. (*With a quick look at* MAJA) The lady and I do not intend to walk different paths from now on.

ULFHEIM: Then you don't know that you've just come up death's road?

RUBEK: We tried it just the same. It wasn't too hard at first.

ULFHEIM: No, not at first. It starts like any other road, but then you get to a point, and PFFT! You can't get up or down, in or out. Deadlocked. And there you stand, Professor, firm as a rock and mountain-fast, as we hunters call it.

RUBEK (*Smiles and looks at him*): Is this supposed to be the warning of the wise?

ULFHEIM: Good God! Save me from sounding wise! (*Urgently pointing up to the mountaintops and whirling mists*) But damn it—it doesn't take genius to see that there's a storm hovering over us right now. Listen to that wind whistling around.

RUBEK (*Listening*): Like the prelude to the Resurrection Day.

ULFHEIM: Bah! Those are storm warnings coming from the very peaks! Look at those black clouds rolling down upon us, singing and pressing lower and lower. They'll soon be wrapped around us like a shroud.

IRENE (*Shivering*): I know that shroud.

MAJA (*Pulling at* ULFHEIM): Let's hurry down!

ULFHEIM (*To* RUBEK): I can't take more than one with me. You two stay in the hut until the storm's over. Later on I'll send somebody up to bring both of you back.

IRENE (*Terrified*): To take us back? No, no!

ULFHEIM (*Harshly*): They'll bring you back by force if they must. It's a matter of life and death up here now, and now you know it! (*To* MAJA, *as he sweeps her up in his arms*) Come, little bird, now you are forced to trust me completely.

MAJA (*Clinging to him*): Oh, how I will sing! How triumphant I will feel if I get down there in one piece!

ULFHEIM (*Begins to descend. Shouts back to the others*): Remember now—wait in the hut until the men come with ropes to bring you down! (*He descends hurriedly into the depths, but with great care, carrying* MAJA.)

IRENE (*Looking for some time at* RUBEK *with frightened eyes*): Did you hear those words, Arnold? Men coming up here to get me! Many men will come!

RUBEK: Irene, be calm.

IRENE: And she—the one dressed in black—she also will come. I know it. She must have missed me by now. She will pounce upon me, Arnold, and put me in that straitjacket! Yes, she carried it with her in the trunk. I've seen it myself—

RUBEK: No one will be allowed to touch you.

IRENE (*With a bewildered smile*): No one! I have means of protecting myself.

RUBEK: What do you mean?

IRENE (*Taking out the knife*): This.

RUBEK (*Trying to seize it*): You have a knife?

IRENE: Always. Night and day I have it, even in my bed.

RUBEK: Give it to me, Irene.

IRENE (*Hiding it in her shawl*): No, you may not have it. I will put it to good use.

RUBEK: How will you use it here?

IRENE (*Looking at him, tensely*): It is destined for you, Arnold!

RUBEK: For me?

IRENE: Yes. When we sat by Lake Taunitzer last evening—

RUBEK: By Lake Taunitzer—?

IRENE: Yes, outside the peasant's cottage. We played with swans and water lilies—

RUBEK: Yes, Irene? Yes?

IRENE: I heard you say with a voice from the grave—icy and cold—that I was just another episode in your life—

RUBEK: *You* were the one who said that, Irene, not I.

IRENE: I took out the knife—I wanted to stab you in the back.

RUBEK (*Somberly*): Why didn't you?

IRENE: Because in my horror I suddenly realized that you were already dead—long ago.

RUBEK: Dead?

IRENE: Yes, dead. Dead. You as well as I. We sat there by the lake last evening—two lukewarm corpses—and played.

RUBEK: I don't call that being dead. But you don't understand me.

IRENE: Where is that burning desire that you felt for me, that you battled and fought against as I stood there before you— the reawakened woman?

RUBEK: Our love is certainly not dead, Irene.

IRENE: Love belongs to life, Rubek. Life on earth. That unbelievable miracle—life on earth! That mysterious puzzle of existence. And that is what is dead in both of us.

RUBEK (*Passionately*): You know very well that my love for you pulsates and burns as passionately in me as ever before.

IRENE: And I? Have you forgotten who I am now?

RUBEK: Be to me whoever and whatever you want to be. To me you are the woman I have dreamed of.

IRENE: I have stood on the turntables of the world—naked— and shown myself to hundreds of men after you.

RUBEK: But I put you there on that pedestal! Blind as I was

then. I put that dead clay image before the live one—yes, even above the happiness of love.

IRENE (*Looking down*): Too late. Too late.

RUBEK: Nothing in your past has lowered you in my eyes even a hairsbreadth.

IRENE (*With raised eyes*): Nor in mine, either!

RUBEK: Well, then, we are free. There is still time for us to live life, Irene!

IRENE (*Looking heavily at him*): The desire to live is dead in me, Arnold. Now I am resurrected. I was searching for you, and when I found you I saw that you and life are lying in state, as I was.

RUBEK: Oh how confused you are! Life is in us and around us, and it is germinating and throbbing as before!

IRENE (*Smiles and shakes her head*): Your young resurrected woman sees all of life lying in state.

RUBEK (*Throwing his arms violently around her*): Then let the two of us dead ones live life one single time to its fullest before we go down to our graves again!

IRENE (*With a scream*): Arnold!

RUBEK: But not here in this misty light. Not here, Irene, with this ugly, wet shroud perpetually flapping over us—

IRENE (*Carried away with passion*): Yes, yes we must go to the light! Into all the frightening grandeur of dawn—up to the promised top of the mountain!

RUBEK: There—up there—we shall celebrate our marriage, Irene. Oh my beloved!

IRENE (*Proudly*): And we shall welcome the sun to look upon us—

RUBEK: We will welcome all the powers of light and all the powers of darkness as well. For you have been reprieved! (*Grasping her hand*) Will you follow me? My bride!

IRENE (*As if in revelation*): I follow you willingly, happily! My lord and master!

RUBEK (*Pulling her along with him*): First we must pass through the mists, Irene, and then—

IRENE: Yes, through all the mists all the way up to the towering mountaintop that is gleaming in the sunrise.

(IRENE *and* RUBEK, *hand in hand, begin to climb the snow-covered mountain path, upward. They soon disappear among the clouds of mist and snow. Mist envelops the scene and for a moment it becomes a soft gray. Wild storm blasts whirl and whistle through the air. The* NURSE *appears from below. She stops and looks around, silent and searching.* MAJA *can be heard singing triumphantly far in the depths below.*)

MAJA: I am free! I am free! I am free!
I am free as a bird! I am free!

(*Suddenly a thundering roar comes from high up on the mountain path where* RUBEK *and* IRENE *have gone. It drowns out the song. Huge snow banks begin to slide and whirl downward with tremendous speed.* RUBEK *and* IRENE *can be dimly seen, high in the distance, being whirled along by the masses of snow, which bury them. The* NURSE *screams and stretches her arms out toward the fallen bodies.*)

NURSE: Irene! (*She stands for a moment, silent. Then she makes the sign of the cross before her in the air.*) Pax vobiscum!

(MAJA's *joyous song resounds from still farther down below. The snow continues to swirl.*)


**CURTAIN**

# THE
# MASTER
# BUILDER

(MASTER BUILDER SOLNESS)
1892

# CHARACTERS

MASTER BUILDER HALVARD SOLNESS

MRS. ALINE SOLNESS   *his wife*

DOCTOR HERDAL   *the family doctor*

KNUT BROVIK   *a former architect, now assistant to Solness*

RAGNAR BROVIK   *his son, a draftsman*

KAJA FOSLI   *his sister's daughter, a bookkeeper*

MISS HILDE WANGEL

SOME LADIES

THE CROWD ON THE STREET


*The action takes place at Master Builder Solness' home.*

# ACT I

A *modestly decorated workroom in the home of* MASTER BUILDER SOLNESS. *At* STAGE LEFT *is a folding door which leads to the hall.* UPSTAGE LEFT *is an iron stove used for heating the room, and* DOWNSTAGE LEFT, *a desk with books, papers and writing materials, and a lighted lamp. At* STAGE RIGHT *a door leads to the rooms of the home.* UPSTAGE RIGHT, *in the corner, are a couch and a table with chairs. On the table are a lighted lamp, a water pitcher, and a glass.* DOWNSTAGE RIGHT, *a rocking chair, an armchair, and a small table. On the* UPSTAGE CENTER *wall there is a door leading to the drafting room, where a work light is on.*

AS THE CURTAIN RISES, KNUT BROVIK *and his son* RAGNAR *are seated in the drafting room working on plans and calculations.* KAJA FOSLI *stands at an upright desk, writing in a ledger.* KNUT BROVIK *is a thin old man with white hair and beard. He is dressed in a slightly worn but well-kept black coat. He wears glasses and a once-white-now-yellowed shirt front.* RAGNAR BROVIK *is in his thirties, a blondish, well-dressed young man with a slight stoop.* KAJA FOSLI *is a frail girl in her early twenties. She dresses carefully and wears a green shade over her eyes, but she seems in poor health. They all work in silence for a moment.*

❦

KNUT BROVIK (*Suddenly stands up and goes to the doorway, breathing with difficulty*): No! I can't stand it any longer!
KAJA (*Going toward him*): Don't you feel well this evening, Uncle?
BROVIK: It seems to get worse day by day.
RAGNAR (*Coming closer to his father*): You should go home, Father. Try to get a little sleep.

BROVIK (*Impatiently*): Back to bed, eh? You really want me to suffocate?

KAJA: Then take a little walk. . . .

RAGNAR: Yes, do that. I'll go with you.

BROVIK (*Violently*): No! I won't leave until he comes back. I'll choke if I don't speak up to him, to the boss himself!

KAJA (*Anxiously*): Oh no, Uncle, wait awhile with that.

RAGNAR: Yes, better wait, Father.

BROVIK (*Breathing with difficulty*): I haven't much time to wait!

KAJA (*Listening*): Sh! He's coming!

(*The three go back to work. There is a short silence.* HALVARD SOLNESS, *the Master Builder, enters from the hall door. He is a middle-aged man of strong health and vigorous physique, with short, wavy hair and dark moustache and eyebrows. He wears a buttoned-up, gray-green jacket with a turned-up collar and wide lapels. On his head he wears a soft gray felt hat, and he carries several rolls of drafting plans under his arm.*)

SOLNESS (*At the door, he points to the drafting room and whispers*): Are they gone?

KAJA (*Quietly, shaking her head*): No. (*She takes off the green eye shade.*)

(SOLNESS *enters the room, throws his hat on the chair, puts the plans on the table in front of the couch, and goes to the desk.* KAJA *writes but seems to be ill at ease.*)

SOLNESS (*Out loud*): What are you putting down there, Miss Fosli?

KAJA: Oh, it's just something that—

SOLNESS (*Coming to her*): Let me see, Miss Fosli. (*Bending over her, whispers*) Kaja!

KAJA (*Softly, still writing*): Yes?

SOLNESS: Why do you always take off your shade when I'm here?

KAJA: Because I look so ugly with it on.

SOLNESS: You don't want to be ugly?

KAJA: It's the last thing in the world I want to be, in your eyes.

SOLNESS (*Gently stroking her head*): Poor little Kaja.

KAJA: Sh! They can hear you!

(SOLNESS *crosses the* STAGE RIGHT *and calls into the drafting room.*)

SOLNESS: Has anyone been in to see me?

RAGNAR (*Standing up*): Yes, the young couple from Lovstrand who want you to build their house.

SOLNESS (*Grumbling*): Oh them! Well, they'll just have to wait. I'm not quite sure what I want to do for them yet.

RAGNAR (*Coming closer to* SOLNESS): They're eager to get the plans as soon as possible.

SOLNESS: God knows *everyone* is in a hurry!

BROVIK (*Looking up*): They said they can't wait to get into a place of their own.

SOLNESS: Oh yes, yes, I know all about that. Can't wait! They'll take the first thing that's offered to them, anything to get a place—a stopover—a make-do, but not a home. No thank you! Let them go to someone else. And you can tell them that for me next time they come here.

BROVIK (*Takes his glasses off and stares*): Would you really give this job to someone else?

SOLNESS: Yes, yes, damn it—if that's the way they want it! I'd rather give it away than build it without rhyme or reason. (*With an outburst*) Besides, I don't even know those people yet!

BROVIK: Oh, they're solid enough. Ragnar knows them. He's a friend of the family. They're solid, all right.

SOLNESS: Oh, solid—solid! That's not what I want to know. Good God, you don't understand me either, eh? I won't have anything to do with strangers. As far as I'm concerned, let them go to whomever they please.

BROVIK: Do you really mean that?

SOLNESS: Yes I do, for once!

(BROVIK *exchanges a look with* RAGNAR, *who gives him a gesture of "not now," but* BROVIK *comes into the front room and goes up to* SOLNESS.)

BROVIK: May I speak to you a moment?

SOLNESS: Of course.

BROVIK: Go in the other room, Kaja.

KAJA: Oh please, Uncle—

BROVIK: Do as I say, child, and close the door after you.

(KAJA *goes toward the other room unwillingly. She looks for help from* SOLNESS, *then closes the door.*)

BROVIK (*Half voice*): I don't want the poor child to know how ill I am.

SOLNESS: Yes. Well, you haven't looked too well lately.

BROVIK: Ah, it'll be over soon for me. My strength gives way little by little. I feel weaker every day.

SOLNESS: Sit down awhile.

BROVIK: Thank you, may I?

SOLNESS: Please do—here. Now?

BROVIK: Well, it's about this business with Ragnar—it's such a worry to me. What's to become of my son?

SOLNESS: He'll stay here with me as long as he wants.

BROVIK: But that's just it. It seems he isn't able to stay here any longer.

SOLNESS: Well now, I think that he's been very well taken care of here, but if he should want more money I wouldn't be unwilling to—

BROVIK: No, no! It has nothing to do with money. What Ragnar has to have now is the chance to build something on his own.

SOLNESS: Do you think he's capable of that?

BROVIK: Well you see, that's the frightening thing. I've begun to doubt the boy. In all these years you've never given him one encouraging word, and yet it seems impossible to me that he's had nothing to offer. He *must* have some talent.

SOLNESS: Has he learned anything? Thoroughly, I mean—anything, that is, except drafting?

BROVIK: You didn't know much about the business side, either, when you worked for me, but you went ahead just the same. You scalped me and many others to get up there—up there at the top.

SOLNESS: Yes—well, that's just how things happened to come my way.

BROVIK: You're so right—everything just came your way. But you can't be heartless enough to let me die before I see what Ragnar can build by himself. Then, too, I want to see them married before I die.

SOLNESS: Does she want that?

BROVIK: No, it's not Kaja. It's Ragnar. He talks about it all the time. Please, please, you must help him get some work on his own.

SOLNESS: Damn it, I can't pick jobs out of the blue for him!

BROVIK: He can get one right now, if you'll let him. A big one.

SOLNESS (*Surprised and unnerved*): He can?

BROVIK: All he needs is your approval.

SOLNESS: What kind?

BROVIK: He can build the house out at Lovstrand.

SOLNESS: I'm going to build that one myself!

BROVIK: You don't have much interest in it.

SOLNESS: How dare you say that?

BROVIK: You said it yourself, just now.

SOLNESS: Don't listen to me when I talk that way. Would they let Ragnar build their house?

BROVIK: Yes. He knows the family and just for the fun of it he's drawn up the blueprints, the calculations—everything.

SOLNESS: And are the young couple pleased? Would they want to live in a house he's designed?

BROVIK: Yes! If you'll only study the plans and give your approval, then he could—

SOLNESS: They'd let Ragnar build their home for them?

BROVIK: They like what he's done so far. They said it was something completely new. It seemed to them to be in all ways—

SOLNESS: New! Not the old-fashioned rubbish I usually build, eh?

BROVIK: They thought it was something different.

SOLNESS (*Bursting out*): So they came here to see Ragnar while I was out!

BROVIK: They came here to see you, to ask you if you'd be willing to back out.

SOLNESS: Back out?

BROVIK: If they find Ragnar's plans more—

SOLNESS: —Back out for your son!

BROVIK: From the original agreement, I meant.

SOLNESS: It's the same thing! (*Smiling bitterly*) Well then, Halvard Solness shall now begin backing out, giving room to the young ones—to babies, perhaps! Just move over, make room. Room!

BROVIK: Good God, there must be room for more than one!

SOLNESS: So now, suddenly, there isn't enough room here, eh? Well, this is the way it's going to be—I'm not going to back out for anyone. Never!

BROVIK: Then you want me to die without any pride or faith in my son? Without the happiness of seeing a single building of his own making? Is that what you want?

SOLNESS (*Turns and mumbles*): Let's not talk about it any more.

BROVIK: No! Give me an answer! Am I to die such a pauper? Am I?

SOLNESS (*Seeming to battle with himself. Finally, in a low, firm voice*): You may die as you see fit.

BROVIK (*Crossing to leave*): May *that* be so!

SOLNESS (*Crossing after him, half in desperation*): Don't you understand? I can't do anything about it! That's the way I am, and I can't change myself.

BROVIK: No, no, I suppose you can't. (*Begins to faint but supports himself with the table*) May I have a glass of water?

SOLNESS (*Pouring him a glass of water*): Of course.

BROVIK (*Drinks and puts the glass down*): Thank you.

SOLNESS (*Crosses to the door of the drafting room, opens it, and calls*): Ragnar, come take your father home.

(RAGNAR *and* KAJA *stand quickly. They both come into the front room.*)

RAGNAR: What is it, Father?

BROVIK: Take my arm and let's go.

RAGNAR: Very well. You come too, Kaja.

SOLNESS: Miss Fosli will have to stay a minute. I have a letter that must be written.

BROVIK: Good night. Sleep well, if you can.

SOLNESS: Good night.

(BROVIK *and* RAGNAR *leave through the hall door.* KAJA *crosses to the desk.* SOLNESS *stands with lowered head.*)

KAJA: Is there a letter?

SOLNESS: Of course not. (*Looking sternly at her*) Kaja.

KAJA: Yes.

SOLNESS (*Pointing commandingly at the floor*): Come here. Immediately.

KAJA: Yes.

SOLNESS: Closer.

KAJA: What do you want?

SOLNESS: Are you the one I can thank for all this?

KAJA: No, no, don't think that of me.

SOLNESS: But this getting married—do you want that?

KAJA: Well, we've been engaged for four or five years now, and—

SOLNESS: And so you thought it was about time, is that it?

KAJA: Both Ragnar and my uncle say we should marry, and I'll have to do as they say.

SOLNESS: Kaja, isn't it also true that deep down you like Ragnar a little?

KAJA: Once I liked Ragnar very much, before I came here to you.

SOLNESS: But not any more? Not even a little bit?

KAJA: You know that I'm fond of only one person now. There's no one else in the whole world for me. I'll never care for anyone else.

SOLNESS: Yes, that's what you say, and yet you leave me just the same. Leave me here all alone with all this!

KAJA: Couldn't I stay here with you after Ragnar and I are married?

SOLNESS: No, absolutely not! Besides, if Ragnar leaves me to work on his own, he'll need you.

KAJA: I can't be separated from you! It would be impossible for me.

SOLNESS: Then see to it that Ragnar changes some of his stupid ideas. Marry him as much as you please, but I— (*Changing his voice*) I mean—get him to stay here with me. Then I can keep you here, my dear Kaja.

KAJA: Oh yes, how lovely it would be if it would all work out that way!

SOLNESS (*Holding her head between his hands, whispers*): Because I can't be without you, you know that. I must have you here with me every day.

KAJA: Oh my God, my God!

SOLNESS (*Kissing her hair*): Kaja—Kaja!

KAJA: How good you are to me! How unbelievably good you are!

SOLNESS (*Sternly helping her to her feet*): Stand up! Stand up, for God's sake. I think I heard something.

(KAJA *stumbles to the desk.* MRS. ALINE SOLNESS *enters from the door* RIGHT. *She is thin and wasted, but there are traces of a past beauty in her face. Her blond hair is arranged in long hanging curls and she is elegantly dressed in black. She speaks slowly and in a mournful tone.*)

ALINE: Halvard—

SOLNESS: Oh it's you, my dear?

ALINE: Perhaps I'm intruding.

SOLNESS: Not at all. Miss Fosli just has a short letter to write for me.

ALINE: Yes, I can see that.

SOLNESS: What do you want, Aline?

ALINE: I just want to tell you that Doctor Herdal is in the living room. Perhaps you will join us, Halvard?

SOLNESS: Hmm. Did he want to talk to me about something in particular?

ALINE: No. Nothing urgent. He came by to visit with me, but as long as he's here he would like to see you.

SOLNESS: I might have known. Well then, ask him to wait awhile, please.

ALINE: You'll join us in a few minutes?

SOLNESS: Maybe, maybe, dear—later—in a moment.

ALINE (*As she leaves, closing the door*): Now don't forget, Halvard.

KAJA: Oh dear, I'm sure Mrs. Solness thinks something nasty of me.

SOLNESS: Oh, not at all, my dear. At least not more than usual. But perhaps it would be best if you left now, Kaja.

KAJA: Yes, yes, I must go.

SOLNESS (*Pointedly*): And straighten out that other situation as soon as you can for me. Do you hear me, Kaja?

KAJA: If it were only up to me—

SOLNESS: I said I want it straightened out, and by tomorrow!

KAJA: If I can't do it any other way, I'll call the marriage off.

SOLNESS: Call it off? Are you crazy? You want to call it off?

KAJA: Yes—rather than lose you. I must be close to you. I just can't leave you . . . I just can't . . . I—

SOLNESS: Damn it! What about Ragnar? It's mostly because of him that I want you to—

KAJA (*Staring at him in fright*): It's mostly because of Ragnar— that you—?

SOLNESS (*Controlling himself*): Oh no, of course not. Don't you understand me either? (*Gently*) It's you I want most of all. You of course, Kaja. But because of that you must get Ragnar to stay here and work for me. There, there, now. Go home.

KAJA: Yes. Well, good night then.

SOLNESS: Good night. Oh by the way, are Ragnar's drawings in there?

KAJA: If he hasn't taken them home.

SOLNESS: Get them for me, will you? Maybe I'll look them over after all.

KAJA (*Happily*): Oh yes, please do.

SOLNESS: For your sake, Kaja dear. Now get them quickly!

(KAJA *hurries to the drafting room, searches anxiously in* RAGNAR's *desk, and brings back several rolls of drafting plans.*)

KAJA: Here they are.

SOLNESS: Good. Put them on the table.

KAJA (*Putting down the rolls*): Well, good night again. And Mr. Solness, think kindly of me.

SOLNESS: Ah, I always do, dear little Kaja. (*Glancing at the living room door*) Now go!

(MRS. SOLNESS *and* DR. HERDAL *enter. He is a stoutish, elderly man with a round, friendly face. He has thin, light hair, is clean-shaven, and wears gold-rimmed glasses.*)

ALINE (*From the doorway*): Halvard, I can't keep the Doctor any longer.

SOLNESS: Come in.

ALINE (*To* KAJA, *who is turning down the lamp on the desk*): Finished with the letter, Miss Fosli?

KAJA: The letter?

SOLNESS: Yes, it was a short one.

ALINE: Yes, well—it must have been very short.

SOLNESS: You can go now, Miss Fosli, and be on time again tomorrow.

KAJA (*As she is leaving*): I will. Good night, Mrs. Solness.

ALINE: Halvard, it must be good for you having that girl around.

SOLNESS: Indeed it is. She's useful in many ways.

ALINE: Yes, it looks that way.

DOCTOR: Handy at bookkeeping, too?

SOLNESS: Well, she's learned quite a bit in the two years she's been here. She's always amiable and willing to do whatever is demanded.

ALINE: Yes, that must be a great pleasure.

SOLNESS: It is, especially when one is not accustomed to that kind of response.

ALINE: How can you say that, Halvard?

SOLNESS: Oh dear me, Aline—please forgive me.

ALINE: Think nothing of it. Well then, Doctor, you'll come back later and have tea with us?

DOCTOR: I only have one call to make, and I'll be back.

ALINE: That will be perfect. (*Exits.*)

SOLNESS: Are you in a hurry, Doctor?

DOCTOR: No, not at all.

SOLNESS: Good. I want to talk to you.

DOCTOR: My pleasure.

SOLNESS (*Sits and waves the* DOCTOR *into the rocking chair*): Well then, let's sit down. Tell me, did you notice anything about Aline?

DOCTOR: Just now, you mean?

SOLNESS: Yes. The way she behaved toward me. Did you notice anything?

DOCTOR (*Smiling*): Damn right I did. One couldn't help but notice. She doesn't—uh—

SOLNESS: Well?

DOCTOR: She doesn't seem to be overly fond of this Miss Fosli.

SOLNESS: Yes, yes, I've noticed that myself. Anything else?

DOCTOR: But then, that's not so surprising, is it?

SOLNESS: What?

DOCTOR: No wife exactly enjoys having another woman around her husband all the time.

SOLNESS: It's a situation I can do nothing about.

DOCTOR: Couldn't you hire a male bookkeeper?

SOLNESS: Just anyone who comes along, eh? No thank you. I wouldn't be satisfied with that.

DOCTOR: Not even with things as they are now, with your wife in such—uh—delicate health? Having this girl around all the time seems to be a strain on her.

SOLNESS: By God, that's the way it is, and I'm not going to change it! I must have Kaja Fosli, and I can't use anyone else except her.

DOCTOR: No one else?

SOLNESS: No, no one else.

DOCTOR: Now listen here, my dear Solness. May I be allowed to ask you a question in confidence?

SOLNESS: Yes, go right ahead.

DOCTOR: Well, as you know, women have a damn good intuition, a kind of "scent."

SOLNESS: That they have.

DOCTOR: Now your wife absolutely can't endure this Kaja Fosli—

SOLNESS: So?

DOCTOR: Hasn't she a reason, in a way, for this intense dislike?

SOLNESS: Oh?

DOCTOR: Now don't be offended. Hasn't she?

SOLNESS: No.

DOCTOR: Absolutely no reason whatsoever?

SOLNESS: Only her own suspicions.

DOCTOR: Well, I know that you've known quite a few women in your life—

SOLNESS: Yes, I have.

DOCTOR: And you were fond of every single one of them.

SOLNESS: Yes, I was.

DOCTOR: But with this Miss Fosli there's nothing of that sort going on?

SOLNESS: Nothing whatsoever—from my side.

DOCTOR: From hers, then?

SOLNESS: I don't think you've got the right to ask me about that.

DOCTOR: True. However, we're discussing your wife's "scent."

SOLNESS: That we are. (*Lowering his voice*) And as far as that's concerned, it has proved itself to some degree.

DOCTOR: Is that so?

SOLNESS: Doctor Herdal, I want to tell you a strange story, if you'd like to hear it.

DOCTOR: Good. I'm always eager to hear strange stories.

SOLNESS: Very well, then—you remember I took Knut Brovik and his son into my employ after the old man's business had completely gone downhill.

DOCTOR: I seem to remember something like that.

SOLNESS: The two of them are really quite bright, each in his own way. But one day the son got engaged and wanted to get married and start out on his own. They think in those directions, those young ones.

DOCTOR (*Smiling*): Yes, they all seem to have that bad habit of getting together.

SOLNESS: I didn't want it to happen. I had use for Ragnar myself, and for the old man too. He's very clever at making estimates and calculating bearing-strains and cubic contents —all that technical hocus-pocus.

DOCTOR: Oh yes, that's part of it too, isn't it?

SOLNESS: Indeed it is. Now, Ragnar was determined to build on his own and there was no stopping him.

DOCTOR: But he's still with you!

SOLNESS: Yes, but now just listen to this. One day she came here on an errand—Kaja Fosli. She had never been here before, and when I saw how deeply taken they were with each other the thought struck me: If I could get her to work in my office perhaps Ragnar would stay.

DOCTOR: That was a fairly good conclusion.

SOLNESS: I didn't breathe a word about it to anyone at the time. I just stood and looked at her and wished very strongly inside myself that I had her here—working. I spoke to her in a friendly manner about this and that, and then she left.

DOCTOR: Well?

SOLNESS: The next day toward evening, when old Brovik and Ragnar had gone home, she came here and behaved as if I had made an arrangement with her.

DOCTOR: What kind of arrangement?

SOLNESS: Exactly the kind I'd been wishing for. But remember, I hadn't spoken a word of it to anyone!

DOCTOR: That *is* rather strange.

SOLNESS: Yes, isn't it? She wanted to know what her duties here would be and if she could begin work the next morning.

DOCTOR: Don't you think she did it so she could be here with her sweetheart?

SOLNESS: I thought so at first, but no, it wasn't that way. As soon as she came here she drifted away from him and grew close to me.

DOCTOR: She grew close to you, then?

SOLNESS: Completely. I've noticed that she even feels my gaze if I look at her back. She shivers if I just come near her. What do you think of that?

DOCTOR: Hmm—I could probably explain that.

SOLNESS: But how about the other thing? When she came here that day she actually thought I'd told her what I had only wished secretly inside myself. Can you explain a strange thing like that, Doctor?

DOCTOR: No, and I'd rather not go into it.

SOLNESS: I should have known. That's why I never wanted to talk about it before. But now this situation is such a damn bother day after day, and it's a shame for me to treat little Kaja this way, poor thing. But I can't do otherwise, because if she left me, Ragnar would too.

DOCTOR: And you haven't told your wife any of this?

SOLNESS: No.

DOCTOR: Why in the world haven't you?

SOLNESS: I find a kind of chastisement—like a self-inflicted pain—a penance, really, in letting Aline think this wrong of me.

DOCTOR: I don't understand that kind of reasoning.

SOLNESS: It's almost like paying off an immeasurable debt.

DOCTOR: To your wife?

SOLNESS: Yes, and it always gives my mind a relief. I can breathe freely for a while. Do you understand?

DOCTOR: No, by God, not a single word!

SOLNESS: Well then, let's not talk about it any more. (*There is a short pause. Then* SOLNESS *turns to the* DOCTOR *and looks at him steadily and with a sly smile.*)

SOLNESS: Well, Doctor, I guess you think you caught me a bit off-guard, eh?

DOCTOR: Off-guard? Not in the least, Mr. Solness.

SOLNESS: Oh, just say it right out. I've been very conscious of it.

DOCTOR: Of what?

SOLNESS: Of you—going around here quietly keeping an eye on me.

DOCTOR: Oh I do? Why in the world would I do that?

SOLNESS: You think that I—well, damn it to hell—you think the same as Aline does.

DOCTOR: And what is that?

SOLNESS: She's begun to think that I'm—in a way—in a way—sick.

DOCTOR: Sick? You? Come now, she's never said a single word about anything like that to me. What should be ailing you, my friend?

SOLNESS: Aline believes that I'm mad. Yes, she does.

DOCTOR: Oh come now, Solness!

SOLNESS: Yes, she does, I swear it! And she's made you believe it, too. It's written all over you, Doctor, I can assure you. You see, I'm not so easily fooled.

DOCTOR: Never, Solness! Nothing like that even occurred to me.

SOLNESS: Is that so? Honestly?

DOCTOR: Nor to your wife—I can vouch for her.

SOLNESS: Well, you'd better not do that. She may have a valid reason for believing it.

DOCTOR: Oh really, I must—

SOLNESS: Very well, dear Doctor, let's not get into that. We'll each stay with his own problems. But—

DOCTOR: Yes?

SOLNESS: Since you don't think I'm mad, or anything like that, then you must imagine I'm a very happy man, eh?

DOCTOR: Is that just imagination?

SOLNESS: No—God knows! Just think . . . to be Master Builder Solness! Halvard Solness himself! Well, well, imagine that—that must be something very special!

DOCTOR: It seems you were always unusually lucky.

SOLNESS: I can't complain there.

DOCTOR: To start with, that ugly old barn of a house burned down. That certainly was a stroke of good luck.

SOLNESS: That was Aline's family home, remember?

DOCTOR: Yes—it was a great tragedy for her.

SOLNESS: She's not over it yet, and it's been twelve or thirteen years.

DOCTOR: True. But what followed was the greatest shock for her.

SOLNESS: Yes. One thing right after the other.

DOCTOR: But you—for you it was a springboard! You started out life a poor country boy and now you're the first man in your field. Oh yes indeed, Mr. Solness, you've had good luck on your side.

SOLNESS: That's what tortures me the most.

DOCTOR: Tortures you? Your good luck?

SOLNESS: It terrifies me constantly because someday my luck will change. Won't it?

DOCTOR: Nonsense! What would change it?

SOLNESS: Youth!

DOCTOR: Youth? Nonsense! You're far from being old yourself, and I should think your position here is stronger than ever.

SOLNESS: But the change is coming, Doctor—I sense it. Every day it's coming closer. At first only one or two will begin to demand, "Get out of my way," and then all the rest will burst ahead, threatening me and screaming, "Give room— move over—we want room!" Yes! Just watch out, Doctor. One day Youth will come and knock on the door—

DOCTOR: Well good God, what of it?

SOLNESS: What of it? It'll be the end of Master Builder Solness! (*A knock is heard at the door leading to the outside.*)

SOLNESS: What's that? Did you hear anything?

DOCTOR: Someone's knocking.

SOLNESS (*Calling*): Come in!

(HILDE WANGEL *enters. She is of medium height, with a delicate and trim build. She is lightly suntanned. She wears a complete hiking outfit, with her outer skirt pinned up, a sailor collar open at the neck, and a small sailor hat with a turned-up brim. A carpetbag and a bedroll are strapped on her back, and she carries a long alpine walking stick. She walks over to* SOLNESS *with sparkling eyes.*)

HILDE: Good evening!

SOLNESS (*Looking at her, uncertainly*): Good evening.

HILDE (*Smiling*): I almost think you don't recognize me.

SOLNESS: No—I must admit that for the moment—

DOCTOR: But I recognize you, miss.

HILDE: Oh no! It's you!

DOCTOR: Of course it's me.

HILDE (*To* SOLNESS): We met at a lodge in the mountains this summer.

DOCTOR: Where are all the other ladies?

HILDE: Oh, they took the inland route home.

DOCTOR: I don't think they particularly liked the rumpus we made every night.

HILDE (*Laughing*): No, I don't think they liked that at all!

DOCTOR (*Shaking a warning finger at her*): And you were guilty of flirting with us, too!

HILDE: Well, it was more fun than sitting with those old ladies and knitting.

DOCTOR (*Smiling*): I completely agree with you.

SOLNESS: Did you just get into town this evening?

HILDE: Just now.

DOCTOR: Are you all alone, Miss Wangel?

HILDE: Yes.

SOLNESS: Wangel? Is your name Wangel?

HILDE: Of course.

SOLNESS: Are you from Lysanger? (HILDE *nods yes.*) Are you the Doctor's daughter?

HILDE: Who else?

SOLNESS: Then we've met before, too—the summer I was in your town to build a tower on the old church.

HILDE: Yes.

SOLNESS: Yes. Well, that was a long time ago.

HILDE: Exactly ten years.

SOLNESS: You must have been just a child then.

HILDE (*With pride*): I was twelve or thirteen at least!

DOCTOR: Is this the first time you've been to this town, Miss Wangel?

HILDE: Yes, it is.

SOLNESS: Do you know anyone here?

HILDE: No one except you and—oh yes, your wife.

SOLNESS: Ah, so you know her, too?

HILDE: A little. We were together for a couple of days at the sanitarium.

SOLNESS: Oh, up there.

HILDE: She said I should visit her if I ever came to town, but it wasn't necessary for *her* to tell me.

SOLNESS: Strange . . . she never mentioned it to me.

HILDE (*Leaning the walking stick against the stove, she takes off the carpetbag and bedroll and puts them on the couch. The* DOCTOR *helps her. She crosses to* SOLNESS.): Now. May I stay here overnight?

SOLNESS: That certainly can be arranged, I should think.

HILDE: —Because I haven't any other clothes than the ones I'm wearing. Oh yes, and a change of underwear in my bag. But all that has to be washed. I'm afraid it's all very dirty.

SOLNESS: Oh well, we'll take care of that! I'll just see where my wife is.

DOCTOR: Well, I'm off. I have a call to make.

SOLNESS: You'll be back, won't you?

DOCTOR (*With a playful glance to* HILDE): Yes, yes, damn right I will. (*To* SOLNESS) Your prediction was right after all, Solness.

SOLNESS: What do you mean?

DOCTOR: Youth did come and knock on your door.

SOLNESS: Yes, but in a different way!

DOCTOR: So it was. No question about that.

(DOCTOR HERDAL *leaves through the hall door.* SOLNESS *opens the door leading into the house and calls.*)

SOLNESS: Aline! Will you come in here, please? There's a Miss Wangel in here. You know her.

ALINE (*Entering*): Who did you say it was? (*Seeing* HILDE) Oh, it's you, Miss Wangel. (*Crosses to* HILDE, *extends her hand*) So you came to town after all?

SOLNESS: Miss Wangel has just arrived, and she's asked if she may stay overnight.

ALINE: Here with us? You're more than welcome.

SOLNESS: —To get her clothes and things straightened out.

ALINE: Well, I'll do the best I can. It's only my duty. Will your trunk arrive later?

HILDE: I don't have a trunk.

ALINE: Oh well, we'll work something out. I'll get your room ready. In the meantime you talk to my husband.

SOLNESS: How about one of the nurseries? They're ready to be used.

ALINE: Oh yes. There's plenty of room there. (*To* HILDE) You just sit down now and rest a bit. (*She exits to the* RIGHT.)

(HILDE, *with her hands behind her back, drifts around the room and looks at various things.* SOLNESS, *also with his hands behind his back, watches her movements.*)

HILDE (*Stopping*): Have you more than one nursery?

SOLNESS: There are three of them in this house.

HILDE: That's a lot—you must have quite a few children.

SOLNESS: No. We have no children, but you can be the child for now.

HILDE: All right—for tonight, anyway. And I won't cry. I promise to sleep like a log!

SOLNESS: I should think you'd be awfully tired.

HILDE: Not at all. But when I am, it's so wonderful to lie in bed and dream.

SOLNESS: Do you dream often?

HILDE: Oh yes, almost every night.

SOLNESS: And what do you dream about mostly?

HILDE: I won't tell you that tonight. Later, maybe. (*She paces the room and stops at the desk. She fingers through the papers and the books.*)

SOLNESS: Are you looking for something?

HILDE: No, I'm just looking at all this. (*Turning to him*) Perhaps it's not allowed?

SOLNESS: You're welcome.

HILDE: Do you write in this big book?

SOLNESS: No, she does—the bookkeeper.

HILDE: A woman?

SOLNESS: Yes.

HILDE: Does she work here all the time?

SOLNESS: Yes.

HILDE: Is she married?

SOLNESS: No, she's single.

HILDE: I see.

SOLNESS: But she's getting married soon.

HILDE: Well, that'll be nice for her.

SOLNESS: But not so good for me! I'll have no one to help me then.

HILDE: Can't you find someone else just as good?

SOLNESS: Maybe you'll stay here and write in the big book for me?

HILDE: No, thank you. None of that! There must be better things for me to do around here . . . don't you think?

SOLNESS: Yes, of course. To start with, I should think you'd like to look around the shops and spruce yourself up a bit.

HILDE: No, I think I'll stay away from all that.

SOLNESS: Really?

HILDE: Well, you might just as well know—I've spent all my money.

SOLNESS: Aha! Neither trunk nor money, eh?

HILDE: Neither. But then, things like that don't matter to me anyway.

SOLNESS: Now I really like you for that.

HILDE: Only for that?

SOLNESS: Among other things. Is your father still alive?

HILDE: Yes.

SOLNESS: Are you planning to study here in town?

HILDE: No, I hadn't planned on that.

SOLNESS: But you'll stay here for a while, won't you?

HILDE: That all depends on what happens.

(HILDE *sits for a while looking at him half seriously, half-smiling. She takes off her hat and puts it on the table.*)

HILDE: Master Builder Solness?

SOLNESS: Yes.

HILDE: Are you a very forgetful person?

SOLNESS: Forgetful? Not as far as I know.

HILDE: Then don't you want to talk about what happened the last time we were together?

SOLNESS (*Indifferently*): Up at Lysander? Well, there doesn't seem to be much to talk about.

HILDE: How can you say a thing like that?

SOLNESS: Well then—you tell me about it.

HILDE: When the tower was finished our whole town celebrated!

SOLNESS: Yes, I won't forget that day so easily.

HILDE: You won't? That's nice of you.

SOLNESS: Nice?

HILDE: There were hundreds and hundreds of people and a big band waiting outside the church. We schoolgirls were dressed in white, and we all had little flags in our hands.

SOLNESS: Oh yes, the flags—I remember.

HILDE: You climbed straight up to the top of the tower—right up to the very top. You were carrying a huge wreath, and you flung it over the spire.

SOLNESS: Yes, I used to do that then. It was an old custom.

HILDE: It was so exciting to stand down there and look up at you. I kept imagining what would have happened if you had fallen down—you, the Master Builder himself!

SOLNESS: Yes, and it could have happened that day. One of those little devils dressed in white kept screaming up at me—

HILDE (*Calling out, radiant with happiness*): Hurrah for Master Builder Solness! Hurrah!

SOLNESS: And she kept waving her flag so hard that I—I—well, it made my head spin to look at it.

HILDE: I was that little devil!

SOLNESS: Of course, it must have been you!

HILDE: It was so thrilling, and it frightened me so terribly! In my wildest dreams I could not imagine that there could be a master builder in all the whole world who could build such immeasurably high towers, and then, that he should stand on the very top of them, himself, in the flesh! And that he didn't get the least bit dizzy—it made me dizzy just to think of it.

SOLNESS: How were you so sure I wasn't?

HILDE: Oh, shame on you! Of course you weren't—I knew it inside. Besides, if you *had* been, you couldn't have stood way up there singing.

SOLNESS: Singing? I sang?

HILDE: Yes, indeed you did.

SOLNESS: I never sang a note in my life.

HILDE: Maybe, but you sang that day. It sounded like harp music in the wind.

SOLNESS: There is something mysterious about all this—

HILDE: But then, *after* that came the important thing.

SOLNESS: The important—

HILDE: Yes! But I don't have to remind you of that.

SOLNESS: Oh yes, please do. Remind me a little of that, too—

HILDE: Can't you remember the big dinner that was held in your honor at the club?

SOLNESS: Yes. It was that same evening, wasn't it? I remember leaving the next morning.

HILDE: And after the club you were invited home with us.

SOLNESS: That's quite correct, Miss Wangel! Exrtaordinary how well you have remembered those little details.

HILDE: Little details! Well, that's a good one! Was it only a little detail, then, that I was alone in the house when you arrived?

SOLNESS: Oh?

HILDE: You didn't call me a little devil that night.

SOLNESS: No, I suppose not.

HILDE: You said I was beautiful in my white dress and that I looked like a little princess.

SOLNESS: You did, Miss Wangel. And besides, I felt so happy that night, so light and carefree—

HILDE: And you said that when I grew up I should become your princess.

SOLNESS: Well, well, did I say that? Did I say all that?

HILDE: Yes, you did, and when I asked you how long I should have to wait, you said that you would return in ten years as a troll and take me away to Spain or some place like that. And you promised to buy me a kingdom.

SOLNESS: Well, after a good dinner, one doesn't count the pennies!

HILDE: You also told me what my kingdom should be called.

SOLNESS: Is that so?

HILDE: You said it should be called the "Kingdom of the Orange."

SOLNESS: Well, that was an appetizing name!

HILDE: I didn't like it. It sounded as if you were making fun of me.

SOLNESS: That wasn't my intention—

HILDE: I know, particularly after what you did next.

SOLNESS: What in the world did I do next?

HILDE: Well, that's the last straw, if you've forgotten that! You've just got to remember things like that.

SOLNESS: Well, give me a little hint, then maybe—

HILDE: You kissed me, Master Builder Solness.

SOLNESS: I did?

HILDE: Yes, you did. You took me in your arms and bent me back and kissed me. Many times.

SOLNESS: But my dear Miss Wangel—!

HILDE: You don't deny it, do you?

SOLNESS: Yes, I certainly do!

HILDE (*Looking scornfully at him*): Well, then. (*She walks to the stove, remains motionless, hands behind her back. There is a short silence.*)

SOLNESS (*Crossing to her, cautiously*): Miss Wangel—
   (HILDE *remains motionless.*)

SOLNESS: Don't stand there like a statue. You must have dreamed all this! (*Putting his hand on her arm*) Now listen to me. (HILDE *moves her arm away from his touch.*)

SOLNESS: Ah, wait a minute! Perhaps there's something else here—something much deeper. Eh? I must have thought all this, I must have wanted it to happen—wished it—actually willed it to happen, and it did! Perhaps that explains it.
   (HILDE *remains silent.*)

SOLNESS (*Impatiently*): Yes, yes, damn it all—then I did do it?

HILDE: Finally you're admitting it.

SOLNESS: Yes, whatever you want.

HILDE: That you took me in your arms?

SOLNESS: Yes.

HILDE: And bent me back?

SOLNESS (*Enjoying the game by now*): Very far back.

HILDE: And kissed me?

SOLNESS: Yes, yes I did!

HILDE: Many times?

SOLNESS: As many as you want!

HILDE: Well, I finally got it out of you!

SOLNESS: Can you imagine I could have forgotten a thing like that!

HILDE: Oh, I suppose you've kissed so many girls in your life.

SOLNESS: You mustn't think that of me. (*After a short pause, looking intently at her*) Miss Wangel?

HILDE: Yes?

SOLNESS: Did anything else happen between us?

HILDE: You know very well nothing else happened. Just then the other guests arrived, and so—

SOLNESS: Yes, that's right, the others arrived. How did I forget that, too?

HILDE: Ah, you didn't forget anything. Maybe you're just a little ashamed, but one doesn't forget things like that.

SOLNESS: You wouldn't think so, anyway!

HILDE: Have you also forgotten what day it was?

SOLNESS: What day?

HILDE: Yes. What day was it when you put the wreath on the church tower? Well? Tell me—quickly!

SOLNESS: Hmm. The very day? Well, I must admit I've forgotten that. I only know it was ten years ago, early in the autumn.

HILDE (*Nodding several times*): It was ten years ago, the nineteenth of September.

SOLNESS: Yes, it must have been around that time. You see, you remember that too? Wait a minute—yes! Today is the nineteenth of September!

HILDE: And ten years have passed. You didn't come for me as you promised.

SOLNESS: Promised? Threatened, you mean!

HILDE: I didn't think it was a threat.

SOLNESS: It wasn't. I was just having some fun with you, I suppose.

HILDE: Was that what you were doing? Having some fun with me?

SOLNESS: A little, yes. Or maybe I was playing a little game— God help me, I don't remember! It must have been something like that. You were only a child.

HILDE: Or maybe I wasn't such a child. At least not the babe in arms you took me for.

SOLNESS: Did you honestly believe I'd return?

HILDE: Yes I did! I expected you to keep your word.

SOLNESS: That I'd come to your home and carry you away?

HILDE: Yes, exactly like a troll.

SOLNESS: And make you into a princess?

HILDE: Wasn't that what you promised?

SOLNESS: And that I'd give you a kingdom, too?

HILDE: Why not? It didn't have to be an ordinary kingdom.

SOLNESS: But something just as good?

HILDE: Yes, at the very least. I used to think that if you could build the highest church tower in the world, you'd surely be able to create some kind of kingdom for me.

SOLNESS: I can't quite figure you out, Miss Wangel.

HILDE: Can't you? It seems simple enough to me.

SOLNESS: I can't be sure if you're serious or if you're—

HILDE: Just having some fun with you, perhaps?

SOLNESS: Yes, exactly! When did you find out I was married?

HILDE: I knew that from the beginning. Why do you ask me that?

SOLNESS: No special reason—it just occurred to me. Why have you come here?

HILDE: I want my kingdom, Master Builder. Your time of grace is up.

SOLNESS (*Smiling*): Well, aren't you something!

HILDE: Give me my kingdom, Master Builder! My kingdom on the table!

SOLNESS: Honestly, now, why have you come here? What do you want?

HILDE: Oh, to start with, first thing tomorrow I'll go around the town and see all the things you've built.

SOLNESS: That'll give you plenty of running around.

HILDE: Yes, you've built so much!

SOLNESS: And most of it in the last few years.

HILDE: Many church towers? Unbelievably high?

SOLNESS: No. I don't build church towers any more. No churches, either.

HILDE: Then what do you build?

SOLNESS: Homes for people.

HILDE: Don't you build towers on them?

SOLNESS: What do you mean?

HILDE: I mean something that points straight up in the air with a huge spire on top—high, high up!

SOLNESS: Strange that you say that. That's precisely what I want to do most of all.

HILDE: Why don't you, then?

SOLNESS: People don't want them any more. It's not fashionable.

HILDE: Imagine—they don't want them.

SOLNESS: But I'm building myself a new home. It's almost finished and it has a tower.

HILDE: A high tower?

SOLNESS: Yes.

HILDE: Very high?

SOLNESS: People will say it's too high for a house.

HILDE: Well! I'll look at that tower the very first thing.

SOLNESS: Tell me, Miss Wangel, what's your name? Your first name, I mean.

HILDE: Hilde.

SOLNESS: Hilde? Oh.

HILDE: You don't remember that? You called me Hilde that day when you were naughty.

SOLNESS: Did I?

HILDE: But you said "little Hilde" then, and I didn't like that.

SOLNESS: Oh, so you didn't like that, Miss Hilde?

HILDE: No, not then. And yet . . . "Princess Hilde." That will sound quite impressive, don't you think?

SOLNESS: Very impressive! Princess Hilde of, of—what was the name of that kingdom again?

HILDE: Oh, that silly old kingdom! I don't want to have anything to do with that one—I want quite a different one now!

SOLNESS: Strange, isn't it? The more I think of it now, the more it seems to me that I've tormented myself for years with . . .

HILDE: With what?

SOLNESS: . . . with trying to remember something that happened once, something I've half forgotten and have never been able to grasp entirely. I often wondered what it could have been.

HILDE: You should have tied a string around your finger, Master Builder.

SOLNESS: I would have wondered all these years what the string meant!

HILDE: Well, it takes all kinds of trolls to make a world!

SOLNESS: It's a good thing that you have come to me now.

HILDE: Is it good?

SOLNESS: I've been so alone here. Sometimes I sit gazing helplessly at everything around me. (*Slowly*) I want you to know something. I'm beginning to be afraid—so dreadfully afraid of youth.

HILDE: Pooh! Is youth anything to be afraid of?

SOLNESS: Yes, it is. That's why I've locked myself in. (*Mysteriously*) One day Youth will come and pound on my door and break into my place.

HILDE: I should think you'd go unlock your door for them.

SOLNESS: Unlock the door?

HILDE: Yes—so that Youth can be allowed in here with you, in friendship.

SOLNESS: No, no, no! Youth will come in here to judge me, and it will be my doom! Don't you see? They're taking the place up front and they'll march under a new banner.

HILDE: Can I be of any use to you, Master Builder?

SOLNESS: Indeed you can. It seems to me that you, too, have come in here under a new banner. Youth against Youth.

(DOCTOR HERDAL *enters through the hall door.*)

DOCTOR: Well, I see you and the young lady are still here.

SOLNESS: Yes. We had many things to talk about, the two of us.

HILDE: Both old and new.

DOCTOR: Oh did you?

HILDE: It's been so very pleasant. You see, Mr. Solness has such an unbelievable memory. He remembers things down to the smallest detail.

ALINE (*Entering from the door* RIGHT): Your room is ready, Miss Wangel.

HILDE: How very kind you are!

SOLNESS (*To* ALINE): The nursery?

ALINE: Yes, the middle one. But first let's all go in and—

SOLNESS (*Nodding to* HILDE): And Hilde? She's going to sleep in the nursery—so there!

ALINE: Hilde?

SOLNESS: Yes, Miss Wangel's first name is Hilde. I knew her when she was just a little girl.

ALINE: Oh did you, Halvard? Well, won't you all please come in? The tea is served. (*She exits with the* DOCTOR.)

HILDE (*Holding all her belongings, speaks softly and rapidly*): Is it true what you said? Can I really be of any use to you?

SOLNESS (*Taking her things from her*): It's true. You are the very thing I've been missing.

HILDE (*Looks at him happily and claps her hands*): But then— sweet heaven!

SOLNESS: Then what?

HILDE: Then I have my kingdom . . .

SOLNESS: Hilde.

HILDE: . . . almost!


CURTAIN

# ACT II

*An attractively decorated, medium-sized drawing room in* SOLNESS'
*house. On the* UPSTAGE *wall is a door leading to a porch and garden.
At* STAGE RIGHT *there is a bay window on the diagonal, with many
flowers in pots on the window sills. In front of the window is a
small table with chairs.* DOWNSTAGE *from it there is a door; farther
down, a console table with a large mirror over it. There are cut
flowers and plants in profusion on both tables. The* STAGE LEFT *wall
is also on the diagonal.* UPSTAGE *from it there are bookshelves;*
DOWNSTAGE, *a flush door covered with matching wallpaper, and
farther down from it, another door. At* STAGE LEFT *are a couch, a
table, and some chairs.*

AS THE CURTAIN RISES, SOLNESS *is seated at the small table looking at*
RAGNAR BROVIK'S *plans, which are spread out in front of him. He
studies the plans and stops occasionally to scrutinize one of them.*
MRS. SOLNESS *walks silently around with a small watering can, taking
care of the flowers. She is dressed in black. Her hat, coat, and parasol
are on the chair near the mirror.* SOLNESS *looks at her several times
without her noticing. Neither speaks.* KAJA FOSLI *enters quietly
from the door* LEFT.

🔥

SOLNESS (*Turns his head and speaks in an off-hand manner*):
  Oh, it's you.
KAJA: I only want to report that I'm here.
SOLNESS: Yes, yes, that's good. Is Ragnar here, too?
KAJA: No, not yet. He had to stay and wait for the doctor, but
  he'll be here soon.
SOLNESS: How is the old man today?
KAJA: Not well at all. He's very sorry and wants to apologize for
  having to stay in bed today.

SOLNESS: By all means let him rest. Now get to your work.

KAJA: Yes. (*Stopping at the door*) Do you want to talk to Ragnar when he gets in?

SOLNESS: No—I haven't anything particular to say to him.

(KAJA *exits* LEFT. SOLNESS *goes back to studying the drawings.*)

ALINE: God knows, he'll probably die, too.

SOLNESS: What do you mean, "too"? Who else?

ALINE (*Not answering*): Yes, old Brovik. I'm sure he's going to die too. You'll see, Halvard.

SOLNESS: Aline, dear, shouldn't you go out for a little walk?

ALINE (*Not stopping her work*): Yes, I suppose I should.

SOLNESS: Is she still asleep?

ALINE: You mean Miss Wangel? Are you sitting there thinking about her?

SOLNESS (*Indifferently*): I just happened to remember her.

ALINE: Miss Wangel has been up for a long time.

SOLNESS: Has she?

ALINE (*Slowly starting to put on her hat*): I looked in on her and she was straightening out her things.

SOLNESS (*After a short pause*): So we found some use for the nursery after all, eh?

ALINE: Yes, so we did.

SOLNESS: Well, it's better than having them all empty.

ALINE: You're right. The emptiness is dreadful.

SOLNESS (*Puts the plans aside, goes to her*): You'll see, Aline, from now on things will be better for us—much better. Life is going to be easier, especially for you.

ALINE (*Looking directly at him*): From now on?

SOLNESS: Yes, you'll see—you'll see.

ALINE: Do you mean because *she's* here?

SOLNESS: I mean when we move into the new house.

ALINE (*Taking her coat*): And you believe that, Halvard? That it'll be better then?

SOLNESS: I won't believe anything else, and I'm sure you think so too.

ALINE: I just don't think about the new house at all.

SOLNESS (*Dejectedly*): It's upsetting to hear you say that. It was mostly for you that I built it. (*Offers to help her with her coat*)

ALINE (*Moving away from his help*): You really do far, far too much for me, Halvard.

SOLNESS (*Vehemently*): Don't talk that way, Aline! I can't bear to hear things like that from you.

ALINE: Very well, then, I won't talk that way, Halvard.

SOLNESS: Just trust me—you'll see! Everything will come out all right in the new place.

ALINE: Oh God—everything all right—for me!

SOLNESS (*Enthusiastically*): Yes—yes! I can assure you of that. You won't believe how many things there will remind you of your own things.

ALINE: All those things that were father's and mother's and all of them burned up—all of them!

SOLNESS: There, there, poor Aline. It was such a dreadful blow for you.

ALINE: You can build from here to doomsday, Halvard, but you'll never build another real home for me.

SOLNESS: Then, for God's sake, let's not talk about it any more!

ALINE: Very well then, as usual we won't discuss it. You always avoid it.

SOLNESS: Do I? Now why should I avoid talking about it?

ALINE: Oh I understand you so well, Halvard. You want to spare me . . . yes, and excuse me, too, whenever possible.

SOLNESS (*Surprised*): I want to excuse you? You?

ALINE: Yes. Who else? I *must* be the one.

SOLNESS (*To himself*): That too!

ALINE: Because as far as the old house is concerned, why, that was fate! Good God, once misfortune had struck, there was nothing for us to do.

SOLNESS: That's very true. Misfortune is not man's doing, so they say.

ALINE: And the dreadful thing that happened after the fire, that was the worst—that—that—

SOLNESS: Don't think about it, Aline.

ALINE: But I must think about it—and talk about it, too, for once! I can't keep quiet any longer, Halvard. I can't bear my own silence, and I know I'll never forgive myself if I don't speak out.

SOLNESS: Forgive yourself?

ALINE: Yes, myself. I had duties on both sides. Both to you and to the babies, but I should have made myself hard and strong and not let fear overpower me—and grief. Yes, grief for the old home that had burned down. Oh Halvard, if I'd only had the strength; if I'd been able to—

SOLNESS: Aline, please don't. Promise me that you'll never think about all this again. Please promise me that.

ALINE: Promise? Oh God—promise! What good would that do?

SOLNESS: How desperate we are! Never a ray of sunlight, never so much as a glimmer of light in this home!

ALINE: This is not a home, Halvard.

SOLNESS: You're right about that, and God knows you're probably right about how things will be in the new house, too.

ALINE: Nothing will change. It will be just as empty—just as desolate there as here.

SOLNESS: Then why in the world have we built it? Can you tell me that?

ALINE: You must find the answer to that yourself.

SOLNESS: What are you getting at, Aline?

ALINE: What am I getting at?

SOLNESS: Yes, damn it! You meant something just then—something else. You had some ulterior motive.

ALINE: No, I assure you.

SOLNESS: Well, thank you very much for that, at least. But I know what I know, Aline, and I can see and hear, too. You can be sure of that.

ALINE: What do you mean?

SOLNESS: Now don't deny it. You have a way of finding hidden meanings in my most innocent remarks—in anything I happen to say.

ALINE: I do that to you? Well!

SOLNESS: Oh yes. Yes, but then, of course, it's understandable with you, Aline—you have to deal with a sick man.

ALINE: Sick! Are you sick, Halvard?

SOLNESS: A halfway insane man, then. Call me whatever you want!

ALINE: Halvard, for God's sake, I—

SOLNESS: But you're mistaken, both of you. You as well as the Doctor! When you come right down to it, there's nothing in the world wrong with me—nothing!

ALINE: Of course not.

SOLNESS: Just sometimes—sometimes I feel that I'll fold up under the weight of this dreadful debt.

ALINE: You're not in debt to anyone, are you, Halvard?

SOLNESS: I am in boundless debt to you, Aline.

ALINE: What do you mean by that? Now don't beat around the bush, Halvard. Tell me at once.

SOLNESS: I've never done you any harm, Aline—not knowingly, anyway, not intentionally. And yet I carry a heart-sickening guilt toward you that is pressing me down, crushing me.

ALINE: Guilt toward me?

SOLNESS: Mostly toward you.

ALINE: Then you *are* sick, Halvard, very sick.

SOLNESS: I might be, in a way.

(HILDE *enters, looking washed and bright. She has changed her dress and let the skirt down.*)

SOLNESS: Ah! Some light is breaking through!

HILDE: Good morning, Master Builder.

SOLNESS: Sleep well?

HILDE: Wonderfully well! As if I were in a cradle. I lay there and stretched out like a—a princess.

SOLNESS: Everything as you wanted it—eh?

HILDE: Very much so.

SOLNESS: And did you dream?

HILDE: Yes I did, but the dream was dreadful.

SOLNESS: Was it?

HILDE: Yes. I dreamed I fell down an awfully steep mountain-side. Do you ever dream things like that?

SOLNESS: Oh yes, from time to time.

HILDE: It's terribly exciting when you're sailing down and down—

SOLNESS: It makes the blood run cold.

HILDE: Do you tuck your legs up under you while it's happening?

SOLNESS: Yes, as tight as I can.

HILDE: Me too!

ALINE (*Taking her parasol*): I'd better go now. I'll look for a few things you might need.

HILDE: Oh dear, sweet Mrs. Solness, you are much too kind to me, really!

ALINE: Not at all. It's my duty; that's why I'm more than happy to do it.

HILDE: Now that I think of it, there's no reason why I shouldn't go myself. I look all right, don't I?

ALINE: Quite honestly, I think some people would stare.

HILDE: Just stare? That might be fun!

SOLNESS: But people might think you were just a bit mad, too.

HILDE: Mad? Oh, are there *that* many mad people in this town?

SOLNESS (*Pointing to his forehead*): Yes. And you see one of them here.

HILDE: You, Master Builder?

ALINE: For God's sake, Halvard!

SOLNESS: Haven't you noticed it yet?

HILDE: No, I haven't. Oh yes! Perhaps I have—in one thing.

SOLNESS: Well, well—did you hear that, Aline?

ALINE: And what is that one thing, Miss Wangel?

HILDE: No—I won't tell you that.

SOLNESS: Oh yes, please do!

HILDE: No thank you. I'm not that mad!

ALINE: When you and Miss Wangel are left alone she'll probably tell you, Halvard.

SOLNESS: You think so?

ALINE: Of course. Remember—you told me you've known her ever since she was a child. (*Exits.*)

HILDE: Your wife can't stand me, can she?

SOLNESS: Why. Did you notice anything?

HILDE: Didn't you notice it yourself?

SOLNESS: Aline has become very withdrawn these last few years.

HILDE: Oh? Has she?

SOLNESS: If you'd only get the opportunity to really know her— She's so kind and good, such a solid person deep down.

HILDE: Is she? Then why did she say that about duty?

SOLNESS: Duty?

HILDE: Yes. She said she'd do some shopping for me because it was her *duty*. I can't bear that disgusting word!

SOLNESS: Why not?

HILDE: It sounds so cold and austere. Don't you think so? Duty, duty. Doesn't that word almost stab you?

SOLNESS: Well now, I can't say I've given it that much thought.

HILDE: Oh well, then. You tell me she's so kind and everything. Why should she say a thing like that?

SOLNESS: But good God, what should she have said?

HILDE: She could have said that she wanted to do it for me because she liked me so much, or something like that. Something warm and sincere.

SOLNESS: Is that how you want things to be?

HILDE: Oh yes, indeed! (*She wanders about the room, looking at bookshelves.*) You have a great many books here.

SOLNESS: Yes, I've collected quite a few.

HILDE: Do you read them all?

SOLNESS: In the beginning I used to try. Do you read much?

HILDE: Never any more. I can't find anything coherent in any of it.

SOLNESS: Ah—my feelings exactly.

HILDE (*Wandering around the room*): Did you do all these drawings?

SOLNESS: No. A young man who is my helper did them.

HILDE: Your apprentice?

SOLNESS: Well, yes, he *is* an apprentice in a way. I suppose he has learned something from me.

HILDE: Then I suppose by now he's very bright and clever. Is he?

SOLNESS: Not particularly. But then, I use him in such a way that he seems—

HILDE: I knew it! He must be very clever.

SOLNESS: Can you tell from his drawings?

HILDE: Oh—that rubbish! But if he's been studying with you, why then—he—

SOLNESS: Ha! There have been many who've studied with me and who've managed to remain unskilled and unsuccessful, as far as that goes.

HILDE: No! If I had to stake my life on it, I wouldn't believe you could be so stupid.

SOLNESS: Stupid?

HILDE: If you're willing to teach all these young fellows and—

SOLNESS: And why not?

HILDE: Oh no, no Master Builder Solness! What good is that? No one else but you should be allowed to build. You alone should do it, and you should do all of it by yourself. There— I've said it!

SOLNESS: Hilde.

HILDE: Well?

SOLNESS: How in the world did you start thinking like that?

HILDE: Why? Was it wrong of me?

SOLNESS: No, not at all. But now, I'll tell you something.

HILDE: What?

SOLNESS: I've lived here so long, alone and silent, and all the time my mind was filled with that very same thought.

HILDE: Well, that seems reasonable to me.

SOLNESS: Then you have noticed—eh?

HILDE: No, I haven't noticed anything.

SOLNESS: But before, you said that you thought I was mad in a way.

HILDE: Oh, I was thinking of something quite different.

SOLNESS: What was it?

HILDE: I don't think you'd be interested.

SOLNESS: No? Well, as you wish. Come here—I'll show you something.

HILDE: What is it?

SOLNESS (*At the window*): You see there—over there past the garden?

HILDE: Yes.

SOLNESS: Just above the stone quarry?

HILDE: You mean that new house?

SOLNESS: Yes, the one that's almost finished.

HILDE: It looks as if it has a very high tower.

SOLNESS: The scaffolding is still up.

HILDE: Is that your new house?

SOLNESS: Yes.

HILDE: The one you're moving into?

SOLNESS: Yes.

HILDE: And are there nurseries in that house too?

SOLNESS: Yes, three—the same as there are here.

HILDE: And no children.

SOLNESS: And never will be.

HILDE: Well, it's just as I said, then.

SOLNESS: What?

HILDE: You are just a bit mad.

SOLNESS: Then that's what you were referring to!

HILDE: Yes—all your empty nurseries, like the one I slept in.

SOLNESS: We had children, Aline and I.

HILDE: You did?

SOLNESS: Two boys the same age.

HILDE: Twins?

SOLNESS: Yes, twins. It was eleven—twelve years ago.

HILDE: And both of them are . . . you don't have the twins any more?

SOLNESS: We only had them for two weeks, and hardly that. Oh Hilde, I can't believe my good fortune that you came here! Finally, I have someone I can talk to.

HILDE: Can't you talk to her?

SOLNESS: Not about this—not the way I want to. (*Continuing ponderously*) And that's true about most subjects.

HILDE: Was that the only thing you meant when you said you needed me?

SOLNESS: Yesterday it was. It was the most urgent thing. Today, I'm not so sure. Come here and let's sit down, Hilde. You sit here on the couch so you can see the view over the garden. Do you feel like listening to something?

HILDE: Yes, I like sitting here and listening to you.

SOLNESS: Then I shall tell you all of it.

HILDE: I have both the garden and you before my eyes, Master Builder. Now tell me things, quickly.

SOLNESS: Over there on the hill where you see the new house . . .

HILDE: Yes.

SOLNESS: . . . that is where Aline and I lived the first years of our married life. There was an old house up there that once belonged to her mother. We inherited it from her—the house and a huge garden.

HILDE: Was there a tower on that house too?

SOLNESS: Not a sign of anything like that. It was a large, ugly, wooden box from the outside, but inside it was warm and friendly.

HILDE: Did you tear down the old rubbish?

SOLNESS: No, it burned down.

HILDE: All of it?

SOLNESS: Yes.

HILDE: Was it a terrible misfortune for you?

SOLNESS: That depends on how you look at it. I became a master builder because of that fire.

HILDE: Oh?

SOLNESS: The two boys had just been born—

HILDE: The poor little twins—yes—

SOLNESS: They came into the world healthy and full of life, and they grew so much from day to day that I could almost see it.

HILDE: Yes, babies grow so fast the first couple of days.

SOLNESS: It was the most beautiful sight in the whole world to see Aline lying there with the two of them on either side of her. Then that night came—the night of the fire.

HILDE: Oh tell me what happened! Was anyone burned in it?

SOLNESS: No. Everyone was rescued from the house.

HILDE: Well then, what happened?

SOLNESS: The fright put Aline into a state of shock—the smell of the smoke, the alarm, leaving the flaming house, and then being exposed to the ice-cold air. To make things worse, they were all carried out just as they lay there in bed, Aline and the babies.

HILDE: And they couldn't endure the cold weather?

SOLNESS: No, it wasn't that. Aline caught a fever and it affected her milk. She insisted upon feeding the babies herself—it was her duty, she said. So both our little boys—oh!

HILDE: They didn't survive?

SOLNESS: No. That's how they were taken from us.

HILDE: It must have been terribly difficult for you.

SOLNESS: Yes, but it was ten times worse for Aline. To think that something that horrible can actually happen in this world! From that day on I built churches with more and more reluctance.

HILDE: And now you won't build a church tower like the one we have in our town?

SOLNESS: No, never again. I remember how happy and relieved I was when that tower was finished.

HILDE: I know that.

SOLNESS: Now I only build homes for people, Hilde.

HILDE: But homes with high towers and spires?

SOLNESS: Yes, possibly.

HILDE: Why don't you call yourself an architect as the others do?

SOLNESS: I haven't studied enough for that. What I know I've found out for myself.

HILDE: But nevertheless, you are a master builder!

SOLNESS: Thanks to the fire, I am. When the house was destroyed, I took most of the garden and laid it out in lots for a housing project. I had the freedom to build as I wanted, and it all went very smoothly for me. My success was sure and fast.

HILDE: You must be a very happy man with things as they are now.

SOLNESS: Happy? Are you going to say that, too, like everybody else?

HILDE: Well, it seems to me you should be happy. —If you'd stop thinking about the babies.

SOLNESS: The two boys— Ah, it's not so easy to get away from them, Hilde.

HILDE: Does their loss still torment you after so many years?

SOLNESS (*Staring at her*): You think I should be a happy man, Hilde?

HILDE: Yes, in some respects.

SOLNESS: When I told you all about the fire . . .

HILDE: Yes?

SOLNESS: . . . was there one thought in particular that stayed with you?

HILDE: No. Should there have been?

SOLNESS: Do you remember that I said it was only because of the fire that I was able to build those homes for people? Well, I built friendly, comfortable, lovely homes where fathers and mothers and a whole flock of children could live in safety and happiness together, with a feeling of what a wonderful thing it is to be alive in this world and to belong to each other—in the big things as well as in the small things.

HILDE: Isn't it a source of great happiness for you to know that you created these beautiful homes?

SOLNESS: Yes, but the price, Hilde! The dreadful price I had to pay!

HILDE: There must be some way you can make the best of it.

SOLNESS: No. In order to get the chance to build homes for others, I had to give up for all time the building of a home for myself—I mean a home for children and a father and a mother.

HILDE: Did you have to give it up forever?

SOLNESS: That was the price of my happiness. Happiness—ha! It didn't come cheap.

HILDE: Couldn't things be better now?

SOLNESS: Never. Never in this life. That's another repercussion of the fire. That, and Aline's illness.

HILDE: And still you build nurseries.

SOLNESS: Ah! Have you never noticed how the impossible always beckons us, Hilde?

HILDE: The impossible—oh yes! Do you feel that, too?

SOLNESS: Yes, I do.

HILDE: Then there is some of the troll in you after all!

SOLNESS: Why troll?

HILDE: Well, what do you call it, then?

SOLNESS: Perhaps you're right. Perhaps there is some troll in me after all. Things have always happened to me so strangely.

HILDE: How do you mean?

SOLNESS: Listen carefully to what I'm going to tell you, Hilde. Everything I've ever desired or created, everything I've ever built for either beauty or comfort or security—yes, all my artistic achievements— Oh—it's dreadful to think of!

HILDE: What?

SOLNESS: —I've had to weigh them on a scale and pay for them. Not with money but with human happiness, and not only mine but with the happiness of others. Can you see that, Hilde? That is the price my position as an artist has cost me and those dear to me. Every single day I live I have to pay the price all over again, and again, and again.

HILDE: Now you're thinking of her.

SOLNESS: Yes, mostly of Aline. She had her vocation in life, too, you know, just as I had mine. But it had to be pushed aside, crushed and thwarted, so that mine could move forward to a kind of great victory. You must know, Hilde, that she too had a talent for building.

HILDE: She did?

SOLNESS: Not for the things that I slave away at—houses with towers and spires—

HILDE: For what, then?

SOLNESS: She built children's souls, Hilda. She built them up so that they could grow in perfect balance to be noble and beautiful and elevate themselves into erect, mature souls. That was Aline's talent, but she let it go fallow and now it lies wasted. It's of no worldly use to anyone, like the heap of burned out ashes after a fire.

HILDE: Even if this were true—

SOLNESS: It is! It's true all right.

HILDE: But you're not responsible for it!

SOLNESS: Well, that is the horrifying question—the question that gnaws away at me day and night.

HILDE: Only that?

SOLNESS: Suppose I was in a way responsible for what happened?

HILDE: For the fire?

SOLNESS: For all of it! And then suppose that I was completely innocent at the same time.

HILDE: Oh, Master Builder, when you talk like that you *do* sound mad after all.

SOLNESS: Hmm. Perhaps on this one point I'll never get my mental balance.

(RAGNAR BROVIK *quietly enters from the* LEFT.)

RAGNAR: Oh, excuse me, Mr. Solness. (*He starts to leave.*)

SOLNESS: No, no—stay a minute, now that you're here. Let's get it over with.

RAGNAR: Yes, if we only could.

SOLNESS: I hear your father is not much better.

RAGNAR: He's getting worse. That's why I've come to ask this of you. Please write a few words—something kind or complimentary—on one of my drawings so that father can read it before he—

SOLNESS (*Vehemently*): Don't talk to me again about your drawings!

RAGNAR: Have you looked at them?

SOLNESS: Yes, I have.

RAGNAR: And they're not worth much? Then I'm worthless, too.

SOLNESS: Stay here with me, Ragnar, and you can have things just the way you want them. You'll marry Kaja and live without a care, perhaps even happily. Just don't expect to build on your own.

RAGNAR: Yes. Now I have to go home to father and tell him what you said. I promised him I would. Is this what you want me to tell him before he dies?

SOLNESS: Oh, tell him—tell him whatever you want. As far as I'm concerned, it doesn't matter. Say anything to him—good God, Ragnar, I can't act any other way!

RAGNAR: May I at least take the drawings with me?

SOLNESS: Yes, take them. Just take them away. They're over there on the table.

RAGNAR: Thank you.

HILDE: No. No, leave them here.

SOLNESS: Why?

HILDE: I want to look at them.

SOLNESS: But you've already looked at—well, leave them, then.

RAGNAR: I will be happy to.

SOLNESS: And go home to your father immediately.

RAGNAR: Yes—I've got to.

SOLNESS: Ragnar, you mustn't make impossible demands of me. You must not ask for things you know I can't give you. Do you understand? You simply must not.

RAGNAR: No, no. Forgive me. (*He exits* DOWNSTAGE RIGHT.)

HILDE: That was very nasty of you. Very ugly.

SOLNESS: You think so too?

HILDE: Yes, very. It was disgusting and cruel and evil.

SOLNESS: Of course you'd say that. You can't know how I feel.

HILDE: Just the same, you shouldn't behave like that.

SOLNESS: You said yourself I was the only one who should be allowed to build.

HILDE: It's all right for me to say things like that, but you mustn't.

SOLNESS: I most of all should be able to say and do these things, since I am the one who has paid the price.

HILDE: Oh yes, with a little domestic comfort—or something like that.

SOLNESS: That, and with any peace my soul might have found.

HILDE (*Rising*): Peace for your soul! Oh you are so right about that, poor Master Builder! You imagine yourself—

SOLNESS: Sit down again, Hilde. This time I'll tell you something very amusing.

HILDE: Yes?

SOLNESS: It might sound like a ludicrous thing, but the whole tragedy hinged on a small crack in the chimney.

HILDE: A crack?

SOLNESS: Yes, at the beginning. I had noticed it before. It was in the flue, and I had seen it often before the fire. Every time I went up to the attic I would look for it and check to see if it were still there.

HILDE: And was it?

SOLNESS: No one else knew about it.

HILDE: You said nothing?

SOLNESS: I said nothing.

HILDE: Didn't you intend to repair it?

SOLNESS: I thought about it, but every time I wanted to go and repair it, something like a hand kept me from it. I thought "not today, tomorrow." But I never got around to it.

HILDE: Why did you keep procrastinating?

SOLNESS: I was brooding over something else, but everything was tied up with that dark crack in the chimney. I seemed to see it as my way out and up. Up to the top, as the Master Builder.

HILDE: It must have been exciting.

SOLNESS: Quite irresistible! At the time it seemed so simple to me, so absolutely practical. I wanted it to happen during the wintertime shortly before dinner. I would be out driving with Aline in the sleigh, and at home the servants would be making roaring fires in the stoves and fireplaces.

HILDE: Yes, for it was to be unbearably cold that day.

SOLNESS: —A cold so cutting that every preparation would be made to keep Aline extra warm when she got home.

HILDE: She's thin-blooded by nature, isn't she?

SOLNESS: Yes, she is. And then on the way home both of us— at the same time—would notice the smoke rising.

HILDE: Just smoke?

SOLNESS: Yes, just the smoke at first, but when we got to the garden gate we would see the old wooden box heaving in a mass of flames. That's how I wished it to be.

HILDE: Good God! But why wasn't it just that way?

SOLNESS: We may very well wonder why, Hilde.

HILDE: But listen, Master Builder, are you sure the fire started from that little crack in the chimney?

SOLNESS: No. I'm quite certain that the crack had nothing whatsoever to do with the fire.

HILDE: What?

SOLNESS: It was undeniably established that the fire started in a clothes closet on the opposite side of the house.

HILDE: Then why all the fuss about that crack in the chimney?

SOLNESS: Let me tell you a bit more, Hilde.

HILDE: All right, if you talk sense.

SOLNESS: I'll try.

HILDE (*Sitting*): Let's have it then, Master Builder!

SOLNESS: Do you think, Hilde, that there are certain select people who have special powers? People who are blessed with the ability to actually wish something into being? Do you believe that?

HILDE: If there are, we'll find out one of these days whether or not I'm one of these select people.

SOLNESS: One does not accomplish these great things alone. There are helpers and servants who must play their parts too, if anything is to come of it. And they won't help unless they are called persistently, from deep inside one's inner self.

HILDE: Who are these helpers and servants?

SOLNESS: We'll talk about that later. I want to tell you about the fire.

HILDE: You don't think there would have been a fire if you hadn't wished it?

SOLNESS: If old Knut Brovik had owned that house, it never would have burned so conveniently for him. I'm certain of that! He has no idea how to employ these helpers and servants. You see, Hilde, after all is said and done, the death of my boys rests upon my shoulders and I alone must bear the guilt. It's my fault, too, that Aline never fulfilled herself as a woman.

HILDE: Perhaps all of it is the work of your helpers and servants—

SOLNESS: Ah. But who employed them? Who called them so recklessly? I did! They came and subjugated themselves to my will. And this is what the good people call having "luck on your side"! Well, I'll tell you what it really feels like to be a man with that kind of luck. It's like living every day with a great open wound in your chest. The helpers and servants keep pulling skin off others to put over your wound, trying to heal it, but the festering never stops. It will never heal, never. Ah! If you could only feel how it tears and burns sometimes.

HILDE: You are ill, dear Master Builder, very ill. I'm almost certain of it.

SOLNESS: Say "mad," Hilde—that's what you mean.

HILDE: No. There's nothing missing in your brain.

SOLNESS: Well then, out with it!

HILDE: God only knows! Unless you came into this world with a very weak conscience.

SOLNESS: A weak conscience? What deviltry is this?

HILDE: I mean your conscience seems to be so delicately built that it can't hold up under the load you've given it.

SOLNESS: Hmm. And just how should a conscience be built, if I may ask?

HILDE: Well, for you—I should like for you to have a really robust conscience.

SOLNESS: Oh, a robust conscience! Is that it? And is that what you have, Hilde?

HILDE: Yes, I believe I have. I've never noticed anything else.

SOLNESS: Perhaps it hasn't been put to the test yet.

HILDE: Oh, it wasn't as easy as you may think for me to leave my father and come here. I love him very much. He's very dear to me.

SOLNESS: But what's a month or two?

HILDE: I'm never going home again.

SOLNESS: Never? Did you have to leave home?

HILDE: Have you forgotten again that the ten years are up?

SOLNESS: Nonsense. Something was wrong at home, eh?

HILDE: No. It was something inside me. It drew me on and swept me along and insisted that I land here.

SOLNESS: That's it! That's it, Hilde! There's a troll in you too, just as there is in me. He's the one who calls on the powers from beyond—and we give in whether we want to or not.

HILDE: I could almost believe you're right, Master Builder.

SOLNESS: There are innumerable devils in this world, Hilde, which are never seen.

HILDE: Devils, too?

SOLNESS: Good devils and evil ones. The blond devils and the swarthy ones. If we only knew which had a hold on us—the dark or the light—then it would be easy!

HILDE: —Or if one had a really robust conscience, one could dare to do what he wants to do the most.

SOLNESS: In that respect most people are just as weak as I am!

HILDE: That might be.

SOLNESS: In all the old sagas about the Vikings . . . have you read any of them?

HILDE: Oh yes! When I used to read, that is. I—

SOLNESS: Well, in all those sagas the Vikings were always sailing to foreign lands and plundering and burning the villages and killing the men . . .

HILDE: . . . and carrying off the women . . .

SOLNESS: . . . and keeping them prisoners . . .

HILDE: . . . then taking them home on their ships . . .

SOLNESS: . . . and behaving with them like—like the most horrid trolls.

HILDE: I think it must have been very exciting!

SOLNESS: Carrying off women?

HILDE: No. To be carried off!

SOLNESS: Is that so?

HILDE: But what's the point in all this Viking business?

SOLNESS: Well, now, those men had robust consciences. When they came back home they could eat and drink and be as happy as children. Their women would welcome them and never want to part from them. Can you understand that, Hilde?

HILDE: Yes, I can understand those women.

SOLNESS: Ah! Perhaps you could do the same thing?

HILDE: Why not?

SOLNESS: You would live, of your own free will, with such a brute?

HILDE: If it were a brute I had truly fallen in love with.

SOLNESS: But could you fall in love with such a man?

HILDE: Good God, one hasn't much control over things like that —you know that!

SOLNESS: I suppose so. It's the troll inside who's responsible for that, too.

HILDE: And all those blessed devils that you seem to know so well—the light haired ones and the dark ones. . . .

SOLNESS (*Warmly and quietly*): I hope for your sake, Hilde, that those devils will choose wisely for you.

HILDE: They've already chosen for me once and for all.

SOLNESS: Hilde, you're like an untamed bird in the forest.

HILDE: Far from it—I don't hide in the thicket.

SOLNESS: Well, that's true. There's more of the bird of prey in you.

HILDE: Maybe. And why not a bird of prey? Why shouldn't I go hunting and take any prey I want? If I could truly get my claws in it and be its master— Ah!

SOLNESS: Hilde, do you know what you are?

HILDE: Yes. You just said I'm some kind of strange bird.

SOLNESS: You are the moment when day breaks. When I look at you it's like looking into the sunrise.

HILDE: Tell me, Master Builder, did you ever call to me from deep, deep inside yourself?

SOLNESS: I think I must have.

HILDE: And what did you want with me?

SOLNESS: You are youth, Hilde.

HILDE: Youth? The very thing you're so afraid of?

SOLNESS: And that I long for deep down.

HILDE: Are these the drawings that—

SOLNESS: Put them away! I've seen enough of them.

HILDE: Yes, but you're going to write on them for him.

SOLNESS: Write on them? Never!

HILDE: But the poor old man is dying! Can't you make them both happy before they part forever? With your comments on these drawings he could build that house.

SOLNESS: That's exactly what would happen and he knows it, the sniveling good-for-nothing.

HILDE: Good God, if he's that incompetent, why don't you lie a little?

SOLNESS: Lie? Take those damn drawings away from me, Hilde!

HILDE: Well, don't bite my head off! You—you who talk about

trolls—now you behave like one! A mean, old, miserly troll. Where do you keep the pen and ink?

SOLNESS: I haven't got any in here.

HILDE: But the girl out there—she has some, I suppose?

SOLNESS: Stay where you are, Hilde! I should lie, eh? For his old father's sake I suppose I could do it. At one time I did crush him and throw him aside.

HILDE: Him, too?

SOLNESS: I wanted some room for myself. I needed to grow. But Ragnar mustn't be allowed to get ahead at any price!

HILDE: Poor thing. He won't get ahead, you can be sure of that. When a young man doesn't have any talent—

SOLNESS: If Ragnar Brovik moves up front, he'll knock me back to the ground. Oh yes, he'll crush me just as I did his father.

HILDE: Crush you! Is he good enough to do that?

SOLNESS: Yes, he is. He's a part of that new generation that stands ready to knock down my door and trample Master Builder Solness!

HILDE (*Quietly*): And still you want to hold him back? Shame, Master Builder.

SOLNESS: I've lost so much of my heart's blood in this battle of mine. And now I've lost my helpers and servants. They don't listen to me any more.

HILDE: Then get along without them.

SOLNESS: It's hopeless, Hilde. The change is coming sooner or later, and the law of retribution has no pity.

HILDE: Don't talk like that! Do you want to kill me? Yes! Do you want to take away what I cherish more than my life?

SOLNESS: And what is that?

HILDE: To see you a great man! To see you with a wreath in your hand, high up on a church tower! Now give me a pencil. You have one, haven't you?

SOLNESS (*Taking a pencil from his sketchbook*): Here's one.

HILDE: Good. And so the two of us will sit down here, Master Builder—

(SOLNESS *sits at the table*. HILDE *stands behind him and leans over the back of his chair*.)

HILDE: And so we write on the drawings. Very, very nicely now, and very warmly, too. We write to this naughty Roald—or whatever his name is!

SOLNESS (*Writes a few lines. Turning to her*): Tell me one thing, Hilde.

HILDE: Yes.

SOLNESS: While you were waiting for me those ten years . . .

HILDE: Yes?

SOLNESS: . . . didn't you ever think of writing to me? I would have answered you.

HILDE: No, no! That's just what I didn't want.

SOLNESS: Why not?

HILDE: I was afraid you'd go all to pieces if I wrote. But we were supposed to be writing on the drawings, Master Builder.

SOLNESS: Oh yes, so we were.

HILDE: So nice and heart-warming. Oh how I hate—how I hate this Roald!

SOLNESS: Have you never really cared for anyone, Hilde?

HILDE (*Coldly*): What did you say?

SOLNESS: . . . if you've ever cared for anyone?

HILDE: For anyone else, I suppose you mean.

SOLNESS (*Looking up at her*): For anyone else, yes. Have you? In these ten years? Ever?

HILDE: Oh yes, every now and then when I was really angry at you for not coming to me.

SOLNESS: Then you did care for others.

HILDE: Oh, a little bit, maybe for a week or so. Good God, Master Builder, you must know how *those* things happen!

SOLNESS: Hilde, why have you come here?

HILDE: Don't waste time talking! The poor old man could be dying right now.

SOLNESS: Answer me, Hilde. What do you want of me?

HILDE: I want my kingdom.

SOLNESS: Hmm.

(SOLNESS *quickly looks at the door* LEFT *and continues to write on the drawings.* MRS. SOLNESS *enters, carrying some packages.*)

ALINE: Here are a few things I got for you, Miss Wangel. They'll deliver the large packages later.

HILDE: How very kind of you!

ALINE: Just my duty, nothing else.

SOLNESS (*Reading what he has written*): Aline?

ALINE: Yes?

SOLNESS: Did you notice if she—the bookkeeper—is out there?

ALINE: Yes, of course she's out there.

SOLNESS (*Putting the drawings in a portfolio*): Hmm.

ALINE: She was standing at her desk as usual when I passed by.

SOLNESS: Then give her this and tell her—

HILDE (*Taking the portfolio from him*): Oh no, let me have the pleasure. What's her name?

SOLNESS: Miss Fosli.

HILDE: Oh, that sounds so cold. I meant her first name.

SOLNESS: Kaja, I think.

HILDE (*Opens the door and calls*): Kaja, come in here! And hurry up. The Master Builder wants to talk to you.

KAJA (*Enters, looking frightened*): Yes?

HILDE (*Handing her the portfolio*): Look, Kaja, you can take this home to them. Master Builder Solness has written on it!

KAJA: At last!

SOLNESS: Give it to the old man as quickly as you can.

KAJA: I'll run straight home.

SOLNESS: Yes, do. It means Ragnar can build on his own now.

KAJA: Oh! May he come in and thank you for all this—this—?

SOLNESS (*Sternly*): I don't want any thank you's. Tell him that for me.

KAJA: Yes—I will.

SOLNESS: And tell him that from now on I won't have any more use for him. That goes for you, too.

KAJA (*Softly*): For me, too?

SOLNESS: You'll have other things to think of, and that's as it should be. Now go home with the drawings, Miss Fosli. Hurry. Do you hear me?

KAJA: Yes, Mr. Solness. (*Exits*)

ALINE: God! What cruel eyes she has!

SOLNESS: Her? That harmless little creature?

ALINE: Ah, well, I see what I see, Halvard. Are you really letting them go?

SOLNESS: Yes.

ALINE: Her, too?

SOLNESS: Aren't you the one who wanted that?

ALINE: But can you do without her? Oh well, I suppose you have someone else in mind, Halvard.

HILDE (*Mischievously*): Not me! I'm no good at standing at a desk.

SOLNESS: Well, we'll make some arrangements. Now you should be concentrating all your efforts on moving into the new house. The sooner the better. Tonight we'll hoist up the wreath. (*Turning to* HILDE) Far up on the very top of the tower. What do you think of that, Miss Hilde?

HILDE (*With eyes sparkling*): It'll be dreadful and wonderful to see you so high up again.

SOLNESS: Me?

ALINE: Oh my God, Miss Wangel, don't imagine anything like that. My husband gets dizzy so easily.

HILDE: Dizzy? No, he doesn't get dizzy.

ALINE: Oh, yes he does!

HILDE: But I've seen him myself, way up on a church tower.

ALINE: Yes, I've heard people talk about that, but now it's absolutely impossible for him.

SOLNESS (*Flaring up*): Impossible? Yes! But just the same—once —I stood up there!

ALINE: How can you say a thing like that, Halvard? You can't even stand on the second-floor balcony! You've always been that way.

SOLNESS: Perhaps you'll be seeing something different tonight.

ALINE: No! Oh no! With God's help I hope I never see that. I'll send a message to the Doctor and he'll certainly be able to stop you from doing anything that foolish, Halvard.

SOLNESS: Now Aline. . . .

ALINE: You're not well, Halvard. It must be that—oh God— Oh God—

(*She leaves hurriedly by the door* RIGHT.)

HILDE (*Looking intensely at him*): Is that really how it is with you? Is it?

SOLNESS: That I get dizzy?

HILDE: That my Master Builder doesn't dare! That he can't climb as high as he builds.

SOLNESS: Does it look that way to you?

HILDE: Yes.

SOLNESS: You seem to look straight through me. Soon none of my thoughts will be safe from you.

HILDE (*Looking toward the bay window*): Up there, then—all the way up?

SOLNESS (*Coming closer to her*): There's a room in the top of the tower, Hilde. You could live there like a princess.

HILDE (*Half-serious*): Yes, that's what you promised me.

SOLNESS: Did I actually do all that?

HILDE: Shame on you, Master Builder! You said I should become a princess and that you'd give me a kingdom. Then you took—oh—no!

SOLNESS (*Carefully*): Are you quite sure it wasn't a dream? A fantasy that you've relived all these years?

HILDE (*Sharply*): Are you trying to tell me you didn't do it?

SOLNESS: I don't know myself. (*Softer*) But now I do know for certain that I . . .

HILDE: That you—? Tell me!

SOLNESS: . . . that I should have done it.

HILDE (*Brightly*): Never in the world could a height make you dizzy.

SOLNESS: Tonight, then, we will hoist the wreath, Princess Hilde.

HILDE (*With a bitter expression*): Over your new home, yes.

SOLNESS: Over the new house that will never be a home for me. (SOLNESS *leaves through the garden door.* HILDE *looks straight ahead with a glassy look on her face. She whispers to herself. Only a few words are audible.*)

HILDE: Terribly . . . exciting . . . !

CURTAIN

# ACT III

*A large porch on* SOLNESS' *house. At* STAGE LEFT *is the house, with a door leading to the inside and a garden bench alongside.* DOWNSTAGE *is a long narrow table. To the left of it there is a wicker armchair and several matching stools. At* STAGE RIGHT *a porch railing looks out between the trees and to the lower part of the new house. The scaffolding is still around the part of the tower that is visible.* UPSTAGE *at the end of the porch are several steps leading to the garden. It is enclosed by a wooden fence, and beyond is seen a street with low, ill-kept houses. Several large old trees in the garden spread their branches over the porch and into the house.*

AS THE CURTAIN RISES *it is late afternoon. The clouds are lit with the last rays of the sun.*

MRS. SOLNESS *sits in the armchair staring toward the* RIGHT. *She is wrapped in a large white crepe shawl. Shortly after the curtain rises* HILDE *enters from the garden. She is dressed as before and is wearing her hat. A small bouquet of wild flowers is tucked into her bosom.*

ALINE (*Turning her head slightly to* HILDE): Have you been out in the garden, Miss Wangel?

HILDE: Yes, I've been looking around down there.

ALINE: You found some flowers, I see.

HILDE: Oh yes—there are so many of them in the bushes.

ALINE: Still? My, my—I never get down there.

HILDE (*Coming closer*): Why? Don't you ever go to the garden to escape?

ALINE (*Smiling faintly*): I don't escape at all, any more.

HILDE: Don't you go down there every now and then just to visit all the lovely things?

ALINE: It's grown so unfamiliar to me—all of it. I'm almost afraid to look at it now.

118

HILDE: Your own garden?

ALINE: It doesn't seem to be mine any more.

HILDE: Oh? Why not?

ALINE: Well, it's not really, Miss Wangel. It's not the same as in father's and mother's time. They've taken so much of it away that it's pitiful. Just imagine—they've divided it all up and built houses for strangers on it. People I don't even know, who can sit and look at me from their windows.

HILDE (*Pleasantly*): Mrs. Solness.

ALINE: Yes?

HILDE: May I stay out here with you for a while?

ALINE: Yes of course, if you want to.

HILDE (*Moves a stool nearer the armchair and sits down*): One can really sit out here and sun oneself like a cat.

ALINE (*Putting her hand very lightly on the back of Hilde's neck*): It's so kind of you to want to sit here with me. I thought you were on your way to see my husband.

HILDE: Why should I want to see him?

ALINE: I thought you were helping him.

HILDE: No thank you! Besides, he's over there with the workmen. He looked so ferocious I didn't even dare speak to him.

ALINE: Oh, he's really gentle and sweet underneath all that.

HILDE: Is he?

ALINE: Oh yes. You don't really know him yet, Miss Wangel.

HILDE (*Warmly*): Will you be happy to move into the new house?

ALINE: I should be. It's what Halvard wants.

HILDE: I shouldn't think that would be the only reason. It's not only because of Mr. Solness, is it?

ALINE: Oh but it is, Miss Wangel. It's my duty to submit to his will. But often it's difficult to force one's mind into obedience.

HILDE: Yes, it must be very difficult.

ALINE: Believe me, it is. —When one is not a better person than I am.

HILDE: You've gone through a great deal. . . .

ALINE: How do you know that?

HILDE: Your husband told me.

ALINE: He never talks to me about those things. Yes, believe me, I've been through a great deal in my lifetime, Miss Wangel.

HILDE (*Nodding slowly with sympathy*): Poor Mrs. Solness. First of all your house burned down—

ALINE (*Sighing mournfully*): Yes, everything I had burned.

HILDE: And then the worst came.

ALINE: Worst?

HILDE: Yes, the worst loss.

ALINE: What do you mean?

HILDE (*Softly*): Your two little boys.

ALINE: Oh yes—them. Oh that was something else. Yes. Well, *that* was the will of God. Sometimes we have to bow under His will and even be grateful to Him for such things.

HILDE: But how can you do that?

ALINE: One can't always, and that is unfortunate, I'm afraid. I know so well that it is my duty, but I can't always do it.

HILDE: Well, that's only natural.

ALINE: And every now and then I have to tell myself that it was a just punishment for me.

HILDE: Why?

ALINE: Because I didn't have the stamina to endure the disaster.

HILDE: I don't understand.

ALINE: Oh, Miss Wangel, let's not talk about the little boys any more. We should only feel happiness for them. They must be blissfully content where they are now. They're in good hands. So good. No, no, it's the little losses in life that tear the heart in two. Losing those things that other people don't value at all.

HILDE (*Puts her arms on* ALINE's *lap and looks up at her warmly*): Dear Mrs. Solness, tell me—tell me what those losses were.

ALINE: As I said, just little things. All the old portraits on the walls were burned, and all the lovely silk dresses that had been in the family for so many years. And all of mother's and grandmother's laces. Imagine—they all burned! And the jewelry! And all the dolls!

HILDE: The dolls?

ALINE (*Stifling a cry, almost breaking*): I had nine beautiful dolls!

HILDE: And they burned too?

ALINE: All of them. It was such a tragedy—such a tragedy for me.

HILDE: Had you saved those dolls from your childhood?

ALINE: Not just saved them. I lived with my dolls every day.

HILDE: Even after you'd grown up?

ALINE: Yes, long after that.

HILDE: Even after your marriage?

ALINE: Oh yes, when he didn't see me. But then they all burned —the poor little dears. No one thought to rescue them. Isn't that a pitiful thing to think about? You mustn't smile, Miss Wangel.

HILDE: I'm not smiling.

ALINE: Because in a way there was life in them, too. I carried them under my heart like unborn children. . . .

(DR. HERDAL, *holding his hat, enters from the door of the house. He sees the women.*)

DOCTOR: Well, well, so you are out here, Mrs. Solness! Catching yourself a cold, eh?

ALINE: I thought it was so nice and warm today.

DOCTOR: Oh yes, so it is! Tell me now—what's wrong? I received your note.

ALINE (*Standing*): There's something I want to talk to you about.

DOCTOR: Good! Let's go inside. (*To* HILDE) Oh! Still dressed for mountain climbing, eh?

HILDE (*Standing up, cheerfully*): Yes indeed! In my full finery! But today I'm not the one who's planning to climb and break my neck. We two shall be standing comfortably below, watching.

DOCTOR: And what are you going to be watching?

ALINE (*Quietly to* HILDE, *frightened*): Quiet, quiet, for God's sake—he's coming. See to it that you get that notion out of his head. Let us try to be friends, Miss Wangel, shall we?

HILDE (*Throwing her arms violently around* MRS. SOLNESS' *neck*): Oh if only we could!

ALINE (*Drawing away gently*): There, there. (*To the* DOCTOR) Let's go inside.

DOCTOR: It's about him, then?

ALINE: Yes, of course it is. Come inside.

(MRS. SOLNESS *and* DOCTOR HERDAL *go into the house.* SOLNESS *enters from the garden a moment later.* HILDE *has a serious expression on her face.*)

SOLNESS (*Seeing the door close*): Have you noticed, Hilde, as soon as I come near she goes away?

HILDE: I've noticed as soon as you come near her you make her go away.

SOLNESS: Perhaps. But there's nothing I can do to change that. Are you freezing, Hilde? You look it.

HILDE: I just came out of a grave.

SOLNESS: What do you mean by that?

HILDE: I've been frostbitten to the bone.

SOLNESS: I think I understand.

HILDE: Why did you come up here?

SOLNESS: I saw you from over there.

HILDE: You must have seen her, too.

SOLNESS: I knew she'd leave as soon as I got here.

HILDE: Does it hurt you very much when she does that?

SOLNESS: In a way it's a relief.

HILDE: Not to have to look at her?

SOLNESS: Yes.

HILDE: Not to be reminded over and over again how she grieves for the little boys?

SOLNESS: Yes, mostly because of that.

(HILDE *crosses to the porch railing, hands behind her back. She looks over the garden.*)

SOLNESS: Did you talk to her long?

(HILDE *stands motionless.*)

SOLNESS: I said, did you talk to her for a long time?

(HILDE *is silent.*)

SOLNESS: Poor Aline! I suppose it was about the two little boys.

(HILDE's *body quivers. She gives several nods, short and definite.*)

SOLNESS: She'll never get over it. Never in her life—never. (*Going to* HILDE) Now you're standing like a statue again, as you did last night.

HILDE (*Turns, speaks seriously*): I'm leaving.

SOLNESS: Leaving?

HILDE: Yes.

SOLNESS: I won't let you!

HILDE: What should I do here?

SOLNESS: Just be here, Hilde.

HILDE: Oh thank you, but it wouldn't stop there.

SOLNESS (*Impulsively*): So much the better!

HILDE (*Flaring up*): I can't harm someone I know! I can't take away anything that belongs to her.

SOLNESS: Who said that you would?

HILDE: A stranger . . . well . . . yes, that would be different. Someone I'd never seen. But a person whom I've learned to know— No, never!

SOLNESS: But I've never proposed anything like that.

HILDE: Oh Mr. Solness, you know very well what would happen. That's why I'm leaving.

SOLNESS: And what's to become of me when you go? What will I have to live for then?

HILDE (*With an indefinable look in her eyes*): Oh, you'll be all right. You have your duties to her—live for them.

SOLNESS: It's too late for her. These powers, these—these—

HILDE: Devils?

SOLNESS: Yes, devils and the demon trolls—they've drained all the good blood out of her, too. They did it for my happiness, and now she's dead because of me and I'm chained to a dead woman. I—I who cannot live without happiness!

(HILDE *goes around the table and sits on the bench. She puts her elbows on the table and her hands hold her chin. She sits for a moment, staring at* SOLNESS.)

HILDE: What are you going to build next?

SOLNESS: I don't think there'll be a next.

HILDE: Not even a cozy home for a happy mother and father and a flock of children?

SOLNESS: There will be no need for that any more.

HILDE: Poor Master Builder! And you've dedicated the last ten years of your life to just that!

SOLNESS: How true, Hilde—

HILDE (*Crying out*): It seems so wrong, so wrong—all of it!

SOLNESS: All of what?

HILDE: How awful not to dare grasp your own happiness—your own life—just because someone you know is standing in the way.

SOLNESS: One that neither of us has the right to pass by.

HILDE: Only God knows if we have the right or not. Oh, if I could just sleep all this away! (*She stretches her arms on the table, rests her head on them, and closes her eyes.*)

SOLNESS (*Pulling the armchair around to the table*): Did you have a cozy, happy home up there with your father, Hilde?

HILDE (*Vaguely, half asleep*): I had a cage.

SOLNESS: And you don't want to go back again, ever?

HILDE: A wild bird doesn't like to be in a cage.

SOLNESS: You'd rather hunt in the open?

HILDE: The bird of prey was born to hunt.

SOLNESS: If only one could have the Viking spirit to carry on through life!

HILDE (*In a normal voice, her eyes open, but motionless*): Or the other thing—tell me—what was that?

SOLNESS: A robust conscience.

HILDE (*Straightens up, eyes sparkling playfully. Nodding to him*): I know what you're going to build next!

SOLNESS: Then you know more than I do, Hilde.

HILDE: My, my, my. Master Builders are so stupid!

SOLNESS: What's it going to be?

HILDE (*Nodding again*): The castle.

SOLNESS: What castle?

HILDE: My castle, of course!

SOLNESS: You want your castle now?

HILDE: You owe me a kingdom, don't you?

SOLNESS: That's what you said.

HILDE: Well, then, I should think a castle goes with it!

SOLNESS (*With increasing exhilaration*): Yes, I suppose the two are inseparable.

HILDE: Very good! Then build it for me, immediately.

SOLNESS (*Smiling*): Within the hour?

HILDE: Yes! I'm not going to wait any longer—your ten years are up and I'm not waiting. So out with my castle, Master Builder!

SOLNESS: It's not easy to owe you anything, Hilde.

HILDE: You should have thought of that before. It's too late now. Therefore—the castle on the table! My castle, and I want it right now!

SOLNESS (*A bit more solemn. Leaning toward her with his arms on the table.*): How have you imagined your castle?

HILDE (*Her look becomes glazed over as if she is looking deeply within herself*): My castle will be built very high up with nothing around it, so that I can see far, far away in all directions.

SOLNESS: It should have a tower, shouldn't it?

HILDE: A dreadfully high tower! And on the top of the tower there will be a balcony and I will stand there. . . .

SOLNESS (*Clutching his forehead involuntarily*): Do you like to stand at such dizzy heights?

HILDE: Oh yes. Up there I'll stand and look down on all the others. Those who build churches and homes for mothers and fathers and flocks of children. And you, too, shall come up to look!

SOLNESS (*Softly*): Will the Master Builder be allowed to come visit the princess?

HILDE: If the Master Builder *wants* to.

SOLNESS (*More softly*): Then I believe the Master Builder *will*.

HILDE (*Nodding*): The Master Builder—he will come.

SOLNESS: But he'll never build any more—poor Master Builder.

HILDE (*Lively*): Oh yes, the two of us shall build together. We'll build the most wonderful—the most wonderful thing in the whole world.

SOLNESS: Hilde, tell me what kind of thing that is.

HILDE (*Looks at him, shaking her head lightly. Pouts and speaks as if to a child*): Master Builders . . . they are very, very stupid people.

SOLNESS: Yes, of course they are stupid. But tell me what it is— the most wonderful thing in the whole world that the two of us will build together.

HILDE (*Silent for a moment, then with an indefinable look in her eyes*): Castles in the air.

SOLNESS: Castles in the air?

HILDE (*Nodding*): Yes, castles in the air. You know what they are, don't you?

SOLNESS: They say that they're the most wonderful thing in the world.

HILDE (*Stands up suddenly and makes a gesture of refusal*): And so they are! They're so very special to live in and so easy to build—especially for a Master Builder whose conscience is prone to dizziness.

SOLNESS (*Standing up*): After this day, the two of us will build together, Hilde.

HILDE (*Smiles, half-doubting*): A real castle in the air?

SOLNESS: Yes, with a solid foundation.

(RAGNAR BROVIK *enters from the house. He carries a very large green wreath of flowers and ribbons.*)

HILDE: The wreath! Oh, it's going to be so terribly wonderful!

SOLNESS: You've brought the wreath, Ragnar?

RAGNAR: I promised the foreman I would.

SOLNESS: Is your father better?

RAGNAR: No.

SOLNESS: Didn't those things I wrote cheer him up a bit?

RAGNAR: It was too late.

SOLNESS: Too late?

RAGNAR: He wasn't conscious by the time Kaja got there. He's had a stroke.

SOLNESS: You should go home right away and look after him.

RAGNAR: He doesn't need me any more.

SOLNESS: You should be there.

RAGNAR: She's at his bedside.

SOLNESS (*Uncertainly*): Kaja?

RAGNAR (*Looking darkly at him*): Yes, Kaja.

SOLNESS: Go home, Ragnar, to both of them. I'll take the wreath.

RAGNAR (*Suppressing a nasty smile*): You're not going to, yourself?

SOLNESS (*Taking the wreath*): I'll go over with it. We have no further use for you today.

RAGNAR: I know you have no use for me from now on, but I'll stay.

SOLNESS: Then stay if you want to.

HILDE (*At the railing*): I'll be standing here and looking at you.

SOLNESS: At me?

HILDE: It'll be terribly exciting!

SOLNESS (*Goes out with the wreath through the garden*): We'll talk about that later, Hilde.

HILDE (*Looks after him, turns to* RAGNAR): I think you should have thanked him, at least.

RAGNAR: Thanked him? *I* should have thanked *him?*

HILDE: Yes. You certainly should have.

RAGNAR: If I thank anyone around here, it'll be you.

HILDE: Why me?

RAGNAR (*Avoiding her*): And—you'd better watch out, miss, because you don't know him yet.

HILDE: I'm the only one who really does.

RAGNAR (*With a nasty smile*): And you say I should thank him, the man who's held me down year after year! He made my father doubt me—he even managed to make me doubt myself—and all because, because—

HILDE: What? Tell me!

RAGNAR: Because he wanted to keep her for himself.

HILDE (*Approaching him*): The girl at the desk?

RAGNAR: Yes.

HILDE: It isn't true! You're lying about him!

RAGNAR: I didn't want to believe it myself before today. She told me herself.

HILDE (*Uncontrollably*): What did she say? I want to know—now!

RAGNAR: She said he's possessed her whole mind. He's stolen all her thoughts for himself and she can never get away from him. She wants to be here where he is.

HILDE: She won't be allowed to stay.

RAGNAR: Who'll stop her?

HILDE: He will!

RAGNAR: Oh, now I understand! From now on she'd just be in the way, eh?

HILDE: You don't understand *anything* if you say things like that! I'll tell you why he's been keeping her here.

RAGNAR: Why?

HILDE: So that he could control *you!*

RAGNAR: Did he tell you that?

HILDE: No, but that's how it is. That's how it must be—I want it to be that way. I want it—I want—

RAGNAR: When you came here he got rid of her.

HILDE: It was you—you he got rid of! What makes you think he'd care for a girl he doesn't even know?

RAGNAR (*After a moment*): Could he have been afraid of me? Of my work?

HILDE: I don't think you should be quite that conceited!

RAGNAR: He must have known for a long time that I could amount to something. Yes, me! And as far as being afraid—well, that's exactly what he is.

HILDE: You expect me to believe that?

RAGNAR: He, the great Master Builder! Oh, he's not afraid to ruin people's happiness as he did my father's and mine, but when it comes to stepping out on a poor little scaffold—*that,* God bless him, he'll never do!

HILDE: Oh you should have seen him as I saw him once. Way up! So high—

RAGNAR: Have you seen that?

HILDE: Yes, I have. And he stood up there so bold and proud and secure. Then he flung the wreath over the church spire.

RAGNAR: I heard he did that once in his life, one single time. My friends talk about it every now and then. Well! No power on earth could get him to do it again.

HILDE: Today he will do it again!

RAGNAR: I'll believe that when I see it.

HILDE: We will see it.

RAGNAR: None of us will ever see that. He's afraid, you know.

HILDE: I will see it! I will—I will—I *must* see it!

RAGNAR: He won't do it—he doesn't dare. The truth is, he has that weakness—the great Master Builder!

(MRS. SOLNESS *enters from the house. She looks around.*)

ALINE: Oh. He isn't here. Where did he go?

RAGNAR: Mr. Solness is with the workers.

HILDE: He went over with the wreath.

ALINE (*Very frightened*): He did? He took the wreath? Oh my God, my God. Brovik! Brovik, you must go after him and bring him back here.

RAGNAR: Shall I tell him you want to see him?

ALINE: Yes, please do say that. No. No, don't tell him I want him. You can say—well, say that there's someone here who wants to see him and that he must come immediately.

RAGNAR: Very well, I'll do that. (*He leaves through the garden.*)

ALINE: Oh, Miss Wangel, you can't imagine what I go through —what fear I have for his sake.

HILDE: Is there anything to be afraid of?

ALINE: Yes, you know there is. Just imagine if it really happened! If he got it into his head to walk up there on that scaffolding—

HILDE: Do you think he'll do it?

ALINE: Oh, one never knows what he'll do. He's capable of anything.

HILDE: Ah! Then you, too, think he's—?

ALINE: I don't know what to think about him any more. The Doctor's been telling me so many things about him. When I put it all together with the things I know and the things I've seen and heard, then—

DOCTOR (*Looking out through the door*): Will he be here soon?

ALINE: Oh, yes, I think so. At least, I've asked him to come.

DOCTOR: You'd better go inside, Mrs. Solness.

ALINE: No, no, I'll stay here and wait for Halvard.

DOCTOR: Some ladies are here to see you.

ALINE: Oh my God! That too, right now?

DOCTOR: They want to see the ceremony.

ALINE: Well then, I'll just have to see them—it's my duty.

HILDE: Can't you ask them to go away?

ALINE: Oh, no, I couldn't do that. Since they've come here, it's my duty to receive them. But you wait out here for him.

DOCTOR: Talk with him and keep him here as long as possible—

ALINE: Yes, do that, dear Miss Wangel. Make sure he doesn't get away. Hold him here as best you can.

HILDE: Shouldn't you do that yourself?

ALINE: Oh yes, yes, it is my duty, but when one has duties in so many directions—well—

DOCTOR: Here he comes.

ALINE: And to think I have to go inside!

DOCTOR (*To Hilde*): Don't tell him I'm here.

HILDE: No. I'll find something else to talk to the Master Builder about.

ALINE: Be sure to keep him here. I think you're the one who can do it best.

(MRS. SOLNESS *and the* DOCTOR *go into the house.*)

SOLNESS (*Entering from the garden*): Does somebody want to see me?

HILDE: Yes—I do!

SOLNESS: Oh it's you, Hilde. I was afraid it was Aline or the Doctor.

HILDE: You're afraid of them, aren't you?

SOLNESS: Do you think so?

HILDE: Yes. People say you're afraid of crawling around up there on the scaffolding, too.

SOLNESS: Well now, that's an entirely different thing.

HILDE: But you are afraid of it, aren't you?

SOLNESS: Yes, I am.

HILDE: Afraid you'll fall down and kill yourself?

SOLNESS: No. Not that.

HILDE: Of what, then?

SOLNESS: I'm afraid of retribution, Hilde.

HILDE: Retribution? (*Shaking her head*) I can't understand you.

SOLNESS (*Throwing his hat on the table*): When I started out, I built nothing but churches.

HILDE (*Nodding*): I know that very well.

SOLNESS: I came from a small and very religious home in the countryside, and that's why it seemed to me that building churches was the most noble profession I could choose.

HILDE: Yes, yes.

SOLNESS: And so I built all those small, poor churches with such an earnest, sincere warmth, with such a devotion that, that—

HILDE: Yes?

SOLNESS: That I thought He ought to be pleased with me.

HILDE: He? What he?

SOLNESS: Well, He for whom the churches were built, of course. He whom they should serve and honor and obey.

HILDE: Was He pleased with you?

SOLNESS: Pleased? Oh Hilde, how can you ask that? He gave the demon troll full reign to do as he pleased with me. Didn't he invite all of them to stay with me night and day and serve me—all those—those—

HILDE: Devils?

SOLNESS: Yes, all kinds of them. Oh no, I soon found out He wasn't pleased with me. (*Mysteriously*) You see, that was really why He let the old house burn down.

HILDE: Was that why?

SOLNESS: He wanted to give me the opportunity to be a master in my field—to build many glorious churches in His honor. I didn't understand at first what He wanted—then suddenly I did.

HILDE: When?

SOLNESS: When I built the church tower up at Lysanger.

HILDE: I thought so!

SOLNESS: I was alone most of the time up there, in that strange and unfamiliar place, and I had time to think and brood. I could see clearly why He had taken my little children from me. It was so that I wouldn't attach myself to anything. No kind of love, no happiness was to be mine. —Do you understand? I was to be just a master builder and nothing else and live my whole life building for Him. (*Smiling*) But that didn't happen.

HILDE: What did?

SOLNESS: I looked deeply into myself . . .

HILDE: Yes?

SOLNESS: . . . and then I did the impossible! I, like Him!

HILDE: The impossible?

SOLNESS: I could never bear to stand at heights before—in the open air—without support, but that day I could!

HILDE (*Leaping up*): Yes, yes you could!

SOLNESS: And when I stood there on the very top and flung the wreath over the spire, I spoke to Him, "Now listen to me, Almighty God. From this day on I also want to be a free builder—I in my field as You are in yours. I don't want to build any more churches for You—just homes for people!"

HILDE: (*With large, sparkling eyes*): That was the song I heard in the air!

SOLNESS: Yes, but He had the last word.

HILDE: What do you mean?

SOLNESS: Building homes for people is not worth a damn.

HILDE: Do you mean that?

SOLNESS: Yes, I do. People don't use their homes to be happy in. They only exist in them, and if I had owned one I wouldn't have found the proper use for it, either. It's been like that as far back as I can see. Nothing! I've built nothing on a solid foundation and sacrificed nothing to have the right to build nothing. Nothing—all of it.

HILDE: And you'll never build anything new after this?

SOLNESS: Ah, now I'll start!

HILDE: What will it be? Tell me! Tell me!

SOLNESS: I'll build the only thing that can truly house happiness. That's what I want to build now.

HILDE: You mean our castles in the air?

SOLNESS: Yes, castles in the air.

HILDE: I'm afraid you might faint from dizziness before we get halfway up.

SOLNESS: Not when I'll be walking hand in hand with you, Hilde.

HILDE: Just with me? Won't there be others with us?

SOLNESS: What others?

HILDE: Oh that girl—Kaja—at the desk, poor thing. Aren't you going to take her?

SOLNESS: Is that what you and Aline were talking about?

HILDE: Is that how it is, or isn't it?

SOLNESS: I won't answer that. You have to believe in me completely.

HILDE: For ten years I believed in you completely—so completely.

SOLNESS: You shall continue believing in me!

HILDE: Then let me see you up there, bold and proud!

SOLNESS (Heavily): Oh, Hilde, I can't do a thing like that every day.

HILDE: I want it! I want it only once more, Master Builder. Do the impossible again!

SOLNESS: If I try, Hilde, I'll stand up there and talk to Him as I did the last time.

HILDE: And what will you say?

SOLNESS: I'll say, "Hear me, Oh mighty Lord. You may now judge me as You see fit, but from now on I will only build the most wonderful thing in the world . . ."

HILDE: Yes, yes, yes!

SOLNESS: ". . . build it with a princess whom I love."

HILDE: Yes, tell Him that—tell Him that!

SOLNESS: All right. And then I'll tell Him, "Now I'll go down and put my arms around her and kiss her—"

HILDE: Many times! Do say that!

SOLNESS: "Many, many times," I'll say.

HILDE: And then?

SOLNESS: Then I'll wave my hat and come down to earth and do as I told Him I would.

HILDE (*Stretching her arms out to him*): Now I see you again as I did that day when there was a song in the air!

SOLNESS (*Looking at her, his head bowed*): What has made you the way you are, Hilde?

HILDE: How have you made me the way I am?

SOLNESS: The princess shall have her castle!

HILDE: Oh Master Builder—my beautiful, beautiful castle—our castle in the air!

SOLNESS: On a solid foundation.

(*A number of people have gathered at the gate, several more on the street. All are somewhat hidden by the trees. Faint band music is heard.* MRS. SOLNESS *and* DOCTOR HERDAL *enter. She wears a fur collar. The* DOCTOR *carries her white crepe shawl. Several* LADIES *appear.* RAGNAR *enters from the garden.*)

ALINE (*To* RAGNAR): Are they going to be playing music?

RAGNAR: Yes, the workmen's band is playing. (*To* SOLNESS) The foreman wants you to know he's ready to go up with the wreath.

SOLNESS (*Taking his hat*): Very well. I'll go over there myself.

ALINE: Why do you want to go, Halvard?

SOLNESS: I have to be there with the workmen.

ALINE: All right then, below, but just below, with the men.

SOLNESS (*As he leaves*): That's what I'm planning on. Don't I always do that for these everyday affairs?

ALINE (*Calling after him*): But do ask the man to be careful when he goes up! Promise me that, Halvard.

DOCTOR (*To* MRS. SOLNESS): You see, I'm right after all. He's forgotten all about that mad idea of his.

ALINE: Yes, what a relief! It's happened twice, you know. Two men have fallen and both of them died immediately. (*To* HILDE) Thank you, Miss Wangel, for getting such a firm hold on him.

DOCTOR (*Cheerfully*): Yes, yes, Miss Wangel, you certainly know how to get a firm hold on someone when you really want to!

(MRS. SOLNESS *and the* DOCTOR *join the* LADIES *on the steps to the garden.* HILDE *remains standing at the railing.*)

RAGNAR (*Going to* HILDE): Miss Wangel, do you see all those young fellows down there at the gate?

HILDE: Yes.

RAGNAR: They're my friends. They all want to watch the Master today.

HILDE: Why?

RAGNAR: They want to see if he'd dare climb up on his own house.

HILDE: Oh, is that what those boys want?

RAGNAR: Yes. He's held us all down so long, I'd like to see him forced to stay down himself.

HILDE: You won't see *that* this time!

RAGNAR: And where will he be if not on the ground?

HILDE: High, high up on the spire—at the top! That's where you'll see him.

RAGNAR: You expect me to believe that?

HILDE: He wants to climb to the top. He wills it. And if that's what he wants, that's just where you'll see him!

RAGNAR: He *wants* to do it, all right. I believe that. But he just can't. His head will start to spin before he gets halfway up, and he'll have to crawl down on his hands and knees.

DOCTOR (*Pointing*): Look! There goes the foreman up the ladder.

ALINE: And he has that big wreath to carry. Oh, I do hope he'll be careful!

RAGNAR (*Staring in disbelief*): But it's—

HILDE: It's the Master Builder himself!

ALINE (*In terror*): Yes, it's Halvard! Oh my God, Halvard! Halvard!

DOCTOR: Quiet! Don't call to him.

ALINE (*Half beside herself*): I want to go to him. I want to get him down.

DOCTOR: Stand still, all of you! Don't make a sound!

HILDE: He's climbing higher and higher. Look! Still higher! Look!

RAGNAR: Now he'll have to turn back! He'll have to!

HILDE: He's climbing and climbing. He'll be at the top soon!

ALINE: I can't stand it any longer. I'll die of fright!

DOCTOR: Don't look.

HILDE: Now! There he stands on the highest platform—all the way up—at the very top!

DOCTOR: No one move! Do you hear?

HILDE (*Quietly, with exultant intensity*): At last— At last! Now I see him again—great and free!

RAGNAR: But this is—

HILDE: Just as I've seen him for ten years. How securely he stands! It's terrifying and yet—how exciting! Look at him! Now he's flinging the wreath over the spire.

RAGNAR: I'm looking at something that can't be happening.

HILDE: He's doing the impossible! Can you see anyone else up there with him?

RAGNAR: There's no one else up there.

HILDE: Yes! He's quarreling with someone.

RAGNAR: You're wrong—

HILDE: Don't you hear a song in the air?

RAGNAR: It must be the wind in the tree tops.

HILDE: I hear a song! A mighty song! (*She shouts in wild abandon.*) Look! Look! Now he's waving his hat! He's saluting us all down here! Let's salute back! Wave back up to him! For now it's completed! (*She takes the white shawl from the* DOCTOR, *waves it, and shouts up at him.*) Hurrah for Master Builder Solness!

DOCTOR: Keep still! Keep still, for God's sake!

(*The* LADIES *wave their handkerchiefs. The crowd in the street joins in the cheering. Then, suddenly, there is a silence and the crowd's cheering turns to a dreadful screaming. A human body, with some planks and other pieces of wood, is seen falling between the trees.*)

ALINE: He's falling!

ALINE and the LADIES: He's falling!

(MRS. SOLNESS *sways and faints. She is caught by the* LADIES. *General shouting and sounds of confusion are heard as the crowd on the street breaks down the fence and runs through the garden on the way to the scene of the accident.* DOCTOR HERDAL *follows. There is a short pause.*)

HILDE (*Staring upward, trancelike*): My Master Builder.

RAGNAR (*Supporting himself against the railing*): He must be smashed to pieces. Dead on the spot.

A LADY (*As* MRS. SOLNESS *is being carried into the house*): Run for the Doctor.

RAGNAR: I can't move—

ANOTHER LADY: Call to him, then.

RAGNAR: How is he? Is he alive?

A VOICE FROM THE GARDEN: Master Builder Solness is dead.

ANOTHER VOICE: The whole head is crushed. He fell into the stone quarry.

HILDE (*Turning to* RAGNAR, *speaks quietly*): I can't see him up there any more.

RAGNAR (*Turning from her gaze*): Oh how horrible, horrible. So he couldn't do it—he couldn't do it after all.

HILDE (*As in a quiet trance, triumphantly*): But he got all the way to the top! And I heard harps in the air. (*She waves the shawl and screams in wild and heartfelt enthusiasm.*) My— my Master Builder!

CURTAIN

# LITTLE
# EYOLF

1894

## CHARACTERS

ALFRED ALLMERS    *an estate owner, a man of letters, and a former tutor*

MRS. RITA ALLMERS    *his wife*

EYOLF    *their nine-year-old son*

MISS ASTA ALLMERS    *Alfred's younger half-sister*

ENGINEER BORGHEIM

THE RAT-WIFE

The action takes place on ALLMERS' estate, on the fiord some fourteen to eighteen miles from town.

# ACT I

*An attractive, expensively decorated solarium in the* ALLMERS' *house. There is a good deal of furniture, cut flowers, and plants around the room.* UPSTAGE *there are glass doors that open onto a veranda. From there the fiord and some wood-covered hills are seen in the distance.* UPSTAGE RIGHT *is a double door,* DOWNSTAGE RIGHT, *a sofa, and on it some throw pillows and an afghan.* DOWNSTAGE LEFT *is a large table with armchairs around it. On the table is an open suitcase. On the wall* LEFT, *another door. It is an early morning in summer. The sun is shining and warm.*

AS THE CURTAIN RISES, RITA ALLMERS *is standing at the table facing* STAGE LEFT, *unpacking the suitcase. She is an attractive, rather tall, voluptuous blonde about thirty years old. She is dressed in a light morning gown. After a moment* ASTA ALLMERS *enters through the door* RIGHT. *She is dressed in a light brown summer suit with a hat, and she carries a parasol. Under her arm is a rather large portfolio with a lock on it. She is slim, of medium height, with dark hair and deep, solemn eyes, and is about twenty-five years old.*

ASTA: Good morning, Rita dear.

RITA: My goodness, Asta, it's you! You must have left town early to be here already.

ASTA: Yes, I did. I felt restless at home. I just had to come out here and see little Eyolf today—and you too, Rita. (*She lays her portfolio on the table near the sofa.*) So I took the early steamer and here I am!

RITA: And on board you just happened to meet an old friend, didn't you? Merely by chance, of course?

ASTA: No. I didn't meet anyone I know. (*Seeing the suitcase*) What does this mean?

RITA: It's Alfred's. Don't you recognize it?

ASTA: What? Alfred's home?

RITA: Yes, imagine that! He took the night train and arrived totally unexpectedly.

ASTA: Then that's what I felt! Something was drawing me out here. But didn't Alfred let you know he was coming home? Not even a postcard?

RITA: Not a single word.

ASTA: Not even a telegram?

RITA: Well, yes, the telegram arrived an hour before he did. (*With an ironic smile*) It was quite short and sweet. (*Smiling*) That's like him, isn't it, Asta?

ASTA: Oh yes. He always does things in his own quiet way.

RITA: But of course that made it all the more wonderful when I got him back.

ASTA: Yes—I can imagine.

RITA: Two whole weeks before we expected him.

ASTA: And how's he feeling? Not so depressed?

RITA (*Closes the suitcase and smiles*): He looked almost transfigured when he came through that door.

ASTA: And he wasn't the least bit tired?

RITA: Oh yes, he was tired—and I mean really tired. But no wonder, poor thing . . . he'd walked most of the way home.

ASTA: Maybe the mountain air was a little too severe for him.

RITA: Oh no. I don't think so. I haven't heard him cough or anything—not once!

ASTA: Well then, you see! It was a good thing the doctor convinced him to take this trip.

RITA: Well—yes—now that he's home again. But believe me, Asta, it's been a dreadful time for me. I haven't wanted to bother you with it, and you don't come to see me very often, you know, so—

ASTA: I know, it's not very nice of me, but—

RITA: No, no, I understand. You have your teaching in school. (*Smiling*) And besides, our young road builder was away.

ASTA: Let's not talk about him, Rita.

RITA: All right, we'll leave the road builder out of this. Oh, if you only knew how I've been missing Alfred! The place has been so empty, so lonely—it's as if we'd had a funeral in the house.

ASTA: Good heavens, he's only been away for six or seven weeks.

RITA: Yes. But remember, Alfred has never been away from me before. Not even for a night—not once in all these ten years.

ASTA: That's exactly why it was about time for him to go. He should have gone to the mountains every summer. No—he really should have.

RITA (*Half smiling*): That's easy enough for you to say! If I were as . . . as sensible as you, I suppose I might have given him that much freedom before, but somehow I just couldn't. It always seemed to me that I'd never get him back. You can sympathize with *that*, can't you?

ASTA: No, I can't. But then, of course, I've never had anyone to lose.

RITA (*With a teasing smile*): Really? No one?

ASTA: Not that I know of. By the way, Rita, where is Alfred? Is he still sleeping?

RITA: Oh, far from it! He got up early—as usual.

ASTA: Well then, he wasn't so tired after all.

RITA: He was when he got here last night. But this morning he's been working with little Eyolf for over an hour.

ASTA: Oh, that poor, pale little boy! Has Alfred started his lessons already?

RITA (*Shrugging her shoulders*): You know that's the way Alfred wants it.

ASTA: Yes, but I think you should put your foot down, Rita.

RITA (*Somewhat annoyed*): Oh, come now, I can't interfere with that! Alfred certainly understands those things much better than I do. Besides, how else can Eyolf spend his time? He can't run around and play like other children.

ASTA (*With determination*): I'll talk to Alfred about it.

RITA: Oh yes, my dear, please do. Well, look who's here!

(ALFRED ALLMERS *enters through the door* LEFT, *dressed in a summer suit. He is a slender, delicately built man about thirty-six or -seven years old, with kindly eyes, thin brown*

hair, and a beard. His expression is solemn and serious. He is
leading EYOLF by the hand. EYOLF is dressed in a uniform of
some kind, that is trimmed with gold braid and military
buttons with lions on them. He is lame and walks with a
crutch under his left arm. His leg is shrunken and limp. He
is undersized and looks sickly, but his eyes are beautiful and
intelligent.)

ALLMERS (Letting go of EYOLF's hand, extends both this hands to
ASTA): Asta! My dear Asta! How good to see you here—and
so soon!

ASTA: I felt I just had to ... welcome home!

ALLMERS (Shaking her hands): Thank you.

RITA: Doesn't he look well?

ASTA: Wonderful! Just wonderful. Your eyes are so much
brighter. You must have written quite a bit while you were
away. I wouldn't be surprised if the whole book were finished—eh, Alfred?

ALLMERS (Shrugging his shoulders): The book? Oh, that.

ASTA: I knew it would be much easier for you to write once you
got away by yourself.

ALLMERS: I thought so too, but it didn't work out that way. I
haven't written a single word!

ASTA: You haven't...?

RITA: So that's it! I wondered why you hadn't touched the
papers in your suitcase.

ASTA: But Alfred, dear, what have you been doing all this time?

ALLMERS: Just thinking. Thinking and thinking.

RITA (Putting her arm around his shoulder): Did you think a
little about those at home?

ALLMERS: Yes, of course, you know I did—a great deal—every
day.

RITA (Taking her arm away): That's all I want to know. Everything's just as it should be!

ASTA: You really haven't written anything, Alfred? And yet you
look so happy, so satisfied. You're usually so discontented ...
I mean, when your work isn't going well.

ALLMERS: How right you are! You see, I've been very foolish.

Thinking is the best thing man can do, and what one finally puts down on paper is worth very little.

ASTA: Worth very little?

RITA (*Smiling*): Are you out of your mind, Alfred?

EYOLF (*Looking up at* ALLMERS *confidently*): Oh Father, whatever you write is worth a great deal!

ALLMERS (*Smiles and pats his hair*): Well, yes—yes, then, if you say so. But, believe me, someone will come after me who will do it much better.

EYOLF: Who will that be? Oh tell me!

ALLMERS: Just give him time. You'll see! You'll see—he'll make himself known.

EYOLF: What will happen to you then, Father?

ALLMERS (*Seriously*): I'll go up to the mountains again ...

RITA: Oh Alfred, the way you talk!

ALLMERS: ... way up to the mountain peaks and into the great empty places.

EYOLF: Father, will I be well enough to go with you?

ALLMERS (*Painfully*): Oh yes. Maybe so, my boy.

EYOLF: Oh what fun! I'd be so proud of myself if I could go climbing in the mountains with you!

ASTA (*Deliberately changing the subject*): Well now, Eyolf, what a nice suit that is.

EYOLF: Thank you, Aunt Asta. It is, isn't it?

ASTA: Yes indeed! And are you dressed up for your father?

EYOLF: Yes. I begged mother to let me put it on; I wanted him to see me in it.

ALLMERS (*Whispering to* RITA): You shouldn't have given him that kind of suit!

RITA (*Whispering back*): He's been begging for weeks! He was so insistent—he gave me no peace.

EYOLF: Oh, I didn't tell you, Father, Mr. Borghcim bought me a bow and arrow set and he's teaching me to shoot with it!

ALLMERS: That's nice. Sounds like just the thing for you, Eyolf.

EYOLF: And when he comes here again I'm going to ask him to teach me how to swim.

ALLMERS: Swim? Why do you want to learn that?

EYOLF: Well, all the other boys down at the water can swim.
I'm the only one who can't.

ALLMERS (*Touched, takes him in his arms*): You can learn anything you want. Anything you really want to do, Eyolf, you
can!

EYOLF: Do you know what I want most of all, Father?

ALLMERS: No, tell me.

EYOLF: Most of all I want to be a soldier.

ALLMERS: Oh, my little Eyolf, there are so many better things
to do.

EYOLF: Yes, I know, but when I grow up I just *have* to be a soldier—you know that!

ALLMERS (*Wringing his hands*): Yes, yes—well, we'll see.

ASTA (*Sitting at the table* LEFT): Eyolf, come over here, dear, to
me. I have something I want to tell you.

EYOLF (*Going to her*): What is it, Aunt Asta?

ASTA: Guess whom I saw yesterday, Eyolf? I saw the old Rat-
Wife.

EYOLF: Really? You saw her? The real Rat-Wife? Oh, you're
just teasing me!

ASTA: No I'm not. It's true. I saw her yesterday.

EYOLF: Where?

ASTA: On the road just outside the town.

ALLMERS: I saw her, too—farther out—in the country.

RITA: Then maybe we'll see her next, Eyolf!

EYOLF: Aunt Asta, why do they call her the Rat-Wife?

ASTA: Oh, people have always called her that. She wanders
through the countryside and chases away all the rats.

ALLMERS: I believe her name is really Miss Varg.

EYOLF: Varg! That means wolf, doesn't it, Father?

ALLMERS (*Patting his head*): Ah, so you know that, eh?

EYOLF (*Secretively*): Maybe what they say is true—that she
turns into a werewolf at night. Do you think so, Father?

ALLMERS: Oh no, I don't think so. But I do think that now you
should go out and play in the garden.

EYOLF: Shouldn't I take my books and study?

ALLMERS: No. No books from now on. I'd rather you go down
to the water and play with the other boys.

EYOLF (*Shyly*): No, Father, I don't want to go there today.

ALLMERS: Why not?

EYOLF: Not in my new clothes.

ALLMERS: Why? Would the boys make fun of your nice clothes?

EYOLF (*Evasively*): No, they wouldn't dare. I'd hit them!

ALLMERS: Well, then—why?

EYOLF: Well, those boys are horrible. They all say I'll never be a soldier.

ALLMERS (*Suppressing his anger*): Why do you think they say that?

EYOLF: Because they're jealous of me. You know what, Father? They're so poor they never have any new clothes! And no shoes, either.

ALLMERS (*Whispering to* RITA): Oh Rita—it's so pathetic.

RITA (*Rises and speaks soothingly*): There, there—

ALLMERS: Someday those ruffians down there will learn who our young Master Allmers really is!

RITA: Someone's at the door.

EYOLF: Maybe it's Mr. Borgheim.

RITA: Come in—

(*The* RAT-WIFE *comes in slowly and noiselessly through the door at the* RIGHT. *She is a small, thin, shrunken creature, old and gray-haired, with sharp, piercing eyes. She is wearing an old-fashioned, country-style, flowered dress which she covers with a black cloak and a large-brimmed hood, or calash. She carries a large red umbrella, and on her arm is a black bag hanging from a loop.*)

EYOLF (*Quietly, holding* ASTA's *skirt*): Aunt Asta! That must be her!

RAT-WIFE (*Making a curtsy in the doorway*): With all my humble apologies—would you kindly permit me to inquire—are the master and mistress of this house disturbed by any gnawing things?

ALLMERS: We? Here? No, I don't think so.

RAT-WIFE: Well, if you are, I would be more than happy to help you get rid of them.

RITA: Yes, yes, we understand, but we don't have anything of that kind here.

RAT-WIFE: Well, that's a pity, for I'm making a tour of this part of the country and God knows when I'll be back around these parts again. Oh, I'm so tired!

ALLMERS (*Indicating a chair*): Yes, you seem to be.

RAT-WIFE: I suppose one should really never tire of doing good for those poor little ones—so brutally hated and persecuted. But it saps my strength, let me tell you!

RITA: Perhaps you'd like to sit down and rest for a while?

RAT-WIFE (*Sitting on a chair between the door and the sofa*): A thousand thanks. You see, all night long I've been out doing my chores.

ALLMERS: You have?

RAT-WIFE: Yes, over on the islands. (*With a chuckle*) They finally had to send for me. Believe me, they didn't want to! And they took their time about making up their minds, but in the end there was nothing else to do but put on happy faces and take their medicine. (*She looks at* EYOLF *and nods.*) Yes, my little sir, they had to swallow their medicine!

EYOLF: Why did they have to?

RAT-WIFE: What?

EYOLF: Take their medicine?

RAT-WIFE: Because they couldn't live any longer without it. And because of all the rats and all of the little rat babies. Now do you see, my young master?

RITA: Oh, those poor people, did they have so many?

RAT-WIFE: Oh yes, the place was alive and crawling with them. (*Laughing with quiet satisfaction*) All night long they were creeping and crawling all over the beds. They would splash into the milk tubs and then go pitter-pattering all over the floors—left and right—back and forth—up and down.

EYOLF (*To* ASTA): I never want to go there, Aunt Asta!

RAT-WIFE: But then I got there—myself and someone else. We took them all with us, the sweet little creatures! We put an end to every one of them.

EYOLF (*Crying out*): Father, look! Look!

RITA: Good God, Eyolf, what is it?

ALLMERS: What's wrong?

EYOLF (*Pointing to the* RAT-WIFE's *bag*): Look—there's something moving in her bag!

RITA (*Shrieking*): Get her out of here, Alfred!

RAT-WIFE (*Laughing*): My dear, gracious lady, you don't have to be afraid of such a tiny tyke!

ALLMERS: What do you have in there?

RAT-WIFE (*Opening the bag*): Why, it's only my little Puggsie-Wuggsie. Come out of the dark, little loved one. (*A small pug dog, with a wide black snout, pushes his head out of the bag. The* RAT-WIFE *beckons* EYOLF *forward.*) Don't be afraid. Come closer, little wounded soldier, come closer—he won't bite. Come here. Come here, now.

EYOLF (*Clinging to* ASTA): No. I'm afraid to.

RAT-WIFE: Don't you think, little man, that he has a kind, lovable face?

EYOLF (*Pointing*): That thing?

RAT-WIFE: Yes—him.

EYOLF (*Stares fixedly at the dog and whispers*): I think he has the most frightening face I've ever seen.

RAT-WIFE: You'll change your mind. Just give yourself time. It'll come—it'll come—

EYOLF (*Involuntarily draws near and strokes the bag gently*): But he is wonderful—wonderful—just the same.

RAT-WIFE (*In a gentle voice*): Right now he's very tired, very weary, poor little thing. He's absolutely worn out. (*Looking at* ALLMERS) Believe me, this kind of game saps the strength out of anyone. —I don't mind telling you, sir.

ALLMERS: What game do you mean?

RAT-WIFE: The luring game.

ALLMERS: Oh! The dog lures the rats?

RAT-WIFE (*Nodding*): Puggsie and I, we do it together. It all goes so easy—this game—at least that's the way it looks! I just slip a string around his neck and lead him around the house three times while I play on my pipes. When they hear the music they just have to come up out of the cellars and down from the attics and off the shelves and out of their holes—every blessed little creature.

EYOLF: And then he bites them to death?

RAT-WIFE: Oh no! No, far from it! No, we walk down to the boat, he and I, and they all follow us. All the grown ones, and the small tots, too.

EYOLF: And then? What happens then? Tell me!

RAT-WIFE: Then I take the boat and push off. With one hand I wiggle the oar and with the other I play my pipes. (*Her eyes sparkle.*) Puggsie swims behind and all the crawlies and the creepies follow—follow—out, out into the deep water. You see, they have to.

EYOLF: Why do they have to?

RAT-WIFE: Because they don't *want* to! Because they have a deadly fear of water. That's why they have to get out into it!

EYOLF: Do they drown then?

RAT-WIFE: Every single one. (*Softly*) And then it's so quiet and so comfortable in the dark—so much better than they ever could have wished for, the dear little ones. Deep down there, they'll have a long, sweet sleep—all those creatures whom people hate and persecute. (*Standing up*) Well! In the old days I didn't have to use Puggsie. I did all the luring myself —just myself alone.

EYOLF: What did you lure then?

RAT-WIFE: People! One in particular.

EYOLF (*Excitedly*): Who was it? Tell me!

RAT-WIFE: It was my own dearest love . . . (*Smiling at* EYOLF) . . . my little heartbreaker.

EYOLF: But where is he now?

RAT-WIFE (*Sternly*): Down there with all the rats! (*In a mild tone again*) But now I have to get back to my chores. Always on the move! So, my master and mistress, have you any use for me today? If you have, I could take care of it immediately.

RITA: No, thank you, I don't think there's any need.

RAT-WIFE: No, no, of course not, my kind mistress. But one can never be sure! Should the master and mistress notice anything nibbling and gnawing—anything creeping and crawling—just call for me and Puggsie. Good-by! Good-by, and a thousand thanks. (*She exits to the* RIGHT.)

EYOLF (*Softly and proudly to* ASTA): Just imagine, Aunt Asta, now I've seen the Rat-Wife too!

(RITA *goes out on the veranda and fans herself with her handkerchief. Shortly after,* EYOLF *exits* RIGHT, *quietly and unnoticed.*)

ALLMERS (*Noticing* ASTA'S *portfolio*): Is this your portfolio, Asta?

ASTA: Yes. I have some of the old letters in it.

ALLMERS: Family papers?

ASTA: Yes—remember? You asked me to go through them while you were away?

ALLMERS (*Patting her on the head*): And you were dear enough to find time to do it?

ASTA: Oh, yes. I went through some of them out here and some in town at my place.

ALLMERS: Thank you so much, my dear. Did you find anything particularly interesting in them?

ASTA (*Lightly*): Oh, you know how it is. One always finds something or other in old papers like these. (*Slowly and solemnly indicating the portfolio*) I've put the letters addressed to mother in here.

ALLMERS: Well, of course, you should keep those.

ASTA (*With effort*): But I want you to look through them, Alfred. Sometime—maybe even later on in life. I didn't bring the key today.

ALLMERS: That's all right, my dear. Anyway, I wouldn't want to intrude.

ASTA (*Looking at him intensely*): Well then, some quiet evening I'll tell you what's in them.

ALLMERS: Yes, that would be better. Keep them, Asta. You have so few of your mother's things.

(ALLMERS *picks up the portfolio and gives it to* ASTA. *She takes it and puts it on the chair under her coat.*)

RITA (*Entering*): I feel as if that awful woman brought the smell of death with her.

ALLMERS: She *is* awful, isn't she?

RITA: I felt sick while she was in the room.

ALLMERS: And yet I think I know exactly what she meant by an irresistible attraction that pulls someone against his will. There's that same fascination in the loneliness of the mountains and the great empty places.

ASTA (*Looking intently at him*): What happened to you up there, Alfred?

ALLMERS (*Smiling*): Me?

ASTA: Yes. There's something so different about you—it's as if you've been transformed. Rita noticed it too.

RITA: Yes, as soon as you came through the door last night! But it's all for the good, isn't it, Alfred?

ALLMERS: It ought to be for the good. It must be!

RITA (*With an outburst*): You've met someone on your trip! That's it! Alfred, you've had that kind of experience, and don't deny it. I can see it all over you!

ALLMERS (*Shaking his head*): No, I didn't meet anyone—nothing like that. Nothing physical has changed with me—just—

RITA: Just—?

ALLMERS: I've had an experience, it's true, and it has changed me, completely, inside!

RITA (*Sighing*): Oh my God!

ALLMERS (*Patting her hand to calm her*): It'll be for the best, Rita dear. You can depend on that.

RITA (*Sitting on the sofa*): Tell us what this is all about, Alfred. Right now, and all of it!

ALLMERS (*Turning to* ASTA): All right. I'll try as well as I can. Asta, do sit down.

(ALLMERS *sits on the sofa next to* RITA. ASTA *moves a chair close to them and sits. There is a short silence.*)

RITA: Well?

ALLMERS (*Looking straight ahead*): When I think back on my life and my destiny for the last ten, eleven years, it all passes before me as some kind of adventure story—or a dream. Do you feel that way too, Asta?

ASTA: Yes, in many ways.

ALLMERS (*In the same mood*): When I think of where we two came from—we two poor little orphans—

RITA (*Impatiently*): But that was a long time ago!

ALLMERS (*Not listening to her*): And now I sit here in all this security and comfort. I've even been able to follow my vocation, to study and write just as I wished. (*Reaches for* RITA's *hand and holds it*) And all this unbelievable happiness we owe to you, my dear Rita.

RITA (*Slapping his hand half in fun, half seriously*): Stop talking like that!

ALLMERS: I mention it as a kind of prologue.

RITA: Well, skip the prologues!

ALLMERS: Rita, you mustn't believe it was the doctor's advice that made me go to the mountains.

ASTA: Wasn't it?

RITA: What was it, then?

ALLMERS: I was not at peace with my work any more.

RITA: No? Oh, my poor love, who spoiled that for you?

ALLMERS (*Shaking his head*): No one. No one from the outside. I felt that I'd misused my talents or, even worse, that I'd neglected them. I realized I had just been wasting away my time in there.

ASTA (*Incredulously*): While you were writing?

ALLMERS (*Nodding*): Yes. I wasn't intended for writing—*only* writing. There must be something else I can do.

RITA: Is that what you were brooding over?

ALLMERS: Yes, primarily that.

RITA: Is that why you were so dissatisfied with yourself just before you left? And with us, too? Because you were, you know, Alfred.

ALLMERS (*Staring straight ahead*): There I sat, bent over my desk, day in and day out and often half into the night. Writing and writing away on that big, thick book, *The Human Responsibility*.

ASTA (*Putting her hand on his arm*): But my dear Alfred, that's going to be your major work!

RITA: Yes. You've said so often enough.

ALLMERS: And believed it, too—ever since I was a child. Then, my dear Rita, you came along and made it possible for me to write it—

RITA: Oh nonsense!

ALLMERS: —You with your "gold and green forests."

RITA (*Half in fun, half seriously*): If you start all that again, honestly, I'll hit you.

ASTA (*Looking at him with sadness*): But the book, Alfred?

ALLMERS: It began to disappear from my mind. More and more the thought of another duty came to me—a duty that demanded something more of me.

RITA (*Taking his hand hopefully*): Alfred.

ALLMERS: And as I thought of Eyolf, my dear Rita—

RITA (*Dropping his hand, disappointed*): Ah. Eyolf.

ALLMERS: Yes, little Eyolf. His place in my heart has grown deeper and deeper ever since that tragic fall from the table. *And* since we've known he'll never completely recover.

RITA (*Insisting*): But you do everything possible for him.

ALLMERS: I mean that from now on I'm going to use all my strength to make him live with his injury as painlessly as possible.

RITA: Why Alfred, I don't think he feels it that deeply, thank God.

ASTA: Oh yes, Rita, he does.

ALLMERS: I'm sure he feels it very deeply.

RITA (*Impatiently*): What more can you do for him, Alfred?

ALLMERS: I can try to enrich the possibilities that lie in his little soul. I'll encourage his finest potentials to grow and flower and bear fruit. And I want more than that! I want to help his mind achieve a harmony—because right now he's ambitious for all those things which will be forever unattainable to him. I must create some kind of contentment in his life.

(ALLMERS *paces the floor several times,* ASTA *and* RITA *following him with their eyes.*)

RITA: Don't let this upset you so much, Alfred!

ALLMERS: Eyolf will continue my life's work if he wants to, or, if he'd rather, he can choose something that's all his own. Maybe that would be best for him. In any case, I'll let my own work go from now on.

RITA: But my dear Alfred, can't you write and be a father to Eyolf at the same time?

ALLMERS: No, I can't. It would be impossible to divide myself. I'm stepping aside for Eyolf. I'll make it my new major work —to make of Eyolf the perfect man of our family!

ASTA (*Stands up and goes to him*): Alfred, you must have fought a terribly hard battle with yourself.

ALLMERS: I did. Here at home I'd never have managed. I couldn't have forced myself to this sacrifice. Never in this house.

RITA: Was *that* your reason for going away this summer?

ALLMERS (*With shining eyes*): Yes. When I was up there in the infinite solitude, and I saw the glorious sunrises over the mountaintops and felt so close to the stars that we seemed to have an understanding between us—as if we were all related—then and only then did I find strength enough to do it.

ASTA (*Picking up his unfinished book*): And what will happen to this? (*Reading the title*) The Human Responsibility?

ALLMERS: Well, I told you I can't divide myself between two duties. From now on I'll fulfill my theories of human responsibility by living them.

RITA (*Smiling*): Do you think you can live up to such high ideals here at home?

ALLMERS (*Taking RITA's hand*): With you as my companion, I can. (*Giving ASTA the other hand*) And with you too, Asta.

RITA (*Withdrawing her hand*): Both of us? So you *can* divide yourself after all!

ALLMERS: But my dear Rita!

(RITA *walks over to the garden door. There is a short, quick knock on the door* RIGHT. ENGINEER BORGHEIM *enters briskly. He is a young man of about thirty. He is bright and friendly and carries himself with grace.*)

BORGHEIM: Good morning, Mrs. Allmers. (*He stops, pleased to see* ALLMERS.) Whom do I see here? Mr. Allmers home already?

ALLMERS (*Shaking his hand*): Yes, I arrived last night.

RITA (*Happily*): His leave of absence was over, Mr. Borgheim.

ALLMERS: Rita, that's not quite true.

RITA (*Approaching*): Oh, yes it is. His leave was definitely over.

BORGHEIM: So you hold on to your husband's reins that tight— eh, Mrs. Allmers?

RITA: No tighter than a wife is entitled to! Besides, all things must come to an end.

BORGHEIM: Oh, not everything, I hope. Good morning, Miss Allmers!

ASTA (*Aloof*): Good morning.

RITA (*Looking at* BORGHEIM): Not everything, you say?

BORGHEIM: Not everything! I'm convinced there are some things in this world that don't end.

RITA: Now you're thinking of love or something like that.

BORGHEIM (*Warmly*): I was thinking about everything lovely.

RITA: And they won't end? Well, let's think about that, and hope for it, too, all of us!

ALLMERS: I suppose you'll soon be finished with all your road work around here?

BORGHEIM: We're finished already—just yesterday, and it lasted long enough for me. Thank God that particular thing came to an end.

RITA: Is that why you seem so radiantly happy today?

BORGHEIM: That's the reason.

RITA: Well, I like that—!

BORGHEIM: What?

RITA: Well, it's not very nice of you, Mr. Borgheim.

BORGHEIM: What do you mean?

RITA: For one thing, you won't be visiting us very often.

BORGHEIM: That's true. I hadn't thought of it that way.

RITA: I hope you'll come out to see us anyway, at least once in a while.

BORGHEIM: Unfortunately, even that won't be possible.

ALLMERS: Really? Why not?

BORGHEIM: Well, I have a new job—a big one—and I'll be starting right away.

ALLMERS (*Shaking his hand*): Well, congratulations! I'm happy for you.

RITA: Congratulations, Mr. Borgheim.

BORGHEIM: But keep it under your hat! I'm not supposed to talk about it yet, but I just can't keep it to myself. It's a very difficult road job up north, with mountain overpasses to tackle and tremendous difficulties to overcome. Oh, what a wonderful world this is, and aren't I lucky to be a road builder in it?

RITA (*Smiling, teasingly*): Then it's only because of your new job that you're here today and in such high spirits?

BORGHEIM: No, not only that. Other promising prospects seem to be opening for me.

RITA: Aha! Then perhaps you have something even more exciting up your sleeve?

BORGHEIM (*Glancing at* ASTA): Who knows! Let's hope luck is like the spring showers—it never rains but what it pours! (*To* ASTA) Miss Allmers, shall we take our little walk as usual?

ASTA (*Quickly*): No, no thank you. Not now. Not today.

BORGHEIM: Oh, please come. Just for a little walk—we have so much to talk over before I leave.

RITA: So there's something *else* you can't talk about yet, eh?

BORGHEIM: Well, that all depends.

RITA: In that case, we can't stop you from discussing it in private first. (*Softly, to* ASTA) Asta, you just have to go with him.

ASTA: Please, Rita—

BORGHEIM (*Imploring*): Miss Allmers, remember that this will be our last walk for a long, long time.

ASTA (*Taking her hat and parasol*): All right, then. Let's walk around the garden, if you wish.

BORGHEIM: Oh, thank you, thank you so much.

ALLMERS: And while you're there, would you keep an eye on Eyolf?

BORGHEIM: Of course. Where is he? I have something for him.

ALLMERS: He's in the garden, playing.

BORGHEIM: Is that so? So he's started to play now? Good—he's usually indoors studying.

ALLMERS: Well, there'll be no more of that! From now on, Eyolf will be an outdoor boy.

BORGHEIM: Good. I agree with that. Out into the fresh air with

him, poor little thing. He couldn't do better than play out-
doors in God's wonderful world. I really think that life is
meant to be just one long game anyway. Let's go, Miss
Allmers.

(BORGHEIM *and* ASTA *go out to the veranda and down through
the garden.*)

ALLMERS (*Standing looking at them*): Rita, do you think there's
anything serious between them?

RITA: I don't know what to say. I used to think so, but Asta's
become so unpredictable lately—so mysterious.

ALLMERS: Has she? Since I've been away?

RITA: In the last few weeks. At least it seems that way to me.

ALLMERS: And she doesn't seem to care for him any more?

RITA: Well, not seriously enough—not without reservations.
That's how I feel about it! (*Scrutinizing him*) Would you be
against it if she did?

ALLMERS: Not really against it, but it would disturb me, I can't
deny that.

RITA: Disturb you?

ALLMERS: Remember I'm responsible for Asta—for Asta's happiness.

RITA: Oh come now—you and your responsibilities! Surely Asta
is old enough to choose for herself.

ALLMERS: Let's hope so, Rita.

RITA: And I don't think Borgheim is so bad.

ALLMERS: Neither do I, but—

RITA: I'd like to see the two of them get together.

ALLMERS (*Annoyed*): Would you? Why?

RITA (*With growing excitement*): Because then she'd have to go
away with him—far away! And she couldn't come out here
and visit us so often.

ALLMERS (*Staring at her in astonishment*): What? Would you
want Asta to stay away?

RITA: Yes. Yes, I would, Alfred.

ALLMERS: Why on earth—?

RITA (*Throwing her arms passionately around his neck*): Because
then, at last, I'd have you all to myself. Oh God, maybe not

entirely—not completely—for myself, not even then! (*Bursting into convulsive sobs*) Oh Alfred, Alfred—I can't lose you!

ALLMERS (*Gently releasing himself*): My dear Rita, do be sensible!

RITA: I don't want to be sensible! All I care about is loving you —only you! Only you in the whole world! (*Again throwing her arms around his neck*) Just you, you, you. . . .

ALLMERS: Rita, please—you're strangling me!

RITA (*Letting go*): I wish I could! (*She looks at him, her eyes flashing.*) If you only knew how I've hated you!

ALLMERS: Hated?

RITA: Yes! All those hours you sat in there by yourself, locked up in your room, brooding over your work—far, far into the night, so long and so late! Oh Alfred, how I hated your work!

ALLMERS: That's all past now, Rita.

RITA (*With a bitter laugh*): Yes, yes, of course it is. Now you've dedicated yourself to something even worse!

ALLMERS (*Shocked*): You mean our child is worse?

RITA (*Vehemently*): Yes—because he comes between us! At least your work wasn't a living thing! The child is! (*With increasing passion*) But let me tell you this, Alfred: I won't stand for it. I won't!

ALLMERS (*Looking steadily, half whispers*): Sometimes you frighten me, Rita.

RITA (*Darkly*): Sometimes I frighten myself. That's why you must be careful not to bring out the evil in me.

ALLMERS: In God's name, do I do that?

RITA: Yes, you do. When you tear apart the thing most sacred to us.

ALLMERS (*Penetratingly*): Stop it! Think what you're talking about—your own child. Our only child.

RITA: The child's only half mine. (*With another outburst*) But you are entirely mine. And I have a right to demand that much.

ALLMERS (*Shrugging his shoulders*): There's no use demanding, Rita. Everything must be given freely.

RITA: And from now on you won't do that?

ALLMERS: No. I can't. I can't divide myself between you and Eyolf.

RITA: What if Eyolf had never been born? What then?

ALLMERS (*Avoiding it*): Well then, things would be different. I would only have you to love.

RITA (*Softly, her voice quivering*): Then I wish—I wish that he'd never been born.

ALLMERS (*Furious*): Rita! You don't know what you're saying!

RITA (*Lashing out*): I gave birth to him in the most wretched pain. But I endured it all with a deep sense of joy, and all for *you!*

ALLMERS (*Warmly*): Yes, yes, I know that.

RITA (*With decision*): But it ends there. I want to live my life with you, and only you. I can't live here and just be Eyolf's mother, just that and nothing else. I don't want to, I tell you! I can't. I want to be everything to you. To you, Alfred —you, alone.

ALLMERS: But you are, Rita—through our child.

RITA: Oh, what an empty phrase! Is that all I'm going to get from you from now on? Empty phrases and nothing else? No, Alfred, no thank you. That's not going to satisfy me. It was physically possible for me to have a child, but I can't just be its mother. You'll have to accept that, Alfred.

ALLMERS: You used to love Eyolf so much!

RITA: I felt sorry for him. You always let him shift for himself. You kept him reading and grinding away at his books—you scarcely ever saw him.

ALLMERS (*Nodding slowly*): Yes, yes, I was blind. The time hadn't come for me to—

RITA: And now it has, I suppose?

ALLMERS: Yes, finally. Now I can see that the greatest achievement in this world for me is to be a true father to Eyolf.

RITA: And to me? What will you be to me?

ALLMERS (*Gently*): I want to continue being fond of you in a calm and tender way. (*He takes her hands.*)

RITA (*Avoiding him*): I don't care one bit for your calm and your tenderness! I want you—entirely—and only for myself!

Just as I had you in those first wonderful days. (*Harshly, and with vehemence*) I'll never in my life accept being pushed aside and fed the scraps.

ALLMERS (*Gently*): It seems to me there's enough happiness here for three of us.

RITA (*With growing contempt*): Well, aren't *you* easy to please! (*Sitting near the table* LEFT) Now listen to me.

ALLMERS (*Moving closer*): What is it?

RITA (*Looking at him with a dull stare*): When I received your telegram last night . . .

ALLMERS: Yes.

RITA: . . . I dressed all in white . . .

ALLMERS: Yes.

RITA: . . . I unpinned my hair . . .

ALLMERS: Your rich, fragrant hair.

RITA: . . . so that it flowed down over my neck and shoulders.

ALLMERS: Yes, yes, I saw it. You were very beautiful, Rita!

RITA: I put the rose-colored shades on both the lamps, and there were just the two of us. We were the only ones awake in the whole house, and there was champagne on the table.

ALLMERS: And I didn't drink any.

RITA (*Bitterly*): Yes. That's true. (*Laughing scornfully*) "You had champagne, but touched it not," as the poem goes. (*She gets up from the armchair, walks wearily to the sofa, and stretches out in a half-lying position.*)

ALLMERS (*Goes to her and stands above her*): I was engrossed in serious thoughts, Rita. I was determined to talk to you about our future. And first, about Eyolf.

RITA (*Smiling*): That's exactly what you did, dear. You talked.

ALLMERS: But I didn't even get started! You began undressing.

RITA: Yes, and while I did, you talked about Eyolf. Don't you remember? You asked me about his digestion.

ALLMERS (*Reproaching her*): Rita!

RITA: And then you got into your bed and went to sleep, and slept very soundly.

ALLMERS (*Shaking his head*): Rita, Rita.

RITA (*Stretching out completely*): Alfred?

ALLMERS: Yes?

RITA: "You had champagne, but touched it not."

ALLMERS (*Almost harshly*): No, I didn't touch it.

(ALLMERS *walks away from her and stands near the garden door.* RITA *lies for a moment absolutely still, with closed eyes.*)

RITA (*Suddenly jumping up*): I'll tell you one thing, Alfred!

ALLMERS: What?

RITA: You shouldn't be so sure of yourself.

ALLMERS: Sure of myself?

RITA: And of *me!*

ALLMERS (*Coming closer*): What do you mean by that?

RITA (*Her lips trembling*): Alfred, I've never been unfaithful to you. Not for a single moment, not even in one thought.

ALLMERS: No, of course not. I know you well enough for that, Rita.

RITA (*With eyes sparkling*): But if you reject me—

ALLMERS: Reject you? I don't know what you mean!

RITA: You can't begin to know what could happen to me if—

ALLMERS: If—?

RITA: If I should ever find out that you don't care for me any longer, that you don't love me as you used to.

ALLMERS: But Rita, my dear, people change through the years. One day our relationship will change, as it has with so many others.

RITA: Never! Never with me, and I don't want any change in you, either! I couldn't stand it, Alfred. I want to have you all for myself, always.

ALLMERS (*Looking at her, disturbed and concerned*): You have a dreadfully jealous mind.

RITA: I can't change myself into something I'm not. (*Threateningly*) If you divide yourself between me and someone else . . .

ALLMERS: Yes?

RITA: . . . then I'll have my revenge on you, Alfred.

ALLMERS: How could you do that?

RITA: I don't know. Oh yes I do—I know very well.

ALLMERS: How?

RITA: I'll destroy our marriage.

ALLMERS: Destroy our—

RITA: Yes! I'll throw myself into the arms of the first man who comes along!

ALLMERS (*Looking tenderly at her, shakes his head*): You could never do that! Not my proud, loyal Rita!

RITA: Oh, you don't know what I'm capable of—if you don't want anything more to do with me.

ALLMERS: How can you say that?

RITA (*Half laughing, lets him go*): I could very easily get my clutches into that . . . that road builder.

ALLMERS (*Relieved*): Oh, thank God—you're teasing!

RITA: I am? Why not him? He'll do as well as anyone.

ALLMERS: It seems to me that he's already spoken for.

RITA: All the better! I'd be taking him away from someone— exactly what Eyolf has done to me!

ALLMERS: How can you possibly feel that little Eyolf has done that?

RITA (*Shaking her index finger at him*): You see? You see? As soon as I just mention Eyolf's name, you get softhearted and your voice quivers! (*Threatening him with a clenched fist*) I'm tempted to wish that he—oh, no!

ALLMERS (*Looking at her with fear*): What is it you could wish, Rita?

RITA (*Turning away from him furiously*): No, no, I'll never tell you! Never!

ALLMERS (*Going close to her*): Rita! I beg you for your own sake —for both our sakes—don't be tempted to do something evil.

(BORGHEIM *and* ASTA *enter from the garden. They are both obviously controlling their emotion. They are upset and look solemn and dejected.* ASTA *remains on the veranda.* BORGHEIM *comes into the room.*)

BORGHEIM: Well, that's that! Miss Allmers and I have just had our last little walk.

RITA (*With surprise*): Ah! It's not to be followed by a longer trip?

BORGHEIM: For me, yes.

RITA: *Just* for you?

BORGHEIM: That's right.

RITA (*Looking darkly at* ALLMERS): Do you hear that, Alfred? (*To* BORGHEIM) I'll bet anything someone with an evil eye has played a trick on you.

BORGHEIM: An evil eye?

RITA (*Nodding*): Yes.

BORGHEIM: Do you believe in the evil eye, Mrs. Allmers?

RITA: Yes, I do. I've just begun to—especially in the evil eyes of children.

ALLMERS (*Whispering to her, upset*): Rita, how can you?

RITA (*Whispering back*): You've made me hateful, Alfred. (*Suddenly, from far off, confused screams and shouts from the direction of the water are heard.*)

BORGHEIM (*Walking to the veranda door*): What's all the noise?

ASTA (*In the doorway*): Look at all those people running down to the water!

ALLMERS: I wonder what it is! (*Looking out for a moment*) Probably it's some of those hoodlums playing a prank.

BORGHEIM (*Shouting*): Boys! Listen, boys! What's going on down there? What's the matter? (*Several voices answer. The replies are confused and muddled.*)

RITA: What did they say?

BORGHEIM: They say that some child's been drowned.

ALLMERS: Drowned?

ASTA (*Upset*): A little boy?

ALLMERS: But they all swim, every one of them!

RITA (*Screaming in terror*): Where's Eyolf?

ALLMERS: Keep calm, Rita! You know Eyolf's playing in the garden.

ASTA: No, he wasn't in the garden.

RITA: Oh God! Let it not be Eyolf!

BORGHEIM (*Shouting*): Who is it, boys? Who is it? (*More indistinct voices are heard shouting.* ASTA *and* BORGHEIM *suppress their cries and run out through the garden.*)

ALLMERS (*Agonized*): It isn't Eyolf! It isn't Eyolf, Rita!

RITA (*On the veranda, listening*): Quiet! Shhh! Be still! I can't hear what they're saying! (*She runs back into the room with a piercing scream.*)

ALLMERS: What did they say?

RITA (*Falling into the armchair* LEFT): They said, "The crutch is floating. . . ."

ALLMERS (*Almost paralyzed*): No! No! No!

RITA (*Hoarsely*): Eyolf! Eyolf! They have to save him!

ALLMERS (*Wildly*): They have to! They have to! Such a valuable life! Such a valuable life! (*He exits through the garden.*)

CURTAIN

# ACT II

A *narrow glen down near the water on* ALLMERS' *property. At* STAGE
RIGHT *are a few solitary trees through which can be seen the fiord in
the distance. At* STAGE LEFT *several old trees branch out over the
glen. There are several chairs, a bench, and a table, all made of
young birch trees.* UPSTAGE *there is a slope, on which a brook forms
into a waterfall, falls among the stones, and disappears into the
forest. A footpath follows alongside the brook.* DOWNSTAGE *is seen
the corner of a small boat shed. A boat has been drawn up on the
land. It is a misty day; drifting rain clouds hover in the sky.*

AS THE CURTAIN RISES, ALFRED ALLMERS, *dressed as before, is seated
on the bench, his arms resting on the table in front of him. He sits
absolutely still and stares unconsciously out over the fiord. After a
pause,* ASTA *enters, coming down the footpath. She carries an open
parasol.*

🔖

ASTA (*Approaching* ALLMERS *with caution*): You shouldn't be
   out here in this damp air, Alfred.
   (ALLMERS *nods slowly but doesn't answer.*)
ASTA (*Folding her parasol*): I've been walking around for the
   longest time, looking for you.
ALLMERS (*Without expression*): Thank you.
ASTA (*Moves a chair and sits beside him*): Have you been down
   here ever since—?
ALLMERS (*Not answering at first*): No. I can't seem to grasp it—
   it seems so incredible, the whole thing.
ASTA (*Putting her hand compassionately on his arm*): My poor
   Alfred.
ALLMERS (*Staring at her*): Is it really true what's happened,
   Asta? Or have I gone insane? Is all of it a dream? Oh, if it

only were! Just think how wonderful it would be if I could simply wake up.

ASTA: If it were only a dream, Alfred, I would wake you.

ALLMERS (*Looking out over the water*): How unmerciful the fiord looks today—so heavy and lethargic. Lead gray with glimmers of yellow lights . . . a mirror reflecting the rain clouds . . .

ASTA: Oh, Alfred, don't sit here like this staring out over the fiord.

ALLMERS (*Not listening to her*): . . . but only the surface. Deep down there's a fierce undertow.

ASTA (*In terror*): In God's name, don't think of what's lying down there.

ALLMERS (*Looking gently at her*): You probably think he's lying right outside here, don't you? Well, he isn't, Asta, so you mustn't think he is. You must remember how strong the current is. It rushes straight out to the open seas from here.

ASTA (*Throwing herself across the table, sobbing*): Oh, my God! Oh, my God!

ALLMERS (*Heavily*): And that's how little Eyolf has gone—so far, so far away from the rest of us.

ASTA (*Looking at him imploringly*): Oh, Alfred, don't say things like that!

ALLMERS: Well, figure it out yourself. —You who are so clever that way. In twenty-eight, twenty-nine hours . . . let me think, let me think—

ASTA (*Screams and covers her ears*): Alfred!

ALLMERS (*Pressing his hands firmly on the table*): Can you find a meaning in this?

ASTA (*Looking at him*): In what?

ALLMERS: This thing that's been done to Rita and me.

ASTA: A meaning?

ALLMERS: Yes, that's what I said. There has to be one somewhere. Our lives, our existence here, our destinies—they can't be totally without meaning.

ASTA: Oh, who can say anything for certain about these things, my dearest Alfred?

ALLMERS (*Laughing bitterly*): Yes, yes, you may be right. Perhaps these things do happen haphazardly after all. They take care of themselves, like a ship drifting without a rudder. Yes, that might very well be. At least it seems that way.

ASTA (*Thoughtfully*): If it only seems that way, then perhaps—

ALLMERS (*Flaring up*): Can you find a better answer for me? I can't. (*More gently*) Here was Eyolf, so gifted, just ready to enter into life—with so many potentials, rich potentials. He would have filled my life with happiness and pride. Then it just happened that a crazy old woman came our way and showed us a dog in a bag. . . .

ASTA: We're not sure that's what actually happened.

ALLMERS: Yes, we are! The boys down at the water saw her rowing out on the fiord. They saw Eyolf standing alone on the pier, staring after her as if he were in a trance. (*Shivering*) And that's how he went down, down into the water, and disappeared.

ASTA: Yes, but just the same—

ALLMERS: She dragged him into the depths, you can be sure of that.

ASTA: But my dear, why should she want to do that?

ALLMERS: That's just the question, Asta! Why? Why? There wasn't any retribution involved. No debt had to be paid. Eyolf had never done her any harm. He never called her names, made fun of her, threw stones at her dog. He had never even seen her or her dog before yesterday, so how could there be reason for retribution? It's all so without meaning, so completely without meaning, Asta. And yet it seems to me that some universal law demanded that it happen.

ASTA: Have you talked to Rita about this?

ALLMERS (*Shaking his head*): It's easier to talk to you about things like this, Asta. (*Sighing deeply*) And about everything else, too.

(ASTA *takes a sewing kit and a small package from her pocket.* ALLMERS *watches absent-mindedly.*)

ALLMERS: What have you got there, Asta?

ASTA (*Taking his hat*): Some black crepe.

ALLMERS: Oh, what's the good of all that?

ASTA: Rita asked me to do it. May I?

ALLMERS: Well, why not? Go ahead.

(ASTA *sews a black band on* ALLMERS' *hat. He watches her. There is a pause.*)

ALLMERS: Where is Rita?

ASTA: I think she's walking in the garden. Mr. Borgheim is with her.

ALLMERS (*Slightly surprised*): Oh! Is Borgheim out here again?

ASTA: Yes, he came on the afternoon train.

ALLMERS: Strange . . . I didn't think he would.

ASTA (*Sewing*): He was very fond of Eyolf.

ALLMERS: Borgheim's a faithful soul, Asta.

ASTA (*With quiet warmth*): Yes, he is. You're right.

ALLMERS (*Looking directly at her*): You're really fond of him, aren't you—deep down?

ASTA: Yes, I am.

ALLMERS: And still you can't decide?

ASTA: Please, Alfred, let's not talk about that!

ALLMERS: All right, then, if you'll just tell me why you can't—

ASTA: Please don't ask me! You really mustn't. You know how painful it is for me. There now—your hat is finished.

ALLMERS: Thank you.

ASTA: Now your left arm.

ALLMERS: Is it necessary to have it there, too?

ASTA: Yes, it's customary.

ALLMERS: Well then, do as you please.

ASTA (*Moves closer and begins to sew*): Keep your arm still so I won't hurt you.

ALLMERS (*Half smiling*): This reminds me of the old days.

ASTA: Yes, doesn't it?

ALLMERS: When you were a little girl you used to sit like this and mend my clothes.

ASTA: I tried my best.

ALLMERS: The first thing you ever sewed for me was black crepe.

ASTA: Was it?

ALLMERS: On my student cap, when father died.

ASTA: Did I sew then? Strange, I don't remember that.

ALLMERS: Well, of course not—you were so small.

ASTA: Yes. I was very young.

ALLMERS: And then two years later when we lost your mother, you sewed a large black band on my sleeve.

ASTA: I felt it was the right thing to do.

ALLMERS (*Patting her hand*): Yes, yes, that's the way it's supposed to be. And ever since then, we two have been alone in the world. Just the two of us. Finished already?

ASTA (*Gathering up her sewing*): Yes. When I look back on it now, those were happy times for the two of us, Alfred—alone, together.

ALLMERS: Yes, even though it was such a struggle.

ASTA: *You* struggled.

ALLMERS (*Lively*): You did too, in your own way. (*Smiling*) You, my faithful Eyolf!

ASTA: Oh! You shouldn't remind me of all that foolishness about that name!

ALLMERS: If you'd been born a boy your name would have been Eyolf.

ASTA (*Smiling to herself*): Yes, I know, but you were already at the university. Just think how childish you were, even there.

ALLMERS: Was I the childish one?

ASTA: It seems to me you were, looking back on it now. You were actually ashamed of not having a brother—just a sister!

ALLMERS: No I wasn't! You were the one.

ASTA: Well yes, maybe I was a little ashamed, too, but I also felt a bit sorry for you.

ALLMERS: You probably did. So you'd get out my old suit I wore when I was a boy—

ASTA: Yes, your lovely Sunday suit. Remember the blue tunic and the short trousers?

ALLMERS (*His eyes lingering on her*): How well I remember you when you put them on and walked around.

ASTA: But I only did it when the two of us were all alone at home.

ALLMERS: How serious we were. And how important.

ASTA: Alfred, you've never told Rita about any of this, have you?

ALLMERS: Yes, I think I did, once.

ASTA: Oh no. How could you, Alfred?

ALLMERS: Well, you see, a man tells his wife everything—that is, practically everything.

ASTA: Yes, I suppose he does.

ALLMERS (*As if awakening, strikes his forehead and rises quickly*): Oh! How can I sit here and—

ASTA (*Rising, concerned*): What's wrong?

ALLMERS: He almost got away from me, completely away!

ASTA: Eyolf?

ALLMERS: I was reliving all those old memories, and he wasn't with me!

ASTA: But he was. Little Eyolf was the very reason for all those memories.

ALLMERS: No, he wasn't. He slipped out of my mind, out of my thoughts, while we sat here talking. All that time I didn't see him. I forgot him completely for the longest time.

ASTA: Oh—you must rest a little from your grief.

ALLMERS: No, no, no! That's exactly what I can't do! I'm not allowed to—I've no right! And I've no heart for it, either. (*He goes toward the boat shed.*) There's only one thing I must do. I must stay out there where he's drifting, down in the depths.

ASTA (*Physically restraining him*): Alfred! Alfred! Don't go out on the fiord!

ALLMERS: I must go to him! Let me go, Asta. I want to go out in the boat.

ASTA (*In panic*): No, Alfred—please, I beg you! Don't go out there!

ALLMERS: All right, all right, I won't go. Now just leave me alone.

ASTA (*Leading him back to the table*): You must give your thoughts a rest, Alfred. Come here and sit down awhile.

ALLMERS (*Attempting to sit on the bench*): Yes, yes, if you want me to.

ASTA: No, don't sit there!

ALLMERS: Yes, let me.

ASTA: No don't! You know you'll just sit and stare at the water. (*Forcing him into a chair at the* RIGHT) There now. You'll be more comfortable here. (*Sitting on the bench*) And now let's go on talking.

ALLMERS (*Sighing*): It did me good to deaden the sorrow and the loss for a moment.

ASTA: Of course. You must do that, Alfred.

ALLMERS: But don't you think it's callous and unfeeling of me to do that?

ASTA: Not at all. It's impossible for the mind to dwell constantly on a single thing.

ALLMERS: It's impossible for me! Before you came down here I was tormenting myself, and I was in such wretched agony because that terrible grief kept gnawing—

ASTA: Really?

ALLMERS: And can you believe it, Asta—?

ASTA: What?

ALLMERS: In the midst of my horrible grief I caught myself wondering what we were going to have for dinner.

ASTA (*Soothingly*): Yes, yes. Well—as long as it can give you some relief.

ALLMERS: Can you imagine that? And I did feel a kind of relief. (*He holds out his hands to her.*) What a fortunate thing for me to have you, Asta. I'm so happy for that. Happy, in the midst of my sorrow.

ASTA (*Looking solemnly at him*): Above all, you should be happy that you have Rita.

ALLMERS: That goes without saying. But Rita and I are not blood relatives—it's not like having a sister.

ASTA (*Tensely*): Do you mean that, Alfred?

ALLMERS: Yes. Our family is something special. (*Half jokingly*) For instance, all our names begin with vowels! Remember how often we used to talk about that? And all our relatives were equally poor. And we all had the same eyes.

ASTA: Do you think I have them?

ALLMERS: No. You take after your mother. You don't look at all like the rest of us, not even father. But just the same—

ASTA: Yes?

ALLMERS: Well, I think that being children together left us so much alike—in our thinking, I mean.

ASTA: Oh you mustn't say that, Alfred. I copied you, and I owe you everything—everything that's good in the whole world.

ALLMERS: You don't owe me anything, Asta. On the contrary.

ASTA: But I do! I owe everything to you—you must know that! No sacrifice was ever too much for you to—

ALLMERS: Sacrifice? Oh, don't call it that, Asta. I've always been so fond of you, ever since you were a little child. (*There is a short pause.*) I always felt there were so many wrongs being done to you that I had to make up for them.

ASTA: Wrongs? To me?

ALLMERS: Yes, and not only on my account, but . . .

ASTA (*Breathless and tense*): But?

ALLMERS: For father, too.

ASTA (*Half rising*): Father? (*Sitting again*) What do you mean by that, Alfred?

ALLMERS: Father was never very kind to you.

ASTA (*Angrily*): Oh, you can't say that!

ALLMERS: Yes I can. It's true! He didn't love you as he should have.

ASTA (*Evasively*): Well, perhaps not in the same way that he loved you—no. But that's understandable.

ALLMERS: And he was often very harsh to your mother, too. At least in the last years.

ASTA (*Softly*): Mother was so much younger than he was, remember that.

ALLMERS: Do you think it was just because they weren't well suited?

ASTA: Perhaps.

ALLMERS: But father was so warmhearted and kind, so nice to everyone else.

ASTA (*Quietly*): Mother wasn't always what she should have been.

ALLMERS: Wasn't she?

ASTA: No, not always.

ALLMERS: To him, you mean?

ASTA: Yes.

ALLMERS: I never noticed that.

ASTA (*Rises, fighting back tears*): Oh my dear Alfred, let them rest in peace—all those who are gone.

ALLMERS (*Rising*): Yes, let them rest. But those who are gone—the dead—they won't let us rest, Asta, day or night.

ASTA (*Looking warmly at him*): Time will make all this less painful, Alfred.

ALLMERS (*Looking hopelessly at her*): It will, won't it? But how am I to get through these first dreadful days? (*Hoarsely*) I just can't see how.

ASTA (*Holding his shoulders, pleads*): Go up and find Rita. Please do.

ALLMERS (*Freeing himself of her*): No, no, no. Don't ask me to do that! Don't you understand? I simply can't! (*More calmly*) Let me stay here with you.

ASTA: All right, we'll stay here together.

ALLMERS (*Grasping her hand*): Thank you for that. (*Looking over the fiord*) Where is my little Eyolf now? (*Smiling sadly at her*) Can you tell me that? You, my wise, big Eyolf? No one in the world can tell me that. I only know one terrible truth—I don't have him any more.

ASTA (*Looks toward the* LEFT *and takes his hand from hers*): They're coming!

(RITA *and* BORGHEIM *enter from the* LEFT *on the footpath. She leads. She is dressed in dark clothes, with a black veil over her head. He carries an umbrella under his arm.*)

ALLMERS (*Crossing to them*): How are you feeling, Rita?

RITA (*Walking past him*): Must you ask that, Alfred?

ALLMERS: Why have you come here?

RITA: I just wanted to know how you were. What are you doing?

ALLMERS: Nothing. Asta came down here to be with me.

RITA: Yes, but before Asta came? You've been away all morning.

ALLMERS: I've been sitting here looking out over the water.

RITA: Oh, how could you?

ALLMERS: Because I prefer to be alone now.

RITA (*Pacing restlessly*): And to sit here like that—for hours in the same place!

ALLMERS: There's no other place on earth I have any reason to be.

RITA: I can't stand to stay in any one place! —Most of all here, so close to the fiord.

ALLMERS: That's why I like it, because the fiord is so close.

RITA (*To* BORGHEIM): Don't you think he should come up with the rest of us?

BORGHEIM (*To* ALLMERS): I think it would be much better for you.

ALLMERS: No, no, let me stay where I am.

RITA: Then I'll stay here with you, Alfred.

ALLMERS: Yes, do. You too, Asta.

ASTA (*Whispering to* BORGHEIM): Let's leave them alone.

BORGHEIM: Miss Allmers, let's take a little walk along the water, for the last time.

ASTA (*Picking up her parasol*): Yes! Let's walk for a little while. (ASTA *and* BORGHEIM *exit together behind the boat shed.* ALLMERS *paces for a while and then sits on a stone beneath the trees* DOWNSTAGE LEFT.)

RITA (*Standing over him, her arms folded*): Can you get used to the thought that we've lost Eyolf?

ALLMERS (*Looking heavily downward*): We must.

RITA: I can't. I just can't. I have a horrible vision that will never leave me—never for the rest of my life!

ALLMERS (*Looking up*): A vision? What have you seen?

RITA: I haven't seen anything—I've just heard about it.

ALLMERS: Tell me.

RITA: I made Borgheim take me to the pier.

ALLMERS: What did you want to find out there?

RITA: I wanted to ask the boys themselves how it happened.

ALLMERS: But we already knew!

RITA: Well, we found out more.

ALLMERS: Did you?

RITA: It isn't true that he disappeared right away.

ALLMERS: Is that what they're saying now?

RITA: Yes. They all say they saw him lying on the bottom. Deep down in the clear water.

ALLMERS: And they didn't save him?

RITA: I suppose there was nothing they could do.

ALLMERS: They know how to swim—every one of them! Did they say how he was lying when they saw him?

RITA: Yes. He was on his back with his eyes wide open.

ALLMERS: Wide open? And very still?

RITA: Yes, very still. Then something came and swept him away. They said it was an undertow.

ALLMERS (*Nodding slowly*): And that was the last time they saw him?

RITA (*Choking with tears*): Yes.

ALLMERS (*Tonelessly*): And never, never will anyone see him again.

RITA (*Wailing*): Day and night he'll be before me, just as he lay down there under the clear water . . .

ALLMERS: . . . with his eyes wide open.

RITA: Yes, his eyes wide open! I can see them now, staring at me.

ALLMERS (*Rising slowly, looks at her with malice*): Were they evil, those eyes, Rita?

RITA (*Turning pale*): Evil—!

ALLMERS (*Going close to her*): Were they evil eyes staring up at you from the depths?

RITA (*Shrinking away*): Alfred!

ALLMERS (*Pursuing her*): Answer me! Were they the evil eyes of a child?

RITA (*Screaming*): Stop it, Alfred!

ALLMERS: And now it's just as you wished it, Rita!

RITA: I? What did I wish?

ALLMERS: You wished that Eyolf was not here.

RITA: I never wished that in my life! I didn't want him to stand between us—that was all!

ALLMERS: Well, from now on he won't.

RITA (*Quietly to herself, gazing straight ahead*): From now on he'll be between us even more. Oh! That dreadful vision!

ALLMERS (*Nodding*): The evil eyes of a child. Yes.

RITA (*Shrinking back terrified*): Leave me alone, Alfred! I'm afraid of you! I've never seen you like this before.

ALLMERS (*Staring coldly at her*): Sorrow makes one evil and ugly.

RITA (*Afraid, but defiant*): I feel the same way.

(ALLMERS *goes to the* RIGHT *and looks over the fiord.* RITA *sits at the table. There is a short pause.*)

ALLMERS: You never loved him completely, did you?

RITA (*Coldly, with composure*): Eyolf never *let* me love him completely.

ALLMERS: Because you never wanted him to.

RITA: Yes, I did. I wanted that more than anything, but from the very first someone stood in the way.

ALLMERS (*Facing her squarely*): Do you mean me?

RITA: No, not in the beginning.

ALLMERS: Who, then?

RITA: His aunt.

ALLMERS: Asta?

RITA: Yes. She stood right there and barred the way.

ALLMERS: Is that how you felt, Rita?

RITA: Yes. Asta stole his love from me. Ever since the day it happened—the accident, his dreadful fall.

ALLMERS: If she did that, Rita, it was done purely out of love.

RITA (*Violently*): Exactly! I can't bear to share anything with anyone. Certainly not love!

ALLMERS: The two of us should have shared Eyolf's love.

RITA: The two of us? Oh, you know very well that deep down you never really loved him either.

ALLMERS (*In amazement*): Didn't I?

RITA: No, you didn't! At first you were so completely wrapped up in your book about responsibility!

ALLMERS (*Forcefully*): Yes I was! And I sacrificed my book for Eyolf's sake.

RITA: But not because you *loved* him!

ALLMERS: No? Then why?

RITA: You began to doubt yourself, that's why. You were wasting away with mistrust. You doubted whether or not you really did have some great calling in life.

ALLMERS (*Searchingly*): And you were able to see that in me?

RITA: Yes, little by little. It didn't take long before you needed something new to fulfill yourself. I suppose I wasn't enough for you any longer.

ALLMERS: That's the law of change, Rita.

RITA: And that's why it was so important for you to make poor little Eyolf into a child prodigy.

ALLMERS: I didn't insist on that. I only wanted to make him a happy person—that's the only thing I wanted.

RITA: But not because you loved him! (*Shyly, groping for words*) Look into yourself . . . examine everything that lies beneath and behind.

ALLMERS (*Not looking at her*): You're avoiding something. There's something you won't say.

RITA: And you, too.

ALLMERS (*Looking thoughtfully at her*): If what you think is true, then we never really possessed our own child.

RITA: No, never in complete love.

ALLMERS: And yet here we are, both of us, grieving so bitterly over his loss.

RITA (*Bitterly*): Yes, isn't it strange? We're grieving over someone else's little boy. A stranger.

ALLMERS (*With an outburst*): Don't call him that!

RITA (*Shaking her head sadly*): We never won his love, Alfred, neither of us.

ALLMERS: And now it's too late! Too late!

RITA: It's all so hopeless!

ALLMERS (*Suddenly flaring up*): And you're the guilty one!

RITA (*Standing up*): I am?

ALLMERS: Yes you! It's your fault he turned out the way he did. It's your fault he couldn't save himself in the water.

RITA: Oh Alfred, you mustn't blame me.

ALLMERS (*Beginning to lose control of himself*): But I do! You were the one who left that little baby lying on the table alone.

RITA: He was very comfortable on the pillows. He was sound asleep and so sweet. —And you had promised to watch him.

ALLMERS: Yes, I had. (*Lowering his voice*) But then you—you lured me to you.

RITA (*Looking defiantly at him*): Just say that you forgot the baby and everything else.

ALLMERS (*Suppressing his anger*): Yes, how true! I forgot him in your arms!

RITA (*With fury*): Alfred, Alfred! That's detestable of you!

ALLMERS: In that moment you sentenced little Eyolf to death!

RITA (*Wildly*): You did, too! If that's the way it was, you did, too!

ALLMERS: Yes, blame me if you want, but we both committed the crime. And our retribution is Eyolf's death!

RITA: Retribution?

ALLMERS (*More controlled*): Yes. This is our punishment. Now we've got what we deserved. While he was alive we shied away from him because of our secret guilt. We couldn't bear to look at that thing he always had to drag along with him.

RITA (*Quietly*): The crutch.

ALLMERS: Exactly. And what we now call our sorrow—our loss —is only the gnawing of a guilty conscience, Rita, nothing else.

RITA (*Staring helplessly at him*): I think this grief will drive us both mad, completely mad! And there's no way to put things right.

ALLMERS: I had a dream about Eyolf last night. It seemed to me that he was coming up from the pier. And he could run like the other boys, as if nothing had ever happened to him, nothing at all. I thought that all this terrible reality was only a dream. Oh how I thanked and praised— (*He stops short.*)

RITA: Who?

ALLMERS: Who?

RITA: Yes. Who was it you thanked and praised?

ALLMERS: I told you I was dreaming.

RITA: Someone in whom you can't even believe?

ALLMERS: That's the way it happened. I was dreaming.

RITA: You shouldn't have taken my faith away, Alfred.

ALLMERS: Would it have been right of me to let you go through life believing in all those empty ideas?

RITA: It would have been better for me—at least I'd have something to console me now. As it is, I go around not knowing right from wrong. I don't know where I am.

ALLMERS (*Looking closely at her*): Rita, if you had a choice . . . to . . . if you could follow Eyolf to wherever he is—

RITA: Yes? (*Pausing*) Well?

ALLMERS: If you were fully assured that you would find him again, know him, understand him—

RITA: Yes, yes, go on.

ALLMERS: Would you of your own free will go over to him? Of your own free will would you leave all this? Renounce your life on this earth? Would you want to do that, Rita?

RITA (*Slowly*): You mean now? This moment?

ALLMERS: Yes, today. This very hour. Answer me, would you?

RITA (*Hesitating*): Oh, I don't know, Alfred. No, I believe I'd rather stay here with you for a while.

ALLMERS: For my sake?

RITA: Yes. Only for your sake.

ALLMERS: And afterward? Answer!

RITA: Oh, how can I answer such a question? I could never, never live away from you. Never!

ALLMERS: But if I went to Eyolf and you had full assurance that you would meet both of us there, would you come over to us?

RITA: I'd want to—so willingly, so gladly—but—

ALLMERS: Well?

RITA (*Moaning softly*): I couldn't. I just feel I couldn't. No. No, I just couldn't—not for all the glory of heaven!

ALLMERS (*After a pause*): Neither could I.

RITA: It's true, isn't it, Alfred? You couldn't do it, either.

ALLMERS: True. The only place that we living creatures belong is here on this earth.

RITA: The kind of happiness we understand is here.

ALLMERS (*Darkly*): Ah! Happiness—happiness.

RITA: You don't think we'll ever find it again, do you? But suppose— No, no, I don't dare say it. I shouldn't even be thinking it.

ALLMERS: Go on.

RITA: Couldn't we try to . . . to—would it be possible for us to forget him?

ALLMERS: Forget Eyolf?

RITA: I mean, forget this remorse, this painful guilt.

ALLMERS: Is that what you'd want?

RITA (*With an outburst*): Oh yes, if only it were possible! There'll come a time when I won't be able to stand this any longer. Can't we find something to help us escape?

ALLMERS (*Shaking his head*): What kind of thing?

RITA: We could travel for a while.

ALLMERS: Away from home? You know you're not happy in any other place.

RITA: Then let's have lots of people around us. We could keep open house—throw ourselves into something that will deaden our senses and make us completely numb.

ALLMERS: That kind of life is not for me. No, I'd rather try to begin my work again.

RITA: Your work? Oh—the very thing that has always stood like a barrier between us?

ALLMERS (*Coldly*): There'll always be a barrier between us.

RITA: Why? Why must there be?

ALLMERS: Who knows? The wide-open eyes of a child may haunt us forever, day and night.

RITA (*In a low voice, shuddering*): Alfred, what a terrible thing to say.

ALLMERS: Our love has been a consuming fire. Now it must be quenched.

RITA: What?

ALLMERS (*Bitterly*): And it *is* quenched in one of us.

RITA (*As if turned to stone*): You dare tell me that!

ALLMERS: It is dead, Rita. What I feel for you now is something new. We are accomplices in crime, and because of that I feel a kind of—of . . . resurrection.

RITA (*Violently*): Oh! I don't care about any resurrection!

ALLMERS: Rita!

RITA: I'm a warm-blooded human being! I can't go around half-dead with ice water in my veins! I will not be locked up for life in misery and remorse . . . closed in with someone who's no longer mine, and mine alone!

ALLMERS: It must come to that, Rita.

RITA: Must it? Even a love that at the beginning was mutual—an equal reaching out toward each other?

ALLMERS: My love did not reach out for you in the beginning.

RITA: What did you feel for me, then?

ALLMERS: Dread.

RITA: I understand that. How did I ever win you?

ALLMERS (*Quietly*): Your beauty seemed to consume me, Rita.

RITA (*Looking deeply at him*): Was that all? Tell me, Alfred.

ALLMERS (*Reluctantly, but with control*): No, there was something else.

RITA (*Crying out*): Let me guess! It was my "gold and green forests," as you call it—wasn't it, Alfred?

ALLMERS: Yes.

RITA: How could you? How could you do it?

ALLMERS: I had Asta to think of.

RITA (*Angrily and bitterly*): Oh yes, Asta! So Asta was the reason for our getting together!

ALLMERS: But she never knew it, and she still doesn't suspect a thing.

RITA: It was Asta! (*Smiling scornfully*) Or maybe not. Perhaps it was Eyolf. Little Eyolf—that's who it was!

ALLMERS: Eyolf?

RITA: Yes. You used to call *her* your little Eyolf, didn't you? It seems to me you told me that once—once in a very intimate moment. (*Going to him*) Do you remember that? That wonderful moment, Alfred?

ALLMERS (*Shrinking away in horror*): I don't remember. I don't want to remember anything.

RITA: It was at that moment your other little Eyolf became crippled.

ALLMERS (*In a hollow voice, supporting himself on the table*): Retribution.

RITA (*Threateningly*): Yes. Retribution.

(ASTA *and* BORGHEIM *return from their walk. She carries some water lilies.*)

RITA (*Composed*): Well, Asta, have you and Mr. Borgheim been able to talk things over?

ASTA (*Putting some flowers and the parasol on the chair*): Yes—fairly well.

BORGHEIM: She didn't say much as we walked.

RITA: Really? Didn't she? Well, Alfred and I have had a talk that will last us for quite a while.

ASTA (*Looking intently from one to the other*): What does that mean?

RITA: I should say it'll last us for the rest of our lives. But come, let's go up to the house, the four of us. From now on we must have company around us. Alfred and I can't manage alone.

ALLMERS: The two of you go on ahead. Asta, I must talk to you.

RITA (*Looking at* ALLMERS): Really? Very well, then. Mr. Borgheim, you come along with me. (*She and* BORGHEIM *go up the path.*)

ASTA: Alfred, what's the matter?

ALLMERS: I can't stand it here any longer.

ASTA: Here—with Rita, you mean?

ALLMERS: Yes. We cannot go on living together.

ASTA (*Shaking his arm*): Alfred! You mustn't say such dreadful things.

ALLMERS: But it's true. We just make each other evil and ugly.

ASTA: I never thought it would actually come to this.

ALLMERS: I didn't either, until today.

ASTA: And now you want—what do you want, Alfred?

ALLMERS: To get away from my life here, far away.

ASTA: You want to live all alone in the world?

ALLMERS: Just as I did before.

ASTA: You can't live alone.

ALLMERS: Oh yes I can. I did once.

ASTA: But I was with you then.

ALLMERS (*Trying to take her hand*): Yes. I want to come home again to you, Asta.

ASTA (*Avoiding him*): To me? No, no, Alfred, that would be impossible.

ALLMERS (*Looking heavily at her*): Borgheim *does* stand in the way, then?

ASTA: No. No, he doesn't. You're very wrong there.

ALLMERS: Well, then, I'll come to you. My beloved sister. I need to be with you again in your home. It will help refresh and ennoble me after having lived with—

ASTA (*Shocked*): Alfred! That would be a terrible sin against Rita!

ALLMERS: I've already sinned against her, but not in this way. Think carefully, Asta. How was our life together, yours and mine? Wasn't it like a dream from morning to night?

ASTA: Yes it was, Alfred, but we can't relive those years.

ALLMERS (*Bitterly*): Has my marriage ruined me for good, then?

ASTA (*Calmly*): I didn't mean that.

ALLMERS: Well, then, we'll live together again, as we used to.

ASTA (*Firmly*): No. We can't.

ALLMERS: Yes we can! A brother and sister have . . .

ASTA (*Tensely*): Yes? Tell me.

ALLMERS: . . . the only relationship that isn't governed by the law of change.

ASTA (*Slowly*): But if that relationship isn't . . .

ALLMERS: Isn't what?

ASTA: . . . isn't the case with us?

ALLMERS (*Crossing closer to her*): What do you mean? What are you trying to tell me?

ASTA: I think it's better if I tell you now, Alfred.

ALLMERS: Yes, tell me!

ASTA: The letters to my mother—those in the portfolio—

ALLMERS: Yes?

ASTA: Those—you must read them after I leave.

ALLMERS: Why must I?

ASTA: You'll understand.

ALLMERS: Well?

ASTA: That I haven't the right to bear your father's name.

ALLMERS (*In amazement*): Asta! What are you saying?

ASTA: Read the letters and perhaps you'll understand . . . and also forgive my mother.

ALLMERS (*Holding onto the table*): I cannot grasp what you're saying, Asta.

ASTA: You are not my brother, Alfred.

ALLMERS: But this doesn't really change our relationship. Nothing as deeply rooted as that can be changed.

ASTA (*Shaking her head*): But everything is, Alfred. We are not brother and sister.

ALLMERS: But our relationship is just as sacred, and we will always keep it that way.

ASTA: Don't forget that now our relationship is subject to the law of change.

ALLMERS (*Looks searchingly at her*): Do you mean that—?

ASTA (*Quietly, deeply moved*): Not another word, my dearest Alfred. (*Picking up the flowers*) See these water lilies?

ALLMERS: Yes. They're the kind that shoot up from very deep water.

ASTA: I picked them from the edge, just where the water flows out to the fiord. (*Holding them out to him*) Do you want them, Alfred?

ALLMERS (*Taking them*): Thank you.

ASTA (*Tearfully*): They're the last greeting from little Eyolf.

ALLMERS: From Eyolf out there—or from you?

ASTA: From both. (*Picking up the parasol*) Come now, come with me—up to Rita. (*She starts to walk up the path.*)

ALLMERS (*Taking his hat, he begins to follow her. Speaking softly*): Asta. Eyolf. Little Eyolf! (*He walks up the path.*)

CURTAIN

# ACT III

*A hillside covered with shrubs on* ALLMERS' *property.* UPSTAGE *is a slope with a railing and a staircase leading* DOWNSTAGE LEFT. *Near the railing stands a flagpole with ropes but no flag. The fiord can be seen in the distance.* DOWNSTAGE RIGHT *there is a summerhouse covered with clinging plants and wild vines. Outside it is a bench. It is a late summer evening with a clear sky. As the action proceeds, it grows dark.*

AS THE CURTAIN RISES, ASTA *is seen seated on the bench with her hands in her lap. She is dressed for traveling; she wears a coat and hat and has a parasol at her side. A small traveling bag hangs from her shoulder.* BORGHEIM *enters* UPSTAGE LEFT, *also carrying a traveling bag with a shoulder strap. On his arm there is a rolled-up flag.*

BORGHEIM: Oh, so this is where you are.

ASTA: I'm looking at it all for the last time.

BORGHEIM: Then it's a good thing I came up here.

ASTA: Have you been looking for me?

BORGHEIM: Yes. I wanted to say good-by to you for now. I hope it's not for good.

ASTA (*Smiling with restraint*): You are persistent, aren't you?

BORGHEIM: A road builder has to be.

ASTA: Have you seen Alfred or Rita?

BORGHEIM: Yes, I saw them both.

ASTA: Together?

BORGHEIM: No, separately.

ASTA: Together?

ASTA: What are you doing with the flag?

BORGHEIM: Mrs. Allmers asked me to put it up.

ASTA: Did she? Just now?

BORGHEIM: Yes—at half-mast. And it's to stay that way, day and night, she said.

ASTA (*Sighing*): Poor Rita, and poor Alfred too.

BORGHEIM: How do you have the heart to leave them? I see you're all dressed and ready to go—that's why I asked.

ASTA (*In a low voice*): I must leave.

BORGHEIM: Well, if you feel that way, then you have to.

ASTA: You're leaving tonight, too, aren't you?

BORGHEIM: Yes, I also have to leave. I'll be taking the train. And you?

ASTA: The steamer.

BORGHEIM (*Glancing at her*): Separate ways, then.

ASTA: Yes. (*She watches him hoist the flag.*)

BORGHEIM (*Finished, walks to her*): Miss Allmers, you can't imagine how I miss little Eyolf.

ASTA (*Looking up at him*): Yes, I know you do.

BORGHEIM: It's so painful for me. I'm not a sad person by nature, you know.

ASTA (*Looking up at the flag*): It'll all pass away—with time. All the sadness.

BORGHEIM: All of it? You believe that?

ASTA: Yes, like bad weather. When you get far enough away from it, then—

BORGHEIM: I'll have to be very far away.

ASTA: Then, too, you'll have your new job.

BORGHEIM: But I have no one to help me with it.

ASTA: Of course you do!

BORGHEIM (*Shaking his head*): No one. I have no one to share happiness with me. And after all's said and done, happiness is the most important thing in life.

ASTA: What about work? All the work and worry?

BORGHEIM: Those things manage to take care of themselves.

ASTA: But happiness—that has to be shared. Is that what you mean?

BORGHEIM: Yes. Otherwise the real joy is lost.

ASTA: Well, yes, there may be something in that.

BORGHEIM: Of course, you can be happy by yourself for a while, but it's not enough in the long run. No. To be truly happy there must be two people.

ASTA: Only two? Never more? Why not several?

BORGHEIM: Well, that's something different. Miss Allmers, couldn't you make up your mind to share happiness and . . . yes, all the work and worry—with one, but only with one?

ASTA: I did try, once.

BORGHEIM: Did you?

ASTA: Yes, with my brother—all those years that Alfred and I lived together.

BORGHEIM: Your brother! Well now, that's something quite different. I'd call that contentment rather than happiness.

ASTA: Those were the most wonderful years I've ever spent.

BORGHEIM: So there you see for yourself! Even that seemed wonderful to you. Now just think if he had been more to you than a brother.

ASTA (*Wanting to rise but remaining seated*): Then we would never have lived together. I was only a child and so was he, really.

BORGHEIM (*After a short pause*): Were those years that precious to you?

ASTA: Yes, believe me, they were.

BORGHEIM: Did you experience any real happiness during that time?

ASTA: Oh yes, so much—so unbelievably much!

BORGHEIM: Tell me about them, Miss Allmers.

ASTA: Oh, they were just little things, really—

BORGHEIM: Such as what? Tell me.

ASTA: Well, there was that time when Alfred graduated and had done so well. Also, shortly after that when he got a job teaching in another school. Or when he was writing one of his papers and he would read it to me out loud, and then afterward we would see it published in a periodical.

BORGHEIM: I understand. It must have been a wonderfully peaceful life—sister and brother sharing their happiness. But then, I don't understand, Asta, how your brother could have ever let you go.

ASTA (*Suppressing her emotion*): Well, Alfred got married.

BORGHEIM: Wasn't it difficult for you?

ASTA: In the beginning, yes. Suddenly I felt I'd lost him completely.

BORGHEIM: Luckily, you hadn't.

ASTA: No.

BORGHEIM: Just the same, how could he have done it? Get married, I mean—when he could have kept you for himself, always?

ASTA (*Looking straight ahead*): I imagine he was subject to the law of change.

BORGHEIM: The what?

ASTA: That's what Alfred calls it.

BORGHEIM: What a stupid law that must be! Anyway, I don't believe in it.

ASTA (*Standing*): You might have to, someday.

BORGHEIM: Never in the world! (*Insistently*) Listen to me, Miss Allmers. Be sensible, for once—about this, I mean.

ASTA: No, no—let's not start that again.

BORGHEIM: I can't let you go this easily! Your brother has everything he wants now, and he's quite content without you. He doesn't miss you at all. Then, there's this new blow that has changed your entire position in the household.

ASTA (*Startled*): What do you mean?

BORGHEIM: The child's been torn away from you—what else?

ASTA (*Regaining control*): Yes, little Eyolf is gone. Yes.

BORGHEIM: So now, what is there left out here for you to do? You don't have the poor little one to take care of any longer. No duties, no responsibilities in any direction.

ASTA: Dear Mr. Borgheim, I beg you, please don't be so persistent.

BORGHEIM: I have to! I'd be insane if I didn't try my best. I'm leaving today, and I won't be seeing you either in town or anywhere else. Who knows what can happen in the meantime?

ASTA (*Smiling seriously*): So you are afraid of the law of change after all.

BORGHEIM: No, not in the least. (*Laughing bitterly*) Besides, I don't see any change in you. I mean, you don't care any more for me now than you did before—I could always sense that much.

ASTA: You know very well that I do.

BORGHEIM: Yes, but not enough—not as I'd want you to. (*Passionately*) Good God, Asta—Miss Allmers—what you're doing is as wrong as anything could possibly be! Just ahead —ahead of today and tomorrow, perhaps—a whole life of happiness lies waiting for us! And we just leave it there! Won't we live to regret it, Asta?

ASTA (*Quietly*): I don't know. But just the same, we'll have to leave it there with all its bright possibilities.

BORGHEIM: I'll have to build my roads alone then, eh?

ASTA (*Warmly*): Ah, if I—so help me God—if I could be with you, to help you with all your work and worry . . . yes, and to share happiness, too—

BORGHEIM: Would you want to—if you could?

ASTA: Yes I would.

BORGHEIM: But you can't?

ASTA (*Looking down*): Could you be satisfied with only half of me?

BORGHEIM: No. I must have all of you.

ASTA (*Looks at him, then speaks quietly*): Then I can't.

BORGHEIM: Good-by then, Miss Allmers.

(BORGHEIM *starts to leave, but stops as* ALLMERS *enters from* STAGE LEFT *as if coming up the hill. He stops at the top of the stairs and points. He speaks quietly.*)

ALLMERS: Is Rita in there in the summerhouse?

BORGHEIM: No. No one's here but Miss Allmers and me.

(ALLMERS *comes closer.*)

ASTA (*Going toward him*): Shall I go down and look for her? Maybe I can persuade her to come up here.

ALLMER: No, no, no, never mind. (*To* BORGHEIM) Did you put the flag up?

BORGHEIM: Yes, Mrs. Allmers asked me to. That's why I came up here.

ALLMERS: You're leaving tonight?

BORGHEIM: Yes, tonight for sure.

ALLMERS (*Looking at* ASTA): And you've found yourself a good traveling companion, I hope?

BORGHEIM (*Shaking his head*): I'm traveling alone.

ALLMERS (*Surprised*): Alone?

BORGHEIM: Completely.

ALLMERS (*Vaguely*): Oh?

BORGHEIM: And I'll stay that way, too.

ALLMERS: There's something so dreadful about being alone. Just the thought of it sends ice through my veins.

ASTA: But Alfred, you're not alone!

ALLMERS: There's something dreadful in that, too, Asta.

ASTA: Don't talk like that! Don't even think it!

ALLMERS: But if you're not going with—? If there's nothing tying you down, why don't you stay out here with me—and Rita?

ASTA: No, I can't do that! I have to go back to town now, definitely.

ALLMERS: Back only to town. Do you hear me?

ASTA: Yes.

ALLMERS: You promise you'll come back again soon?

ASTA (*Quickly*): No, I don't dare promise you that. Not for a while, at least.

ALLMERS: Very well, as you wish. We'll meet in town.

ASTA: No, Alfred, you must stay here at home with Rita now.

ALLMERS (*Not answering her, turns to* BORGHEIM): Yes. It's probably best you're traveling alone.

BORGHEIM (*Protesting*): How can you say such a thing?

ALLMERS: Well, you never know whom you're liable to meet on the way—later on.

ASTA: Alfred!

ALLMERS: —The real traveling companion. When it's too late ... too late.

ASTA (*Quietly, trembling*): Alfred. Alfred.

BORGHEIM (*Looking from one to the other*): What do you mean? I don't understand.

(RITA *enters from* UPSTAGE LEFT.)

RITA (*In distress*): Now don't all of you go away from me!

ASTA (*Crossing to her*): You said you wanted to be alone.

RITA: Yes, but I don't dare to any longer, dear. It's beginning to get dark and terrifying. It seems that there are wide-open eyes staring at me.

ASTA (*Softly and sympathetically*): And what if there are, Rita? You shouldn't be afraid of them.

RITA: Imagine your saying that! Not afraid!

ALLMERS: I beg you, Asta, by everything that's dear in the world, stay here with Rita.

RITA: Yes, and with Alfred too. Do that—please do, Asta.

ASTA: Oh, I want to . . . so . . . so badly.

RITA: Well, do, then! Because Alfred and I can't go through the sorrow and the dreadful loss alone.

ALLMERS: And the guilt—why don't you say that, too?

RITA: Well, whatever you like to call it, we can't endure it alone, just the two of us. Oh Asta, I beg you—stay here and help us. Take Eyolf's place, and then—

ASTA (*Shrinking*): Eyolf!

RITA: Wouldn't you like her to do that, Alfred?

ALLMERS: If she wants to, and if she can.

RITA: You used to call her little Eyolf— (*Taking* ASTA's *hand*) From now on, Asta, you shall be our little Eyolf—Eyolf—just as you were then.

ALLMERS (*With restraint*): Stay. Share life with us, with Rita and me—with me, your brother.

ASTA (*Resolved, taking her hand back*): No, I can't. (*Turning around*) Mr. Borgheim, do you know what time the steamer leaves?

BORGHEIM: Very soon. It's already overdue.

ASTA: Then I must get on board. Would you like to go with me?

BORGHEIM: Would I like to? Yes, indeed!

ASTA: Well, then, come!

RITA (*Slowly*): Ah, so that's it. You won't stay here with us.

ASTA (*Throwing her arms around* RITA's *neck*): Thank you for everything, Rita. (*Walks over to* ALLMERS *and takes his hand*) Good-by, Alfred. A thousand good-bys.

ALLMERS (*Softly, with intensity*): What does all this mean, Asta? You're running away from something.

ASTA (*In quiet anguish*): Yes, Alfred, I am. I'm escaping.

ALLMERS: From me?

ASTA (*Whispering*): From you, yes . . . and from myself.

ALLMERS (*Taken aback*): Oh!

(ASTA *walks* UPSTAGE *as if going down the hill.* BORGHEIM *waves his hat and follows her.* RITA *leans against the entrance of the summerhouse.* ALLMERS *paces about, obviously upset. He crosses to the railing, where he stands and stares downward. There is a pause.*)

ALLMERS (*Turning around, composed*): Here comes the steamer. Look—you can see it there, Rita.

RITA: I don't dare look.

ALLMERS: You don't dare?

RITA: No. It has a red eye, and a green one. Wide-open eyes that glow and burn.

ALLMERS: Those are the signal lights—you know that.

RITA: From now on they'll be eyes to me, and they'll stare—stare at me out of the darkness . . . yes, and into the darkness, too.

ALLMERS: It's docking now.

RITA: Where? Where are they docking this evening?

ALLMERS (*Close to her*): At the pier as usual, my dear.

RITA (*Rigid*): How can they go in there?

ALLMERS: They have to.

RITA: But that's where Eyolf— Oh, how can they go in there?

ALLMERS: Life is merciless, Rita.

RITA: Human beings are merciless! They have no respect, no consideration, for the living or the dead.

ALLMERS: You're right. Life goes on as if nothing had happened.

RITA (*Staring straight ahead*): Nothing has happened to them—only to the two of us.

ALLMERS (*Anguished, with new pain*): Rita, how useless it was for you to give him birth in so much torment and pain. Now he's gone, and there's not a trace of him anywhere.

RITA: Only the crutch that was pulled out of the sea.

ALLMERS (*Angrily*): Can't you keep quiet! I don't want to hear that word.

RITA (*Wailing*): I just can't bear the thought that we don't have him any more.

ALLMERS (*Coldly and bitterly*): You did very well without him when he was here. A whole day could go by without your setting eyes on him.

RITA: Yes, because I knew I could see him whenever I wanted to.

ALLMERS: And in that way we wasted the short time we had with our little Eyolf.

RITA (*Listening in dread*): Do you hear that, Alfred? It's ringing again.

ALLMERS (*Looking out over the fiord*): That's the bell on the steamer. It's ready to leave.

RITA: Oh, I don't mean the bell. I mean the other sound—the one I've heard in my ears all day. (*After a pause*) Now it's ringing again!

ALLMERS (*Going over to her*): You're mistaken, Rita.

RITA: No I'm not—I hear it distinctly. It sounds just like funeral bells. Slowly . . . oh, slowly, and always the same words.

ALLMERS: Words? What words?

RITA (*Nodding her head in tempo*): "The crutch is floating . . . the crutch is floating." It seems to me you ought to be able to hear it, too.

ALLMERS (*Shaking his head*): I don't hear anything because there's nothing to hear.

RITA: I don't care what you say! I hear it clearly.

ALLMERS (*Looking over the railing*): Now they're on board, Rita. The ship is on its way to town.

RITA: I don't understand why you can't hear it. "The crutch is floating . . . the crutch is floating."

ALLMERS (*Moving closer to her*): You shouldn't stand here and listen to things that don't exist! I tell you, Asta and Borgheim are already on board and on their way. Asta is gone!

RITA (*Looking timidly at him*): Then you'll be going soon, too, won't you, Alfred?

ALLMERS (*Quickly*): What do you mean by that?

RITA: You'll be following after your sister, won't you?

ALLMERS: Did Asta say anything to you?

RITA: No. You told me it was because of Asta that we came together in the first place.

ALLMERS: Yes, but it was you who held me here—with our marriage.

RITA: Ah! Not with my beauty? That beauty that once consumed you?

ALLMERS: The law of change. Perhaps it could be the very thing that will hold us together.

RITA (*Nodding slowly*): Well, there's a change taking place in me. I can feel the pain of it.

ALLMERS: Pain?

RITA: Yes. There's a kind of giving birth in it.

ALLMERS: Yes, there is—or a resurrection. A transition into a higher form of life.

RITA (*Gazing sadly ahead*): Yes, built on the wreckage of this life's happiness.

ALLMERS: That wreckage may be the foundation of our victory, Rita.

RITA (*Vehemently*): Oh! What an empty phrase! Good God— we're human beings meant to live on this earth.

ALLMERS: Yes, but we're related somewhat to the oceans and the skies, too, Rita.

RITA: Maybe you are, but I'm not!

ALLMER: Oh yes you are, more than you realize.

RITA (*Going closer to him*): Tell me, Alfred, couldn't you think of going back to your work again?

ALLMERS: The work that you hated so much?

RITA: It takes less to please me now. I'm willing to share you with your book.

ALLMERS: Why?

RITA: So that I can keep you here with me, close by.

ALLMERS: There's so little I can do to help you, Rita.

RITA: Maybe I could help you.

ALLMERS: With my work, you mean?

RITA: No. With your life.

ALLMERS (*Shaking his head*): I don't think I have any more life to live.

RITA: Well . . . to help you endure it, then.

ALLMERS (*Darkly, staring ahead*): I think it would be best for both of us if we separated.

RITA (*Scrutinizing him*): Where would you go? Perhaps to Asta after all?

ALLMERS: No. From now on I can never go to Asta.

RITA: Where, then?

ALLMERS: Up to the loneliness—the solitude.

RITA: To the mountains? Is that what you mean?

ALLMERS: Yes.

RITA: That's all daydreaming, Alfred. You couldn't live up there.

ALLMERS: And yet, I'm drawn up there just the same.

RITA: Why? Tell me.

ALLMERS: Sit down. I'll try to explain something to you.

RITA: Something that happened to you up there?

ALLMERS: Yes.

RITA: Something you concealed from Asta and me?

ALLMERS: Yes.

RITA: Oh, you keep so quiet about everything! You shouldn't be that way.

ALLMERS: Sit down here, and I'll tell you about it.

RITA (*Sitting on the bench*): Yes, let me hear it.

ALLMERS: I was absolutely alone up there in the midst of the quiet, high white mountains. One day I came to a large, desolate mountain lake, and there was no way to cross it. No people, no boat.

RITA: Well, what happened?

ALLMERS: I decided to go on—entirely on my own—into a side valley. I thought that from that side I could get over the high mountains and between the peaks and down again on the other side of the lake.

RITA: And instead you got lost, Alfred?

ALLMERS: Yes. I made a mistake in the direction. There was no road, you know, no path. I walked on for a whole day and most of the next night. Finally, I felt that I'd never get back to people again.

RITA: Never to come home! But surely you were thinking about us?

ALLMERS: No, I wasn't.

RITA: No?

ALLMERS: No. It was so strange. It seemed that both you and Eyolf had wandered away—far away from me. And so had Asta.

RITA: What did you think of, then?

ALLMERS: I didn't think. I walked on, dragging myself along the edge of the precipice, and I experienced a feeling of peace—even pleasure—at being in the presence of death.

RITA (*Standing up abruptly*): Don't talk about such gruesome things!

ALLMERS: That's how I felt. Just no fear! It seemed to me that there I was with Death as a good traveling companion. It was all so natural, so reasonable and simple—everything! Then I remembered that people in my family didn't live to be old.

RITA: Please don't say things like that, Alfred. After all, you came out of it alive.

ALLMERS: Then all at once I was there, on the other side of the lake.

RITA: And you had simply lived through a horrible experience—a night of terror. You must admit that to yourself, Alfred.

ALLMERS: That night elevated me and enabled me to reach a decision. I turned around and started home to Eyolf.

RITA (*Softly*): Too late.

ALLMERS: Yes. My good companion came with me and took Eyolf away. Only then was I terrified of him. Terrified of it all—all this life that we don't dare to leave. That's how much you and I are bound to this earth!

RITA (*With a glimmer of joy*): Yes. It's true! For you *too*!

(*Going closer to him*) Let's just go on living our lives together as long as we possibly can.

ALLMERS (*Shrugging his shoulders*): Go on living! Oh yes! Yes, by all means! And yet we have nothing to fill this life of ours! It's all empty waste—all of it—wherever I look.

RITA (*Fearfully*): Sooner or later you'll go away from me, Alfred —I feel it! I can see it on your face. You'll go away from me.

ALLMERS: With my good traveling companion, you mean?

RITA: No. Something worse. You'll go of your own free will. It's only here with me that you feel that you have nothing to live for. I know that. Isn't that what you're thinking? Isn't it? Answer me!

ALLMERS (*Looking sternly at her*): If it is? What then? (*From the distance below are heard sounds of people shouting and calling in anger and fear.* ALLMERS *walks to the railing and looks down.*)

RITA: What's that? (*With an outburst*) Maybe they've found him.

ALLMERS: He'll never be found.

RITA: What is it, then?

ALLMERS (*Coming toward her*): Just a fight, as usual.

RITA: Down at the water?

ALLMERS: Yes. That whole filthy waterfront should be cleared away. Done away with! The men are coming home drunk as usual and beating their children. Listen to the boys screaming and the women yelling for help.

RITA: Maybe we should send someone down there to help them.

ALLMERS (*Hard and angry*): Help them? The very boys who did nothing to help Eyolf? No! Let them go under, the way they let Eyolf go under.

RITA: Don't talk like that, Alfred—don't even think it.

ALLMERS: I can't think any other way. Those old dilapidated shacks should be torn down.

RITA: But what would happen to all those poor people?

ALLMERS: They'd have to go somewhere else.

RITA: And their children?

ALLMERS: What difference does it make where they end their miserable lives?

RITA (*Quietly, with reproach*): You're forcing yourself to be this hard, Alfred.

ALLMERS (*Angrily*): I've a right to be hard from now on. In fact, it's my duty.

RITA: Your duty?

ALLMERS: To Eyolf. He mustn't lie down there unavenged—it's as simple as that! Think it over, Rita, and have the whole place leveled to the ground when I'm gone.

RITA (*Intently*): When you're gone?

ALLMERS: Yes. That'll give you a purpose, something to fill your life. And you should have something.

RITA: You're right. I must have that, at least. But can you guess what I'm going to do the moment you leave?

ALLMERS: No. What?

RITA (*Slowly, with resolution*): As soon as you've left me, I'll go down to the waterfront and get all those poor lost children to come up here to our home. All those badly behaved ruffians—

ALLMERS: What will you do with them here?

RITA: I'll take care of them.

ALLMERS: You!

RITA: Yes, I will. I will do just that. The day you leave, they'll be here, all of them, as if they were my very own.

ALLMERS (*Shaken*): In our little Eyolf's place?

RITA: Yes, in our little Eyolf's place. They'll live in Eyolf's room, read his books, play with his toys. And they'll each have a turn to sit in his chair at the table.

ALLMERS: This is madness! And it's madness for me to listen to you. Besides, I don't know a person in the world who would be less suited for this kind of thing than you!

RITA: Then I'll have to elevate myself to it, won't I? I'll have to learn, and train myself.

ALLMERS: Are you serious about this? Then there certainly has been a change in you.

RITA: Yes there has, Alfred, and I have you to thank for it. You've left me with an emptiness in life that I must fill with something—something that resembles a kind of love.

ALLMERS: Well, it's true we haven't done much for those poor people down there.

RITA: We haven't done anything for them.

ALLMERS: We've hardly thought of them.

RITA: Not with compassion, anyway—not with kindness.

ALLMERS: And we had all the "gold and green forests."

RITA: We closed our hands to them, and our hearts too.

ALLMERS (*Nodding*): Then perhaps it's understandable that they wouldn't risk their lives to save little Eyolf.

RITA (*Softly*): Would you have? Be honest, Alfred. Are you sure that we would have risked *ours*?

ALLMERS: You must never doubt that, Rita!

RITA: Why not? We're only human!

ALLMERS: What do you think you can do for all those neglected children?

RITA: To start with, I'll try, if I can, to ease and ennoble their lives.

ALLMERS: If you can do that, little Eyolf was not born in vain.

RITA: Nor taken from us in vain.

ALLMERS (*Looking steadily at her*): You should face one thing, Rita. You are not driven to this by love.

RITA: No, I'm not. At least, not yet.

ALLMERS: Do you know why you are doing it?

RITA: Well, you've spoken to Asta so often about human responsibility—

ALLMERS: The very book you hated?

RITA: I still hate that book. I used to listen while you explained it, and now I'll try—in my own way—to continue your work.

ALLMERS (*Shaking his head*): You're not doing this for the sake of the unfinished book.

RITA: No. I do have another reason.

ALLMERS: What is it?

RITA (*Softly, with a melancholy smile*): I want to win back the affection of those wide-open eyes that stare at me.

ALLMERS: Could I be a part of this? Could I help you, Rita?

RITA: Would you want to?

ALLMERS: Yes, if I only knew how.

RITA (*Hesitating*): You'd have to stay here—with me.

ALLMERS (*Softly*): Let's try and see if it's possible.

RITA (*Hardly audible*): Let's do that, Alfred.

(*Both are silent. After a short pause,* ALLMERS *goes over to the flagpole and puts the flag up to the top.* RITA *stands at the summerhouse and watches him quietly.*)

ALLMERS (*Coming close to her*): We have a full day's work ahead of us, Rita.

RITA: You'll see, Alfred, every now and then a kind of peace—an almost holy tranquility—will descend upon us.

ALLMERS: And perhaps we'll be aware that their spirits are visiting us.

RITA: Their spirits?

ALLMERS: Yes. Perhaps they'll be around us—those dear ones, the ones we've lost.

RITA (*Nodding slowly*): Our little Eyolf . . . and your Big Eyolf.

ALLMERS (*Staring straight ahead*): It may happen, every now and then on our way through life, that we shall seem to have a glimpse of them.

RITA: Where shall we look Alfred?

ALLMERS (*Looking at her fixedly*): Upward.

RITA (*Nodding*): Yes, yes, upward.

ALLMERS: Upward toward the peaks. Toward the stars and into the great silence.

RITA (*Giving him her hand*): Thank you.


CURTAIN

# THE
# WILD
# DUCK

A PLAY IN FIVE ACTS

1884

# CHARACTERS

HAAKON WERLE   *an industrialist*

GREGERS WERLE   *his son*

OLD EKDAL

HJALMAR EKDAL   *Old Ekdal's son, a photographer*

GINA EKDAL   *Hjalmar's wife*

HEDVIG EKDAL   *their daughter, age fourteen*

MRS. BERTHE SORBY   *Haakon Werle's housekeeper*

DR. RELLING

MOLVIK   *a one-time theologian*

GRABERG   *Haakon Werle's bookkeeper*

PETERSEN   *Haakon Werle's butler*

JENSEN   *a footman*

A PASTY, FAT GENTLEMAN

A THIN-HAIRED GENTLEMAN

A NEARSIGHTED GENTLEMAN

SIX OTHER DINNER GUESTS

SEVERAL HIRED WAITERS


ACT ONE takes place in the home of HAAKON WERLE. The remaining acts take place in the studio rooms of HJALMAR EKDAL.

# ACT I

*The home of* HAAKON WERLE, *an industrialist, a richly decorated room furnished with bookcases and comfortable, upholstered furniture. A desk cluttered with papers and account books stands in the center of the room. The lamps have green shades, give it a soft glow.* UPSTAGE, *open folding doors with draperies drawn aside give a glimpse of a more beautiful room in the background. It is a large music room lit by branching candelabras and lamps.* DOWNSTAGE RIGHT *there is a study area and a small concealed door which leads into* WERLE'S *office.* DOWNSTAGE LEFT *is a glowing stove; and* UPSTAGE LEFT, *a double door leading into the dining room.*

AS THE CURTAIN RISES, WERLE'S *servant* PETERSEN, *in livery, and a hired waiter* JENSEN, *in black, are putting the study in order. In the larger room two or three other hired* WAITERS *move about arranging things and lighting lamps. From the dining room comes the hum of conversation and the laughter of many voices. A glass is tapped with a knife and there is a short silence. A toast is proposed. Shouts of "bravo" are heard and the conversation is resumed.*

PETERSEN (*Lights a lamp on the stove and puts a green shade over it*): Be quiet, Jensen, and listen to them. The old man is standing up now. He's proposing a long-winded toast to his Mrs. Sorby.

JENSEN (*Moving an armchair forward*): Do you think there's any truth in what people are saying? Is there something going on between those two?

PETERSEN: The devil knows.

JENSEN: He was quite a lively buck in his young days!

PETERSEN: Maybe.

JENSEN: But you said he's giving this dinner party for his son.

PETERSEN: Yes. He came home yesterday.

JENSEN: Now isn't that something? I didn't even know Mr. Werle had a son.

PETERSEN: Oh yes, he has a son, all right! But he makes himself scarce around here. He's a steady fixture at the Hoydal Works up north. You know, in all the years I've served this house, he's never been in town.

A WAITER (*From the doorway of the next room*): Excuse me, Petersen, there's an old fellow who—

PETERSEN (*Grumbling*): What the devil! Now who?

(OLD EKDAL *appears from the inner room at the* RIGHT. *He is dressed in a threadbare jacket with a high collar, a fur cap, and woolen mittens. He wears a dirty red-brown wig and a little gray handle-bar moustache. He carries a cane and under one arm has a package wrapped in brown paper.*)

PETERSEN (*Hurrying toward him*): Good God! What are you doing here?

EKDAL (*From the doorway*): I've got to get into the office, Petersen.

PETERSEN: It was closed an hour ago.

EKDAL: They already told me that at the front door, but Graberg's still in there and I've got to see him. Oh, be kind, Petersen. Let me sneak in that way. (*He points toward the tapestry, where there is a hidden door.*) I've gone through that way before.

PETERSEN (*Opening the door*): All right, all right then, go ahead. But be sure to go out the front way. We have company tonight.

EKDAL: Yes, I know, I know that. Thanks, Petersen, good old friend! Thanks! (*Mumbling*) Idiot!

(OLD EKDAL *exits.* PETERSEN *closes the door after him.*)

JENSEN: Is he part of the office staff?

PETERSEN: Old Ekdal? Hardly. He does some copying now and then when they need extra help. Did you know that in his time he was a fine gentleman?

JENSEN: Really? He looks like he's had some rough weather since then.

PETERSEN: He has! He was an army lieutenant.

JENSEN: Well, I'll be damned! Was he?

PETERSEN: My God, was he ever! Then he went into business for himself—something to do with the lumber trade. They say he played a nasty trick on Mr. Werle. They were partners up at Hoydal, you know. Oh yes, indeed, I know old Ekdal very well. We've drunk many a good beer and schnapps together at Madame Eriksen's.

JENSEN: He doesn't look like he's able to treat very often.

PETERSEN: Treat? God no, Jensen, but I always think it pays to be generous to people who've seen better days.

JENSEN: Did he go bankrupt?

PETERSEN: No, no—worse than that, much worse. He ended up in prison.

JENSEN: In prison?

PETERSEN: Well, a jail of some kind. Sh! Quiet! They're getting up from the table.

(*Two servants open the dining room door. The* GUESTS *are heard talking.* MRS. SORBY *enters with two* GENTLEMEN. *They are talking. Gradually the whole dinner party enters, including* MR. WERLE. HJALMAR EKDAL *and* GREGERS WERLE *enter last.*)

MRS. SORBY: Petersen, we'll take our coffee in the music room.

PETERSEN: Very well, Mrs. Sorby.

(MRS. SORBY *and the two* GENTLEMEN *go into the inner room and then off to the* RIGHT. PETERSEN *and* JENSEN *follow her.*)

FAT GENTLEMAN (*To the* THIN-HAIRED GENTLEMAN): Whew! That dinner was an exhausting piece of work!

THIN-HAIRED GENTLEMAN: Well, with a little bit of will power one can accomplish quite amazing things in three hours.

FAT GENTLEMAN: But afterwards—afterwards, my dear Chamberlain—the repercussions!

THIRD GENTLEMAN: I believe I overheard that the demitasse and liqueur are to be served in the music room.

FAT GENTLEMAN: Bravo! Then perhaps Mrs. Sorby will be kind enough to favor us with a piece of music.

THIN-HAIRED GENTLEMAN (*Sotto voce*): It's likely to be the only favor we'll get from her tonight!

FAT GENTLEMAN: Oh no! Berthe would never slap the hands of her old friends!

(*The* GENTLEMEN *laugh and go into the inner room.*)

WERLE (*In a low voice, dejected*): Gregers, I don't think anyone even noticed it.

GREGERS: What, Father?

WERLE: You didn't notice either?

GREGERS: What?

WERLE: There were thirteen of us at the table.

GREGERS: There were?

WERLE (*Looking toward* HJALMAR EKDAL): We're normally accustomed to parties of only twelve. (*Speaking to the other* GENTLEMEN) Gentlemen, this way, please.

(MR. WERLE *and the others exit* RIGHT *into the back room.* HJALMAR *and* GREGERS *stay behind.*)

HJALMAR: (*Who has overheard the conversation*): You shouldn't have invited me, Gregers.

GREGERS: Why not? Tonight was supposed to be a dinner in my honor. Shouldn't I ask my oldest and closest friend?

HJALMAR: I don't think your father likes the idea. I'm not usually invited to this house, you know.

GREGERS: So I hear. But I wanted to see you tonight and talk to you. I'll probably be going back soon. We've drifted far apart since our school days, haven't we, old classmate? It's been sixteen—no, almost seventeen years!

HJALMAR: Has it been that long?

GREGERS: Yes, it has. Well now, how are things with you, Hjalmar? You're looking very well. You've filled out—become a little stouter.

HJALMAR: Stout? Hmm. You can hardly call me stout, but I do look more manly than I did at school.

GREGERS: True. Your exterior hasn't suffered at all.

HJALMAR: No. But inside? Oh, that's another story, believe me!

You heard how my life collapsed for me and for my loved ones? It's been so dreadful, since we've seen each other.

GREGERS (*Cautiously*): How are things with your father now?

HJALMAR: Dear Gregers, let's not talk about it. My poor, unhappy father! He lives with me, of course. He hasn't a soul on earth to hold on to but me. Ah, I find all this so horrifying and humiliating. Instead, you tell me how you've been getting along up there at Hoydal.

GREGERS: It's been lonesome—beautifully lonesome at times. I've had more than enough time to brood over many, many things. (*He sits in an armchair near the stove, motioning* HJALMAR *into another chair nearby.*) Come over here and let's make ourselves more comfortable.

HJALMAR (*Sentimentally*): I want to thank you just the same, Gregers, for this invitation to your father's table. I take it as a sign that you don't hold a grudge against me.

GREGERS (*Surprised*): Where did you get that idea?

HJALMAR: Well, you must have felt it, those first years.

GREGERS: What do you mean?

HJALMAR: After the disaster. It would have been quite natural for you to have felt something. Why, your father came within a hair'sbreadth of being drawn into that—that . . . well, that dreadful catastrophe.

GREGERS: Do you think I could have held that against you? Who ever gave you that idea?

HJALMAR: I know how you felt, Gregers. Your father told me.

GREGERS (*In amazement*): My father? Oh—is that why I never heard a single word from you in all these years? Not one single word?

HJALMAR: Yes.

GREGERS: Not even when you left school and took up photography?

HJALMAR: Your father advised me never to write to you. Never!

GREGERS (*Looking straight ahead*): Maybe . . . maybe he was right. Tell me, Hjalmar, are you satisfied with your life now?

HJALMAR (*With a light sigh*): Oh yes, I am. I have no right to complain. I must admit, though, at first it felt a bit strange to me. It was such a complete change. My whole life was totally uprooted—completely different. My father's absolute ruin—the terrible shame, the disgrace—

GREGERS (*Moved*): Yes, yes, I know. I know.

HJALMAR: I couldn't go on with my studies. There wasn't a penny left, anyway. On the contrary, there were debts—mostly to your father, I believe.

GREGERS: Hmm.

HJALMAR: I thought it was best to make a clean break and get away once and for all from the old surroundings—from all my personal contacts. Your father advised me particularly about that. He was very helpful to me at the time—

GREGERS: My father?

HJALMAR: Yes. But you know all that, don't you? Where else could I have acquired enough money to learn photography, to furnish a studio, and get myself established? Believe me, it all costs money!

GREGERS: My father paid for it?

HJALMAR: Yes, my dear friend, he did. Didn't you know? I understood he wrote you everything.

GREGERS: Not a word. At least, not about his part in it. He must have forgotten about that. We've never exchanged anything but business letters. So! It was actually my father who—!

HJALMAR: It certainly was. He didn't want people to know, but he was the one. Also, he was instrumental in my being able to get married. Did you know that?

GREGERS: No, not that, either! (*Shaking him by the arm*) My dear Hjalmar, I can't tell you how happy this makes me—and troubles me, too. You see, maybe I've done father a great injustice in a way—a small way. This proves he's quite generous after all, that he has a heart and a conscience.

HJALMAR: Conscience?

GREGERS: Yes, or whatever you want to call it. I can't find words to tell you how pleased I am to hear this about my father! Well, Hjalmar, so now you're married, eh? That's more than I'll ever be! I hope you've found a lot of happiness as a married man.

HJALMAR: Yes, I have. She's as kind and clever a wife as any man would want. She's not completely without refinement, you know.

GREGERS (*A little surprised*): Why, of course not.

HJALMAR: Life itself is an education, and then there's been our daily companionship—and we have frequent friends and visitors, wonderfully clever and intelligent people who come and visit all the time. I bet you wouldn't even recognize Gina now.

GREGERS: Gina?

HJALMAR: Yes, my dear friend, didn't you remember her name?

GREGERS: Whose name? I—

HJALMAR: Don't you remember her? She lived in this house for a while.

GREGERS (*Looking at him*): You mean Gina Hansen?

HJALMAR: Yes, of course—Gina Hansen.

GREGERS: The one who managed our house the last year mother was so ill?

HJALMAR: Yes! But my dear Gregers, I know for sure your father wrote you about my marriage.

GREGERS (*Standing up*): He did, but he didn't mention that . . . (*Beginning to pace the floor*) Wait a minute—yes, perhaps he did, now that I think of it. My father always writes me such short letters. (*Half sitting on the armrest*) But tell me, Hjalmar—this is most pleasant—how did you happen to meet Gina—your wife?

HJALMAR: Rather simple. At the time, everything in this house was so upset because of your mother's illness that Gina didn't stay here very long. She found it too much to manage, so she gave notice and left. It was a year before your mother's death, or perhaps the same year.

GREGERS: It was the same year. I was away from home—up at Hoydal. What happened then?

HJALMAR: Well, Gina went to live with her mother, who ran a little eating place. She was a large, hard-working, efficient woman. There was a room in the house for rent—a nice, pleasant room—

GREGERS: And I suppose you were lucky enough to get it?

HJALMAR: Yes, indeed I was. In fact, your father suggested it. That's how I happened to meet Gina!

GREGERS: And you became engaged?

HJALMAR: Yes. Love happens so easily to young people.

GREGERS (*Rises and wanders around*): Tell me, when you became engaged, did father suggest that—I mean, was that when you took up photography?

HJALMAR: Just about then, yes. I wanted to get away and make a home, the sooner the better. Your father and I both agreed that the photography business was the most practical, and Gina thought so too. Then there was another thing—luckily, Gina had just learned retouching.

GREGERS: How convenient!

HJALMAR (*Standing up, pleased*): It was a lucky break, wasn't it?

GREGERS: Without a doubt. My father seems to have acted almost like a godfather to you.

HJALMAR (*With emotion*): He didn't forget that his old friend's son needed help through those difficult times. He does have a good heart, Gregers.

MRS. SORBY (*Entering arm in arm with* MR. WERLE): No objections now, Mr. Werle! You shan't remain another moment in there staring at all those lights! It isn't good for you.

WERLE (*Lets go her arm, rubs his eyes*): I'm inclined to believe you're right.

(PETERSEN *and* JENSEN *enter with the refreshment trays.*)

MRS. SORBY (*To the* GUESTS *in the next room*): This way, if you please, gentlemen. If any of you would like a liqueur, you're welcome. You'll just have to come in here and serve yourselves.

FAT GENTLEMAN (*Walking up to* MRS. SORBY): Good God, Mrs. Sorby! Is it true you've abolished our heaven-sent right to smoke?

MRS. SORBY: I have! Here in Mr. Werle's private domain it's strictly forbidden, my dear Chamberlain.

THIN-HAIRED GENTLEMAN: Since when have you enforced these stringent amendments to the cigar law, my dear Mrs. Sorby?

MRS. SORBY: Since the last dinner, Mr. Chamberlain, when a certain individual allowed himself to overstep the line.

THIN-HAIRED GENTLEMAN: And you don't allow anyone to overstep the line—not even the least bit, Berthe? Never?

MRS. SORBY: Not even the least little bit, my dear Chamberlain Balle.

(*Most of the* GUESTS *have assembled in* MR. WERLE's *room. The servants serve the liqueurs.*)

WERLE (*To Hjalmar*): What are you studying, Ekdal?

HJALMAR: Just an album, Mr. Werle.

THIN-HAIRED GENTLEMAN: Ah—photographs! Well, that's right in your line.

FAT GENTLEMAN (*In an armchair*): Haven't you brought any of your own pictures?

HJALMAR: No sir, I haven't.

FAT GENTLEMAN: Ah! You should have. It's good for the digestion to sit and look at pictures.

THIN-HAIRED GENTLEMAN: And it's always a part of the evening's entertainment.

NEAR-SIGHTED GENTLEMAN: And all contributions are received most gratefully!

MRS. SORBY: What the Chamberlains mean is that if one is asked to dinner, one should work for one's food, Mr. Ekdal.

FAT GENTLEMAN: When one has had such a delicious dinner, such an obligation becomes a pleasure.

THIN-HAIRED GENTLEMAN: Good God—if it comes down to obligations and survival, well, then—

MRS. SORBY: You're so right about that!

(*They continue the conversation with laughter.*)

GREGERS (*Softly*): You must join in, Hjalmar.

HJALMAR: What should I say?

FAT GENTLEMAN: Mr. Werle, don't you think that Tokay must be regarded as a comparatively healthful drink for the stomach?

WERLE (*At the stove*): Well, I can safely answer for the Tokay you drank this evening. It's one of the very finest years, but of course you've probably already noticed that.

FAT GENTLEMAN: Yes, it had an unusually delicate bouquet.

HJALMAR (*Uncertain*): What do you mean, finest years? Does the year make any difference with the wine itself?

FAT GENTLEMAN (*Laughing*): Well, indeed it does!

WERLE (*Laughing*): Ha! It doesn't pay to put a noble wine in front of you!

THIN-HAIRED GENTLEMAN: Good Tokay is much the same as good photography, Mr. Ekdal. They both need sunshine. Isn't that so?

HJALMAR: Yes. Light is very important indeed.

MRS. SORBY: Why, it's the same with Chamberlains! They, too, desire sunshine. So much so, they'd do anything to find their little place in the sun, as the saying goes!

THIN-HAIRED GENTLEMAN: Oh, that's a worn-out old sarcasm!

NEAR-SIGHTED GENTLEMAN: Mrs. Sorby is performing . . .

FAT GENTLEMAN (*Reprimanding her*): . . . at our expense! Mrs. Berthe! Mrs. Berthe!

MRS. SORBY: But it's true what they say—vintages do differ tremendously. The old vintages are, of course, the finest.

NEAR-SIGHTED GENTLEMAN: Do you include me among the old ones?

MRS. SORBY: Far from it.

THIN-HAIRED GENTLEMAN: Well then, how about me, my sweet Mrs. Sorby?

FAT GENTLEMAN: Yes, and me too? Into what vintage would you put us?

MRS. SORBY: The sweet vintage, my dear gentlemen! (*She sips from her liqueur glass. The* GENTLEMEN *smile and begin to gather around and make small jokes with her.*)

WERLE: Mrs. Sorby always finds a way out—when she wants to. Hold out your glasses, gentlemen, and Petersen will see to them. Gregers, let's drink a glass together.
(GREGERS *doesn't move.*)

WERLE: Don't you want to join us, Ekdal? I didn't have the opportunity to acknowledge you at the table.

GRABERG (*Looking through the tapestry door*): Excuse me, Mr. Werle, but I can't get out.

WERLE: What? Are you locked in again?

GRABERG: Yes sir. Flakstad took the keys.

WERLE: Well, come through here, then.

GRABERG: There's someone with me.

WERLE: Well, come, come, both of you. Don't be shy.

(GRABERG *and* OLD EKDAL *enter.*)

WERLE (*Involuntarily*): Oh good God!

(*The* GUESTS' *laughter and chattering stop.* HJALMAR, *having lost his composure at the sight of his father, puts his glass down and turns toward the stove.*)

EKDAL (*Not looking up, makes small bows to both sides and murmers*): I beg your pardon. I'm coming through the wrong way. The front door was locked . . . the front door was locked. I beg pardon . . . beg pardon. . . .

(GRABERG *and* OLD EKDAL *exit.*)

WERLE (*Between his teeth*): That damn Graberg!

GREGERS (*Staring at* HJALMAR, *stunned*): He couldn't be your—

FAT GENTLEMAN: What's going on here? Who was that?

GREGERS: No one. Just the bookkeeper and someone else.

NEAR-SIGHTED GENTLEMAN (*To* HJALMAR): Did you know that man?

HJALMAR: I don't know. I didn't look at him.

FAT GENTLEMAN (*Rising*): What the devil is going on, then? (*He walks over to another group who are talking quietly.*)

MRS. SORBY (*Whispering to the servant*): Give something to him—something really nice.

PETERSEN (*As he exits*): As you wish.

GREGERS (*Shaken. To* HJALMAR, *slowly*): That was your father.

HJALMAR: Yes.

GREGERS: You stood there and denied you knew him!

HJALMAR (*Whispering vehemently*): What could I have done?

GREGERS: Your own Father?

HJALMAR (*Painfully*): If you were in my place, what—

(*The subdued conversation between the* GUESTS *begins to take on the tone of forced loudness.*)

THIN-HAIRED GENTLEMAN (*Crossing to* HJALMAR *and* GREGERS *in a friendly way*): Ah! You two are reliving your old school memories, eh? What? Don't you smoke, Mr. Ekdal? May I give you a light? Oh yes, it's true we're not allowed to smoke in here—

HJALMAR: Thank you, it doesn't matter—I don't care—

FAT GENTLEMAN: Don't you have a nice little poem you would like to recite for us, Mr. Ekdal? You used to do it so charmingly.

HJALMAR: Unfortunately, I can't remember any of them now.

FAT GENTLEMAN (*Crossing to the other room*): Oh, that's a shame. Well, what shall we think of to do, Balle?

HJALMAR (*Solemnly*): Gregers, I want to leave. When a man feels that fate has conspired to give him a crushing blow— well, then—tell your father good night for me, please.

GREGERS: Yes, yes. Are you going right home?

HJALMAR: Yes. Why?

GREGERS: Perhaps I'll come over to see you later.

HJALMAR: No, don't do that. You mustn't come to my house. It'll look so gloomy after this splendid banquet. We can meet someplace in town.

MRS. SORBY (*Moving closer, speaks quietly*): Are you leaving us, Ekdal?

HJALMAR: Yes.

MR. SORBY: Give my best to Gina.

HJALMAR: Thank you.

MRS. SORBY: Tell her I shall be visiting her one of these days.

HJALMAR: Oh yes, thank you. (*To* GREGERS) Stay here. I'll manage to disappear unnoticed. (*He saunters casually into the next room and exits* RIGHT.)

MRS. SORBY (*Softly to the servant, who has come back*): Well, did you give the old one something?

PETERSEN: Yes. I slipped a bottle of cognac into his pocket.

MRS. SORBY: Oh dear, couldn't you find something more suitable than that?

PETERSEN: Oh no, that's what he likes best of all, Mrs. Sorby.

FAT GENTLEMAN (*In the doorway, with a sheet of music in his hand*): Shall we play our duet now, Mrs. Sorby?

MRS. SORBY: Yes, of course—let's do just that!

GUESTS: Bravo, bravo!

(MRS. SORBY *and the* GUESTS *exit* RIGHT. GREGERS *stands by the fireplace.* MR. WERLE *looks for something on his desk. He seems to want* GREGERS *to leave. When* GREGERS *remains standing,* WERLE *walks over to the door to the music room.*)

GREGERS: Father, would you wait a moment?

WERLE (*Stopping*): What is it?

GREGERS: I want to talk to you.

WERLE: Can't it wait until we're alone?

GREGERS: No, it can't. We may never be alone again.

WERLE (*Coming closer*): What's that supposed to mean? (*During the following, faint piano music can be heard from the music room.*)

GREGERS: How have you allowed that family to become so miserably destitute?

WERLE: I suppose you mean the Ekdals?

GREGERS: Of course! Lieutenant Ekdal was once very close to you.

WERLE: Unfortunately, yes. Much too close, and I've paid for it for years. I can thank him for the stain that I—yes, I too—have upon my reputation.

GREGERS (*Quietly*): Was he the only guilty one?

WERLE: Whom else do you have in mind?

GREGERS: You both bought that forest property.

WERLE: Yes, but Ekdal drew up the boundary maps. Those misleading maps! He pursued the illegal cutting of timber on government property, and he was the one in charge of everything up there. I wasn't aware of what Lieutenant Ekdal was doing.

GREGERS: He probably wasn't, either.

WERLE: That very well might have been! But the fact is, he was found guilty and I was acquitted.

GREGERS: I know that nothing was ever proved against you.

WERLE: Acquittal is acquittal. Why are you digging up all those old troubles? They gave me gray hairs before my time. Is this the kind of thing you've been brooding about up there all these years? I can assure you, Gregers, here in town the whole incident was forgotten long ago, as far as my reputation is concerned.

GREGERS: And for the Ekdal family?

WERLE: What would you want me to do for them? When Ekdal was released from prison he was a broken man—absolutely beyond help. There are people in this world who, just because they get a few buckshot in them, dive to the bottom and never come up again. You can take my word for it, Gregers, it was impossible for me to stretch myself any further for those people and not arouse gossip and suspicion.

GREGERS: Suspicion? Oh, I see!

WERLE: I've arranged for Ekdal to do the copying work for this office all these years. I've paid him far, far more than the work is worth.

GREGERS (*Without looking at him*): I don't doubt it.

WERLE: Are you laughing? Maybe you don't think it's true. Well, check the books—except I never enter that kind of expense into the accounts.

GREGERS (*Smiling coldly*): No, I'm sure you have certain expenses that it is best not to record.

WERLE (*Startled*): What do you mean by that?

GREGERS (*Gathering courage*): How much did it cost for Hjalmar to become a photographer?

WERLE: How should I know?

GREGERS: You paid for it! And for the entire studio! And I also know how generous you were in setting up their home life, too.

WERLE: Well? And you accuse me of not doing anything for that family? Let me assure you, those people have cost me a small fortune.

GREGERS: Have you kept accounts on that "small fortune"?

WERLE: Why do you ask that?

GREGERS: I have my reasons. Tell me, when you so graciously began concerning yourself with your old friend's son, wasn't that about the same time he was thinking of getting married?

WERLE: How the devil do you expect me to remember that after all these years?

GREGERS: You wrote me a very long letter just about then. A business letter, naturally. You added a postscript—rather concise—that Hjalmar Ekdal had married a Miss Hansen.

WERLE: That's true. Her name was Hansen.

GREGERS: Yes. But you didn't say it was Gina Hansen, our former housekeeper.

WERLE (*Laughing scornfully, with effort*): No. It didn't occur to me you were particularly interested in our former house-maids!

GREGERS: You're right, I wasn't. (*Lowering his voice*) But there was someone in this house who did have a very special interest in her.

WERLE (*Flaring up*): What do you mean? What are you aiming at?

GREGERS (*Quietly and firmly*): I'm aiming at you.

WERLE: How dare you! You have the gall to—! And he . . . that . . . that ungrateful—photographer! How dare he insinuate such things!

GREGERS: Hjalmar didn't say a thing about this—not one word. He hasn't the vaguest suspicion of any of it.

WERLE: Where did you hear it, then? Who could have said such things?

GREGERS: My poor, unhappy mother told me. The last time I saw her.

WERLE: Your mother! I should have known. You two always sided together. She turned you against me from the beginning.

GREGERS: No she didn't. But I saw her suffering and all the humiliations she had to bear. I saw how it all got the best of her and she crumbled away—

WERLE: Oh, she didn't have anything to suffer or endure. No more than anyone else, at least. But it's always that way with sickly, oversensitive people. There's no dealing with them—

I've learned that to my regret! And now you're going around nursing your suspicions, digging up all that old trouble, delving into old rumors about your own father! Listen to me, Gregers. I think at your age you should find something more useful to do.

GREGERS: You're right, I should. It's about time.

WERLE: You may find some peace of mind that way. What's the purpose of slaving away up there at the Works as a common clerk, year in and year out, refusing to take anything but the ordinary monthly wage? It's madness!

GREGERS: If only I could be sure of that!

WERLE: Oh, I understand how you feel. You want to be independent. You don't want to owe me anything. Well, now you have a splendid opportunity to be independent, to be your own master in everything.

GREGERS: Oh? How?

WERLE: When I wrote you to come back to town immediately—

GREGERS: Yes, what did you want? I've been waiting all day to find out.

WERLE: I wanted to propose that you come here and share in my firm.

GREGERS: As a partner?

WERLE: Yes. But it doesn't mean we'd have to be together constantly. You would take over the business here in town and I could move up to Hoydal.

GREGERS: Would you want that?

WERLE: Yes. I'm not able to work as I used to. I have to save my eyes, Gregers—they're becoming very weak.

GREGERS: They've always been weak.

WERLE: It's different now. Besides, other circumstances might make it desirable for me to live up there, at least for a while.

GREGERS: I'd never imagined anything like this.

WERLE: Listen now, Gregers. There are many, many things that separate us. But we are, nevertheless, father and son. I think we ought to be able to come to some kind of arrangement with each other.

GREGERS: For appearances, you mean?

WERLE: At least that would be something! Think it over, Gregers. It's possible, isn't it?

GREGERS (*Looking him coldly in the eyes*): What's underneath all this?

WERLE: What do you mean?

GREGERS: You're going to *use* me somehow.

WERLE: In a relationship as close as ours, I suppose one always makes use of the other.

GREGERS: That's what they say.

WERLE: I want so much to have you here at home with me for a while. I'm a lonely man, Gregers. I've always felt lonely— all my life, but mostly now when I'm getting on in years. I need to have someone near me—

GREGERS: You have Mrs. Sorby.

WERLE: Yes, I have, and she has, so to speak, become indispensable to me. She's witty and sweet-natured—she livens up the house. I feel I need that very much.

GREGERS: Well then, you have everything you want.

WERLE: Yes. But I'm afraid it won't last. A woman in a situation like this can be seen in a false light by the outside world. Yes, and I'll admit it's not very helpful to a man's reputation, either.

GREGERS: Oh, is that so? But surely a man who gives this kind of dinner party can take the risk.

WERLE: What about her, Gregers? I'm afraid she won't tolerate this situation much longer. And even if she, out of her devotion to me, were to . . . well, place herself above the gossip and scandal, don't you think, Gregers, that you, with your strongly developed sense of righteousness—?

GREGERS (*Interrupting*): Tell me one thing—cut and dried you're planning to marry her, aren't you?

WERLE: And if I do—?

GREGERS: That's what I'm asking you.

WERLE: Well, if you're opposed, would there be any way of winning you over?

GREGERS: I'm not opposed. In any way.

WERLE: Well, I—I thought out of respect to your dead mother's memory.

GREGERS: I'm not sentimental.

WERLE: Well, whatever you are, you've just taken a great weight off my mind. I'm delighted that I can count on your support in this matter.

GREGERS (*Looking intently at him*): I see how you plan to use me.

WERLE: Use you? Why do you insist on saying that word?

GREGERS: Oh come now, let's not get particular in our choice of words—not when we're alone! (*Laughing shortly*) Then that's it! Damn it all, that's why it was essential for me to come to town! On Mrs. Sorby's account, a family life will be arranged in this house—a tableau of father and son! Well, this will be something new!

WERLE: How dare you speak like this to me!

GREGERS: When was there ever any family life here? Never, as far back as I can remember. But now, by God, it has to look like it! No doubt it will be unquestionably touching to see the son rush home on the wings of filial piety to attend the aging father's wedding feast! What's to become of all those ugly rumors about his poor dead mother and how she suffered in shame? Not one thing. All annihilated in one stroke by her own son!

WERLE: Gregers, I don't believe there's a man in this world you hate as much as you hate me.

GREGERS (*Slowly*): I've seen you too close.

WERLE: You've seen me through your mother's eyes. (*Lowering his voice*) But let me remind you how often those eyes were . . . clouded over.

GREGERS (*Trembling*): I know what you're getting at! Well, who was responsible for that? Who bears the guilt for that weakness in mother? You do! You and all your—your—the last of them was that woman you paired off with Hjalmar Ekdal after you no longer—

WERLE (*Shrugging his shoulders*): Word for word as though I were listening to your mother.

GREGERS (*Not listening*): And there sits Hjalmar with his big, childlike, unsuspecting mind in the midst of all that deceit! Living under the same roof with such a woman, and never knowing that what he calls his home was built on a lie! (*Taking a step closer*) When I look back on your past, I see a great, bloody battlefield strewn with the broken and destroyed bodies of your victims.

WERLE: The rift between us is too wide.

GREGERS (*Bowing coldly*): I agree. That's why I'm taking my hat and coat and leaving.

WERLE: You're leaving for good?

GREGERS: Yes. I've just discovered I have a mission in life.

WERLE: A mission?

GREGERS: You'd laugh at me if I told you what it is.

WERLE: A lonely man doesn't laugh that easily, Gregers.

GREGERS (*Pointing toward the music room*): Do you know what Mrs. Sorby is playing with those Chamberlains in there? Blindman's buff! Good night and farewell.

(GREGERS *exits* UPSTAGE RIGHT. *Sounds of laughter and merrymaking are heard from the party. Some of the* GUESTS *are visible now from the other room.*)

WERLE (*Mumbling spitefully after* GREGERS): Poor fool! And he says he's not sentimental!

CURTAIN

# ACT II

HJALMAR EKDAL's *attic studio. The room appears to be rather large.
It is plain, but comfortably decorated and furnished. Various instru-
ments and pieces of photographic equipment are scattered throughout the room. At* STAGE RIGHT *are a slanting roof and a skylight
with large panes of glass half-covered by blue curtains. In the* UP-
STAGE RIGHT *corner is a door which leads into the hallway, staircase,
and the street below. Between these two doors stands a sofa, slightly
away from the wall. In front of it are a table and a couple of chairs.
On the table is a lighted lamp with a shade, some photographs, and
several small articles such as pencils, papers, and brushes. On the
wall* LEFT *are two doors with an iron stove in between them. In the
corner by the stove there is an old armchair. On the* UPSTAGE RIGHT
*and* CENTER *walls are wide sliding doors. On the* UPSTAGE LEFT *wall
there is a bookcase full of books, boxes, bottles of chemicals, instru-
ments, tools, and other kinds of equipment.*

AS THE CURTAIN RISES, GINA EKDAL *is sitting on the chair near the
table, sewing.* HEDVIG *is sitting on the sofa, her hands shading her
eyes and with her thumbs in her ears, reading a book.* GINA *glances
several times at* HEDVIG *with a look of concern. She tries to conceal
her emotion.*

🪶

GINA:  Hedvig! (HEDVIG *doesn't hear. Louder*) Hedvig!

HEDVIG (*Dropping her hands, looks up*):  Yes, Mother?

GINA:  My dear Hedvig, you mustn't sit here and read any
longer.

HEDVIG:  Oh Mother, can't I—just a *little* longer? Just a little?

GINA:  No, no. You put that book away now. Your father doesn't
like you to read this late. He never reads at night.

HEDVIG (*Closing the book*):  No, father doesn't like to read much
at all, does he?

GINA (*Puts her sewing aside, picks up a pencil and a small note-book*): Do you remember how much we paid for the butter today?

HEDVIG: It was one crown sixty-five ore.

GINA (*Making a note of it*): Oh yes, that's what it was. It's dreadful how much butter we use in this house. (*Writing*) And then there was the sausage and the cheese, let me see now . . . and then the ham . . . hmm. (*Adding it up*) Yes, that's it.

HEDVIG: Don't forget the beer.

GINA (*Writing*): Oh, of course—I forgot. It adds up so fast, but we have to have the beer.

HEDVIG: Don't forget we didn't have a hot dinner tonight because father was out.

GINA: Well, it all helps! Oh, and I took in eight and a half crowns for the photographs.

HEDVIG: Really? You got *that* much?

GINA: Exactly eight and one-half crowns.

(*There is a silence.* GINA *takes up her sewing again.* HEDVIG *picks up the paper and pencil and begins to draw. She keeps her eyes shaded with her left hand.*)

HEDVIG: Isn't it wonderful to think that father's a guest at a big dinner party at Mr. Werle's?

GINA: Well, you can't exactly say he's Mr. Werle's guest. His son sent over the invitation. (*There is a short pause.*) After all, we don't have anything to do with Mr. Werle.

HEDVIG: I'm so anxious for father to come home. He promised to ask Mrs. Sorby for a treat for me.

GINA: Well, believe me, there are plenty of good things to eat in that house. You can be sure of that.

HEDVIG (*Drawing*): Besides, I'm getting just a bit hungry.

(OLD EKDAL *enters from the hall door with a paper bundle under his arm and another package in his coat pocket.*)

GINA: You're so late tonight, Grandfather!

EKDAL: They closed the office on me! I had to wait for Graberg, and I had to go through—

HEDVIG: Did they give you some more copying, Grandfather?

EKDAL: This whole bundle! Just look at it!

GINA: Well, that's good.

HEDVIG: And you have a package in your pocket, too.

EKDAL: What? Oh, nonsense, nonsense, there's nothing there. (*Putting his cane away in the corner*) This means that I'll have work for a long time, Gina. (*Opening one-half of the door on the back wall*) Sh! (*He looks inside the door for a while and carefully closes it, chuckling.*) All of them are sound asleep. And she has found her way into her basket.

HEDVIG: Are you sure she won't freeze in there, Grandfather?

EKDAL: How can you even think of such a thing? Freeze? In all that straw? (*Walking toward the* UPSTAGE *door* LEFT) I'm looking for matches.

GINA: Matches are on your chest of drawers.

(OLD EKDAL *goes into his room.*)

HEDVIG: What good luck! Grandfather got all that copying work!

GINA: Yes, poor old father. He'll have a little pocket money for a while.

HEDVIG: Now he won't have to spend all his mornings at that awful Madame Eriksen's restaurant.

GINA: Yes, there's that, too.

HEDVIG (*After a short silence*): Do you think they've been seated at the dinner table yet?

GINA: God knows. Probably.

HEDVIG: Just imagine—all that wonderful food father can eat! I'm sure he'll be in a good mood when he gets home. Won't he, Mother?

GINA: I suppose so, but it would help if we could tell him the room was rented.

HEDVIG: Oh *that* won't be necessary tonight!

GINA: Maybe, but good news would be very nice, just the same. Besides, that room's no use to anyone standing empty.

HEDVIG: No—I meant that it won't be *too* necessary to tell him good news tonight because father will be in such a happy mood as it is. It'll be better to have the news about the room some other time.

GINA (*Looking at her*): Does it make you happy if you have something nice to tell your father when he comes home?

HEDVIG: Oh, yes, because then everything here is more pleasant.

GINA (*Thinking it over*): There's something to that.

(OLD EKDAL *re-enters and heads toward the first door to the* LEFT. GINA *turns halfway around in her chair.*)

GINA: Do you want something in the kitchen, Grandfather?

EKDAL: Hmm, yes—yes, I do. But you just stay there, now, don't move. (*He goes out.*)

GINA: I hope he doesn't stir up the burning coals out there. (*She writes awhile.*) Hedvig, go look. See what he's up to.

(OLD EKDAL *enters again with a small pitcher of steaming water.*)

HEDVIG: Did you get some hot water, Grandfather?

EKDAL: Yes, I did. I did. I'm going to use it for something. I'm going to write, and the ink is as thick as porridge.

GINA: But Grandfather, you should eat your supper. I left it out there for you.

EKDAL: Oh, it's all right as it is. We'll let it go tonight, Gina. I'm very busy, I tell you! And I don't want anything brought to my room—not anything. (*He goes into his room.* GINA *and* HEDVIG *look at each other.*)

GINA (*Quietly*): Wonder where he got the money.

HEDVIG: Probably from Graberg.

GINA: No. Graberg always sends the money straight to me.

HEDVIG: Well, he must have gotten a bottle on credit somewhere.

GINA: Poor grandfather! No one gives him anything on credit.

(HJALMAR EKDAL *enters. He is wearing an overcoat and a gray felt hat.*)

GINA (*Throws her sewing aside and stands up*): Ekdal! Are you back already?

HEDVIG (*Running up to him at the same time.*): Oh Father. You're home so soon!

HJALMAR (*Taking off his hat*): Yes. Well, I think most of them had begun to leave.

HEDVIG: So early?

HJALMAR (*Starting to take off his overcoat*): It was a *dinner* party, you know.

GINA: Let me help you.

HEDVIG: Me too.

(*They take off his coat, and* GINA *hangs it on the wall hook.*)

HEDVIG: Were there many people there, Father?

HJALMAR: Oh no, not many. There were about twelve or fourteen of us at the table.

GINA: Did you get to talk to all of them?

HJALMAR: Yes, a little. But Gregers monopolized most of my time.

GINA: Is he as homely as ever?

HJALMAR: Well, I guess he's not much to look at. Isn't the old man home yet?

HEDVIG: Grandfather's in his room writing.

HJALMAR: Did he say anything?

GINA: No. Should he have?

HJALMAR: Didn't he mention anything about—? I heard he went to see Graberg. I'll just go in and see him a moment.

GINA: No, no, you'd better not.

HJALMAR: Why not? Did he say he didn't want to see me?

GINA: He doesn't want to see anybody tonight.

(HEDVIG *makes a sign to* HJALMAR *and clears her throat.*)

GINA (*Not noticing*): He's been in the kitchen to get some hot water—

HJALMAR: Ah! And now he's in there. . . ?

GINA: Most likely.

HJALMAR: Good Lord. My poor old white-haired father. Well, we'll let him just sit there in his room and enjoy what he can.

EKDAL (*Enters from his room in a bathrobe. He carries a lighted pipe.*) You're home? I thought I heard you talking.

HJALMAR: I just got here.

EKDAL: You probably didn't see me, did you?

HJALMAR: No, but they told me you went through. I left so that I could catch up with you.

EKDAL: Hmm. That was very nice of you, Hjalmar. Who were all those people?

HJALMAR: Oh, all different sorts—there was Chamberlain Fors, and Chamberlain Balle, and Chamberlain Kaspersen, and Chamberlain So-and-So, and What's-His-Name, and—oh, I don't know!

EKDAL (*Nodding*): Do you hear that, Gina? He's been dining with all those Chamberlains!

GINA: Yes indeed! That's a very distinguished household now.

HEDVIG: Did the Chamberlains sing, Father? Did they recite anything?

HJALMAR: No. They were just talking a lot of nonsense. Then they wanted *me* to recite something, but they didn't get me to do it!

EKDAL: Ha! And you didn't do it for them, eh?

GINA: Well, you could have done *that*—

HJALMAR: No, one shouldn't be at their beck and call. (*Pacing the room*) At least, I'm not going to be!

EKDAL: No, no! Our Hjalmar is not of that grain!

HJALMAR: I don't know why I should be responsible for their entertainment. When I happen to go out for once, let the others exert themselves. Those fellows go from one feeding place to another and drink, day in and day out. Let them put themselves out and work a little for all the good food they've had.

GINA: But you didn't tell them that?

HJALMAR (*Grunts to himself and mumbles*): Oh didn't I? They certainly got an earful from me.

EKDAL: The Chamberlains?

HJALMAR: And that's not all! (*In an off-hand manner*) We had a little argument about Tokay.

EKDAL: Tokay? Ah, that's a noble wine. Indeed it is.

HJALMAR (*Stops his pacing*): It can be noble, but let me tell you this, not all the vintages are equally good. It all depends on how much sun the grapes have had.

GINA: Oh Ekdal, you know about everything.

EKDAL: Is that what they were arguing about?

HJALMAR: They tried to argue, but they were informed that it's the same with Chamberlain—all vintages are not equally good!

GINA: No! Oh, the things you come right out with!

EKDAL (*Laughing to himself*): So that's what you served up to them, eh?

HJALMAR: Yes—straight in their faces!

EKDAL: Gina, he gave it to them straight in their faces—he said it!

GINA: No! Just think—straight in their faces!

HJALMAR: Yes, but I don't want it repeated. Things like this shouldn't be gossiped about. And naturally, the whole thing happened in a very friendly manner. They were pleasant, congenial people. Why should I offend them? No, no, I wouldn't—of course not. No, by all means.

EKDAL: But straight in their faces?

HEDVIG (*Endearingly*): How nice it is to see you dressed in a tail coat, Father. You look so wonderful in it.

HJALMAR: Yes, don't you think so? And this one really fits me perfectly. It's as if it were made for me . . . well, maybe it's a little tight under the arms. (*Starting to take off the coat*) Help me, Hedvig. I'd rather wear my old jacket. Where's my jacket, Gina?

GINA (*Brings the jacket and helps him on with it*): Here it is.

HJALMAR: (*Indicating the tail coat*): Now then, you have to remember that Molvik downstairs gets this back first thing tomorrow morning.

GINA (*Putting it aside*): Don't worry, it'll be taken care of.

HJALMAR (*Puts his jacket on, then stretches*: Ahh. That's better! Now that feels more comfortable to me. Casual clothes fit my easy-going nature better after all, don't you think, Hedvig?

HEDVIG: Yes, Father.

HJALMAR: Look—when I untie my tie like this so that the ends fly loose—look here.

HEDVIG: It looks so wonderful with your moustache and your big curly head of hair.

HJALMAR: I wouldn't really call it curly. Wavy, maybe.

HEDVIG: But it's so very, very curly.

HJALMAR: Actually, it's wavy.

HEDVIG (*After a moment, pulls him by the coat*): Father.

HJALMAR: Yes, what do you want?

HEDVIG: Oh you know—you know very well.

HJALMAR: No, I don't.

HEDVIG (*Laughs and whimpers*): Oh yes you do, Father. Don't tease me any longer.

HJALMAR: What *is* this all about?

HEDVIG (*Shaking him*): Please don't talk like that. Now—give it to me, Father! You know very well you promised me a treat—

HJALMAR: Oh no! How could I forget that!

HEDVIG: Oh, you just want to play a trick on me, Father. Oh that's so naughty of you! Where have you hidden it?

HJALMAR: No, honestly, I forgot. But just a moment—let me see—I have something else for you, Hedvig. (*He goes over to the tail coat and looks through the pockets.*)

HEDVIG (*Jumping up and down, clapping her hands*): Oh, Mother! Mother!

GINA: There—you see? If you just wait for things—

HJALMAR (*Holding out a paper*): See, here it is.

HEDVIG: That? That's just a piece of paper.

HJALMAR: It's the dinner card. You see—the bill of fare. Look here, it says "Menu." That means the list for the dinner—it's a list of what we had to eat.

HEDVIG: You didn't bring anything else?

HJALMAR: I told you I forgot the other thing. But take my word for it, there's not much pleasure in all those sweet things. Now sit down at the table and read the menu, and then later on I'll describe to you just how all the dishes tasted. There you are, Hedvig.

HEDVIG (*Holding back her tears*): Thank you. (*She sits down but doesn't read. GINA makes signs to her which HJALMAR notices.*)

HJALMAR (*Pacing the floor*): Honestly, it's incredible what the breadwinner of a family is expected to think of! Let him forget the most insignificant trifle, and he's immediately surrounded by sour faces. Well, one has to get used to that, too. (*He stops at the stove beside OLD EKDAL.*) Have you peeked in there tonight, Father?

EKDAL: Yes, you know very well I have. She's gone to bed in her basket.

HJALMAR: In her basket, eh? Well, she's getting used to it, then.

EKDAL: I told you she would. (*Pointing to the sliding doors*) But there are some other little details that we—

HJALMAR: You mean some improvements? Yes.

EKDAL: They have to be done, you know, Hjalmar.

HJALMAR: Yes, certainly. Let's talk awhile about the improvements, Father. Come over here—let's sit down on the sofa.

EKDAL: Yes, let's. I think I'll fill up my pipe first, and then I can clean it at the same time. (*He goes into his room.*)

GINA (*Smiling at* HJALMAR): Clean his pipe, eh?. .

HJALMAR: Yes, yes, Gina. Well, let him do it, the poor shipwrecked old man. Now—those improvements. It's best I get them out of the way tomorrow.

GINA: You probably won't have time tomorrow, Ekdal.

HEDVIG (*Interrupting*): Oh, yes he will, Mother!

GINA: Remember, those prints have to be retouched. They've called for them so many times already.

HJALMAR: Those prints again! They'll be ready. Have any new orders come in?

GINA: No, sad to say. Tomorrow I only have that portrait sitting, but you already know about that.

HJALMAR: Nothing else? Oh well, if one doesn't make an effort. . . .

GINA: What more can I do? I put as many ads in the paper as I possibly can.

HJALMAR: Oh, those papers! You can see how much *they* help. And I suppose no one looked at the room?

GINA: No, not yet.

HJALMAR: Well, that's to be expected. If one isn't industrious . . . well— One *really* has to get a hold on oneself, Gina.

HEDVIG (*Moving toward him*): May I bring you your flute, Father?

HJALMAR: No, not the flute. I don't need that kind of pleasure in this world— (*Walking around*) I will go to work tomorrow—no question about that. I will work as long as my strength lasts.

GINA: But my dear Ekdal, that wasn't what I meant.

HEDVIG: Father, do you want me to bring you a bottle of beer?

HJALMAR: Absolutely not. I don't need anything . . . did you say beer?

HEDVIG (*Lively*): Yes, Father, lovely, chilled beer.

HJALMAR: Well, if you insist, bring me a bottle.

GINA: Go get it, Hedvig! It'll make everything snug and cozy again.

(HEDVIG *runs over to the kitchen door. At the stove* HJALMAR *stops her, looks at her, holds her head between his hands, and presses her to him.*)

HJALMAR: Hedvig! Hedvig!

HEDVIG (*Happy and in tears*): Oh dear, sweet Father!

HJALMAR: No, you mustn't call me that. "There sat I at the rich man's feast and gorged myself at his heavy-laden tables," and I didn't even—

GINA: Nonsense, nonsense.

HJALMAR: But I didn't—it's true! And you mustn't ever rely on me for things like that. You both know that I love you, regardless of everything.

HEDVIG (*Throwing her arms around him*): And we love you so very, very much, Father.

HJALMAR: If I become unreasonable every now and then— then . . . so— Dear God! You must remember that I am a man who is constantly attacked by armies of sorrows. Well . . . (*He dries his eyes.*) this is not the time for beer! Bring me my flute.

(HEDVIG *runs to the bookcase and gets the flute.*)

HJALMAR: Thank you. Well, now. With the flute here and you two beside me—ah!

(HEDVIG *sits down at the table with* GINA. HJALMAR *walks back and forth. He begins to play a Bohemian folk dance in a slow, mournful tempo with sensitivity and growing feeling. He stops playing, reaches out his hand to* GINA, *and speaks with emotion.*)

HJALMAR: It may be that we live here, crowded and plain— —here, under our humble roof, Gina—but it's still home. And I must say, Gina, how good it is to be right here.

(*He begins to play again. After a short while there is a knock at the door.* GINA *stands up.*)

GINA: Sh! Ekdal, I think there's someone at the door.

HJALMAR: Oh no, not again!

(HJALMAR *puts the flute back onto the bookcase.* GINA *opens the door.* GREGERS *stands outside in the hallway.*)

GREGERS: Excuse me.

GINA (*With a start*): Oh!

GREGERS: Is this where the photographer Ekdal lives?

GINA: Yes, it is.

HJALMAR (*Walking toward the door*): Gregers! Is it you? Well —do come in.

GREGERS (*Entering*): I said I'd be visiting you.

HJALMAR: But tonight? And you left the party?

GREGERS: Yes, both the party and my father's house. Good evening, Mrs. Ekdal. I don't know if you recognize me.

GINA: Oh yes, you're young Mr. Werle—you're easy to recognize.

GREGERS: I look like my mother, I suppose, and no doubt you remember her well.

HJALMAR: You left your father's house? Is that what you said?

GREGERS: Yes. I've moved into a hotel.

HJALMAR: You have? Well, since you're here, take off your coat and sit down.

GREGERS (*Takes off his overcoat. He wears a plain gray suit of provincial cut.*) Thank you.

HJALMAR (*Sitting on a stool near the table*): Here—sit on the sofa. Make yourself comfortable.

GREGERS (*Sits on the sofa and looks around*): So this is where you do your work, Hjalmar! And you live here, too?

HJALMAR: Yes. This is the studio room, as you can see—

GINA: But there's so much space in here that we use it for our sitting room.

HJALMAR: We had a better apartment before, but this place has one great advantage—it has many other rooms.

GINA: There's even an extra one across the hall that we can rent out.

GREGERS (*To* HJALMAR): Well, well! You have boarders too!

HJALMAR: Well, not yet. It hasn't happened that quickly. One has to be industrious. (*To* HEDVIG) What happened to that beer?

(HEDVIG *goes out into the kitchen.*)

GREGERS: That's your daughter?

HJALMAR: Yes, that's Hedvig.

GREGERS: She's your only child?

HJALMAR: Yes, the only one. She's the greatest happiness in our lives and . . . (*Lowering his voice*) our deepest sorrow, too.

GREGERS: What do you mean?

HJALMAR: There's a great danger that she might lose her eyesight.

GREGERS: Go blind?

HJALMAR: Yes. So far, we've only noticed the first symptoms, so we know it's in the early stages. She may be all right for a while, but the doctor has warned us that it will come—eventually.

GREGERS: What a terrible tragedy! How did it happen?

HJALMAR (*Sighing*): Inherited, most likely.

GREGERS (*With a start*): Inherited?

GINA: Ekdal's mother had very bad eyesight.

HJALMAR: My father says so. I can't remember her that well.

GREGERS: Poor child! How is she taking it?

HJALMAR: You don't think we've told her, do you? She doesn't suspect any danger. She's happy and carefree—always chirping like a little bird, and all the while flying into everlasting night. (*Overcome with emotion*) Oh it's intolerable, Gregers. (HEDVIG *brings in a tray with beer and glasses on it and puts it on the table.* HJALMAR *strokes her head.*)

HJALMAR: Thank you, Hedvig.

(HEDVIG *puts her arm around his neck and whispers in his ear.*)

HJALMAR: No, no bread and butter now. (*Looking at* GREGERS) Well, perhaps Gregers would like some?

GREGERS: No thank you. No—no.

HJALMAR (*Still downhearted*): Well, you can bring some out all the same. Just the heel of the bread will be fine for me. And put plenty of butter on it, now.

(HEDVIG *nods contentedly and goes into the kitchen.*)

GREGERS (*Watching her until she is gone*): She looks so strong and healthy.

GINA: Yes. Except for her eyes she's perfectly all right, thank God.

GREGERS: She'll look a great deal like you, I think. How old is she now?

GINA: Hedvig is exactly fourteen. Her birthday is the day after tomorrow.

GREGERS: She's quite big for her age.

GINA: Yes, she's grown up so much in the last year.

GREGERS: Somehow, when I see how fast the young ones grow up, it makes me realize how old I am. How long have you two been married?

GINA: We've been married—hmm . . . well, let me see— almost close to fifteen years.

GREGERS: Just imagine that. Has it been that long?

GINA: Indeed it has. (*Suddenly becomes alert, looks at him*) Yes. That's exactly right.

HJALMAR: Yes, of course it is. Fifteen years in a few months. They must have been long years for you, Gregers, up there at Hoydal.

GREGERS: They certainly seemed long at the time. But now when I look back, I hardly know where they've gone.

(OLD EKDAL *comes out of his room without his pipe. He is wearing his old army hat and walks a little unsteadily.*)

EKDAL: Well, Hjalmar! Now we can sit us down and have our little talk about—hmm . . . what was it about now?

HJALMAR (*Walking over to meet him*): Father, there's someone here I want you to meet. Gregers Werle. I don't know if you can remember him or not.

EKDAL (Looking at GREGERS, *who stands up*): Werle? So that's the son, is it? What does he want of me?

HJALMAR: Nothing. He's come to visit me.

EKDAL: So? Is there anything wrong?

HJALMAR: No. By all means, no.

EKDAL (*Waving an arm*): Mind you, now—not that I'm afraid —but—

GREGERS (*Walking over to him*): I wanted to bring you a greeting from your old hunting grounds, Lieutenant Ekdal.

EKDAL: Hunting grounds?

GREGERS: Yes. Up there around the Hoydal Works.

EKDAL: So? Greetings from up there! Well, I used to know every inch of those forests in the old days.

GREGERS: You were a great hunter in your time.

EKDAL: Well, maybe so. That could be, could be. You're looking at my uniform! I don't ask anyone's permission to wear it here at home. It's all right as long as I don't wear it on the street.

(HEDVIG *brings a plate of bread and butter to the table.*)

HJALMAR: Sit down, Father, and have yourself a glass of beer. Won't you please, Gregers?

(OLD EKDAL *mumbles to himself and stumbles over to the sofa.* GREGERS *sits on the chair close to him.* HJALMAR *sits on the other side of* GREGERS. GINA *sits a little away from the table. She is sewing.* HEDVIG *stands beside her father.*)

GREGERS: Do you remember, Lieutenant Ekdal, when Hjalmar used to come up and visit you during the summers and at Christmas time?

EKDAL: Did you? No, no I can't quite remember that. But I must say that I *was* a first-rate hunter. I've shot bears too, I have. I've killed nine of them.

GREGERS (*Looking at him with sympathy*): And now you don't hunt at all, do you?

EKDAL: Oh I wouldn't say that. I hunt at times. Not in the old way, of course—not like in the old days. You see, the forest . . . forest . . . you see, the forest— (*He takes a drink.*) How is your forest up there now?

GREGERS: Not as good as it was in your day. It's been all thinned out.

EKDAL: Thinned out? Thinned out and cleared away? (*Slowly, as if afraid*) That's a dangerous deed. Bad things will follow. The forest will revenge itself—it will get back its own.

HJALMAR (*Filling his father's glass*): Here you are, Father.

GREGERS: How can a man like you—such an outdoor man—live in these close quarters, all cooped up by four walls?

EKDAL (*Smiles a little and glances at* HJALMAR): Oh, it's not so bad here. You'd be surprised. Not so bad at all.

GREGERS: But all those things you're used to—the cool, invigorating air, the free life in the forest, the fields alive with animals and birds—

EKDAL (*Smiling*): Hjalmar, shall we show it to him?

HJALMAR (*Quickly, a little embarrassed*): Oh no, Father, not this evening.

GREGERS: What is it you want to show me?

HJALMAR: Oh it's just something—you can see it some other time.

GREGERS (*Continues to speak to* EKDAL): What I wanted to suggest, Lieutenant Ekdal, is that you should come up to the Works with me. I'll be going back there soon. I'm sure you could get some copying to do, and then, too, there's nothing here to hold you—none of those wonderful things you were so used to in the forest.

EKDAL (*Glaring at him, angrily*): Nothing here to hold me?

GREGERS: Of course you have Hjalmar, but he has his own family. And a man like you, who has always been drawn to a life that's free and wild—

EKDAL (*Striking the table*): Hjalmar, now he's going to see it!

HJALMAR: No, Father! It's not worth the trouble. It's so dark.

EKDAL: Nonsense! There's moonlight tonight. (*Standing up*) He's going to see it, I tell you. Let me pass by. Come on— help me, Hjalmar.

HEDVIG: Oh yes—do, Father.

HJALMAR (*Standing up*): Oh well, then.

GREGERS (*To* GINA): What kind of thing is it?

GINA: Oh, you mustn't expect anything too nice.

(OLD EKDAL *and* HJALMAR *have gone over to the back wall and pushed aside the double sliding doors.* HEDVIG *helps* OLD EKDAL. GREGERS *remains standing at the sofa.* GINA *continues sewing, unconcerned. Through the opening of the door is seen a large, irregular attic room full of dark nooks and crannies. Here and there are a couple of chimneys extending to the ceiling. There are several skylights, through which the bright moonlight shines on various parts of the attic. The rest is in darkness.*)

EKDAL (*To* GREGERS): You're welcome to come in.

GREGERS (*Walking over to them*): What do you have there?

EKDAL: You can come in and see for yourself.

HJALMAR (*A bit embarrassed*): All of this belongs to father, you understand.

GREGERS (*In the doorway, looking into the attic*): You keep chickens in there, Lieutenant Ekdal?

EKDAL: I should say we do keep chickens! They've gone to roost now—but you should see them by daylight!

HEDVIG: And then there's—

EKDAL: Sh! Don't say anything yet!

GREGERS: And you have some pigeons too, I see.

EKDAL: Indeed we do have pigeons! They have their roosting boxes up there under the beams. Pigeons always like to roost high up, you know.

GREGERS: They're not all common pigeons.

EKDAL: Common? I should say not! We have tumblers—and a pair of pouters, too. But come over here. Can you see that barrel over there by the wall?

GREGERS: Yes. What do you keep in there?

EKDAL: That's where the rabbits stay at night.

GREGERS: Rabbits, too?

EKDAL: Damn right—rabbits too! Hjalmar, did you hear that? He asked if we have rabbits. But now I'll show you the most important thing of all. Now it comes! Move over, little Hedvig. Stand there—that's it. Now look down there. Can you see a basket? With straw in it? Eh?

GREGERS: Yes, and I see a bird in it.

EKDAL: Hmm. A bird—!

GREGERS: Is it a duck?

EKDAL (*Offended*): Yes, it just so happens to be a duck!

HJALMAR: But what *kind* of duck do you think it is?

HEDVIG: It's not just an ordinary duck!

EKDAL: Sh!

GREGERS: It's not one of those common Muscovy ducks either, is it?

EKDAL: No. No, Mr. Werle, it isn't a Muscovy duck. This is a wild duck!

GREGERS: No! Is it really? A wild one?

EKDAL: Yes sir! That's just what it is. That bird, as you called it, is a real wild thing. Yes indeed, my son, that's our wild duck!

HEDVIG: *My* wild duck. I own it.

GREGERS: And it can live up here in the attic? Is it happy here?

EKDAL: She's got a whole barrel of water to splash in, I want you to know!

HJALMAR: We change the water every other day.

GINA (*Turning toward* HJALMAR): My dear Ekdal, it's getting icy cold in here.

EKDAL: Yes—well, let's close up, then. It's best we don't disturb their night's sleep. Give me a hand, Hedvig.

(HJALMAR *and* HEDVIG *slide the doors together.*)

EKDAL: Some other time you can really get to see her. (*He sits in the armchair near the stove.*) Oh, they're very strange, these wild ducks, I can tell you!

GREGERS: But how did you catch it, Lieutenant Ekdal?

EKDAL: Aha! I didn't catch it. There's a certain man in town we have to thank for it.

GREGERS (*A bit startled*): That man couldn't be my father, could he?

EKDAL: Yes, to tell you the truth, that's exactly who it is. Your father.

HJALMAR: It seems odd that you should have guessed that, Gregers.

GREGERS: Well, you told me you owed so many things to him that I—

GINA: We didn't get the duck from Mr. Werle himself.

EKDAL: Just the same, Gina, it's Haakon Werle we can thank for it! (*To* GREGERS) He was out shooting in his boat, you see, and he shot at her. But his eyesight is so poor that he just winged her.

HJALMAR: Yes, she was hit a couple of times.

HEDVIG: In her wing! She couldn't fly.

GREGERS: But didn't she dive to the bottom?

EKDAL (*Sleepily, in a thick voice*): I should say so! Wild ducks always dive down like that, they do. They dive as deep as they can and then they bite into the seaweed and long grasses or any damn thing they can get hold of down there. That way they make sure they'll never come up again.

GREGERS: But Lieutenant Ekdal, your wild duck did come up again!

EKDAL: Your father had a first-rate dog. He dived right in after her and brought her to the surface.

GREGERS (*Turning to* HJALMAR): And that's how you got her?

HJALMAR: Not that easily. First, your father took her home, but she wasn't happy there, so Petersen was given orders to put an end to her.

EKDAL (*Half-asleep*): Yes, Petersen—that damn idiot!

HJALMAR (*Speaking softly*): And that was how we got her. Father knows Petersen quite well, so they arranged to bring it here.

GREGERS: And she's living there in your attic and doing very well?

HJALMAR: Yes, unbelievably well. She's gotten fat! You see, she's been in there so long she's probably forgotten all about the real wild life—the one she was born for—and that's the whole secret.

GREGERS: I think you're right about that, Hjalmar. You must never let her see the sky or the ocean. But now I better not stay any longer. I believe your father's asleep.

HJALMAR: Oh well, as far as that's concerned, you're not disturbing him.

GREGERS: Oh, by the way—you said you have a room for rent. Do you?

HJALMAR: Yes! Do you know of someone?

GREGERS: Could I have it?

HJALMAR: You?

GINA: Oh now, not *you*, Mr. Werle!

GREGERS: I'd like to move in first thing tomorrow morning.

HJALMAR: Well, yes. You may have it with the greatest of pleasure.

GINA: But Mr. Werle, it isn't any kind of room for you.

HJALMAR: How can you say that, Gina?

GINA: Well, for one thing, it's not large enough—and it's very dark and—

GREGERS: That doesn't make any difference. It'll be all the same to me.

HJALMAR: I think it's quite a nice room. Not so badly furnished—

GINA: And don't forget those two who live underneath—

GREGERS: Yes? Who are they?

GINA: Well, one was a tutor—

HJALMAR: His name is Mr. Molvik.

GINA: And the other's a doctor. His name is Relling.

GREGERS: Relling? I know him slightly. He had a practice up at Hoydal for a while.

GINA: They're a pair of good-for-nothings, I can tell you! They go out nights and come home very late, and they aren't always—

GREGERS: Oh, one soon gets used to those things. I hope to acclimate myself as well as that wild duck did.

GINA: Just the same, I think you should sleep on it first.

GREGERS: You don't want me in this house, do you, Mrs. Ekdal?

GINA: Oh for heaven's sake, what makes you think that?

HJALMAR: This isn't at all like you, Gina. Tell me, Gregers, do you plan to live here in town?

GREGERS (*Putting on his overcoat*): Yes, from now on.

HJALMAR: But not in your father's house? What do you plan to do?

GREGERS: Oh Hjalmar, if I only knew *that*, things wouldn't look so glum. When one has to bear the cross of having the name Gregers, and with *Werle* attached to it— Well, Hjalmar, have you ever had to live with anything so terrible?

HJALMAR: I don't think it's so terrible.

GREGERS: I'd feel like spitting on anyone who had that name.

HJALMAR (*Laughing*): Well now, if you weren't Gregers Werle, who would you like to be?

GREGERS: If I could choose, I would want—most of all—to be a clever dog.

GINA: A dog!

HEDVIG (*Involuntarily*): Oh, no!

GREGERS: Oh yes! A tremendously clever dog. One of those dogs that plunges in after a wild duck who has dived to the bottom and locked his jaws into the sea grass and mud.

HJALMAR: I must say, Gregers, I don't understand a word you're saying.

GREGERS: Oh, well—there isn't much meaning in it. Early tomorrow morning I'll move in. (*To* GINA) You won't have trouble with me. I do everything for myself. (*To* HJALMAR) We'll talk about everything else tomorrow. Good night, Mrs. Ekdal. (*Nodding to* HEDVIG) Good night.

GINA: Good night, Mr. Werle.

HEDVIG: Good night.

HJALMAR (*Who has lighted a candle*): Wait a moment. I'll have to light your way—it's very dark on the stairs.

(GREGERS *and* HJALMAR *exit.*)

GINA (*Thoughtfully, her sewing in her lap*): Wasn't that strange talk? He wants to be a dog?

HEDVIG: Mother, I want to tell you something. I think—I really think he meant something else.

GINA: What do you mean, something else?

HEDVIG: Well, I don't know what it could have been, but all the time he was talking it was as if he meant something else.

GINA: You think so? Well anyhow, it was strange.

HJALMAR (*Returning, enters the room*): The light was still burning. (*Blows the candle out and puts it away*) Ah! Well! Can one finally get something to eat around here? (*He begins to eat bread and butter.*) You see, Gina? If one is industrious—

GINA: What do you mean, industrious?

HJALMAR: It's certainly lucky we finally got the room rented, isn't it? And to a person like Gregers—a dear old friend.

GINA: I don't know what to say.

HEDVIG: Oh Mother, you'll see—it'll be so nice.

HJALMAR: You're a strange one! You were so anxious to get it rented, and now that it is, you're not pleased.

GINA: Yes I am, Ekdal. If it had only been someone else. What do you think Mr. Werle will say?

HJALMAR: Old Werle? It's none of his business.

GINA: Something must have come up between them again—especially since the young one has decided to move out of the house. You know how those two are with each other.

HJALMAR: That might very well be, but—

GINA: And now maybe Mr. Werle will think you're behind it all.

HJALMAR: Let him believe what he wants! Old Mr. Werle has done a great deal for me, I'll admit, but that doesn't mean I have to be grateful to him forever.

GINA: But my dear Ekdal, he might take it out on grandfather. Maybe he'll lose that measly little income he gets from Graberg.

HJALMAR: I'm almost tempted to say "all to the good!" It's humiliating for a man like me to see his gray-haired father treated like a leper. But soon the time will be ripe. (*Taking more bread and butter*) I have a mission in life, and I want to see it fulfilled.

HEDVIG: Oh yes, Father, you must do that!

GINA: Sh! For heaven's sake, don't wake him up.

HJALMAR (*In a softer voice*): I shall do it, I tell you. The day shall come when—when— And that's why it's a *good* thing we got the room rented. It makes me more independent. A man who has a vision in life must be independent. (*Moving over to the armchair*) Poor old white-haired father! Depend on your Hjalmar—he has wide shoulders, and they're strong, too. One fine day you'll wake up and . . . (*To* GINA) Maybe you don't believe that?

GINA (*Standing up*): Yes, of course I do. But first let's get him to bed.

HJALMAR: Yes. Let's do that.

(*They gently take hold of* OLD EKDAL *and carefully lead him out.*)


**CURTAIN**

# ACT III

HJALMAR EKDAL's *studio. It is morning. Daylight is streaming through the large windows in the slanted roof. The draperies are drawn aside.* HJALMAR *is seated at the table retouching a photograph. Several other pictures are in front of him.*

SHORTLY AFTER THE CURTAIN RISES, GINA *enters through the hall door. She wears her hat and coat, and on her arm she carries a basket with a lid.*

HJALMAR: Are you back already, Gina?

GINA: Oh yes, one has to hurry. (*She puts down the basket and takes off her coat.*)

HJALMAR: Did you look in on Gregers?

GINA: Yes, I did. His room looks very pretty, I'll tell you! He made himself nice and comfortable as soon as he got in.

HJALMAR: Oh, did he?

GINA: Well, he said he wanted to take care of himself. He put wood in the stove, and then he went and closed the damper and filled the whole room with smoke. Oh, there was such a stink!

HJALMAR: Oh, no!

GINA: Wait till I tell you the rest! It's even better. He decided to put out the fire, so he threw all the water that he had washed with right into the stove! Now the floor is flooded and the whole place looks like a pigpen.

HJALMAR: What's he been doing in the meantime?

GINA: He said he was going out for a while.

HJALMAR: I went in there myself, for a moment, after you left.

GINA: Yes, I heard. You invited him to lunch, didn't you?

HJALMAR: Just a light lunch, you know. After all, it's his first

245

day here. We really have to do it. You must have something
in the house.

GINA: I'll see if I can find something.

HJALMAR: And just this once, don't make it too skimpy. I think
Relling and Molvik may be coming up, too. I met Relling
on the stairs and I just had to—

GINA: So we're having the two of them, too, eh?

HJALMAR: Oh good God! A couple more or less won't make
that much difference.

EKDAL (*Opens his door and looks in*): Listen here, Hjalmar!
(*Seeing* GINA) Oh, well.

GINA: You want something, Grandfather?

EKDAL (*Going inside again*): Oh no. It doesn't matter.

GINA (*Taking up the basket*): Watch him carefully so he doesn't
go out.

HJALMAR: Yes, yes, I will. Now Gina, listen—a little herring
salad would be good. Relling and Molvik more than likely
were out on the town last night.

GINA: All right. Just so they don't all get in my way too soon.

HJALMAR: They won't. Give yourself time.

GINA: And in the meantime you can get a little work done.

HJALMAR: What? I *am* working! I'm working with all the
strength I have.

GINA (*Going into the kitchen*): I only meant that then you'd
have it out of the way.

(HJALMAR *sits for a while and brushes slowly and reluctantly
at the photograph.* OLD EKDAL *peeks in, looks around the
room, then whispers.*)

EKDAL: Are you busy, Hjalmar?

HJALMAR: Yes—I'm here struggling with these pictures.

EKDAL: Oh, well. God knows, if you're as busy as all that—well
then. . . .

(*He goes into his room again, leaving the door open.*)

HJALMAR (*Continues to work in silence awhile. Putting the
brush down, goes to the door*): Father, are you busy?

EKDAL (*Grumbling*): Well, if you're busy, then I'm busy, too!
Hmm!

HJALMAR (*Going back to his work*): Very well, then—by all means!

EKDAL (*Shortly afterward, coming to the door*): You see, Hjalmar, I'm not all *that* busy!

HJALMAR: Well, it looked to me as if you were writing.

EKDAL: Damn it all! Old Graberg can wait for his copy a day or two! Life doesn't depend on it, for God's sake!

HJALMAR: No. You're not his slave, are you?

EKDAL: And then there *is* that thing in there—

HJALMAR: Yes! Maybe you want to get in there, eh? Shall I open it for *you*?

EKDAL: I didn't really want to disturb you.

HJALMAR (*Standing up*): I only meant that if we finish it now, we'd have it out of the way.

EKDAL: Yes, that's true. It has to be finished early tomorrow morning, anyway. It *is* tomorrow, isn't it?

HJALMAR: Yes, of course—it's tomorrow.

(HJALMAR *and* OLD EKDAL *both push aside the sliding doors. The morning sun shines through the skylight. A couple of pigeons fly back and forth, and others are cooing on their perches in the background. The chickens are cackling farther back in the room.*)

HJALMAR: There. Now you can go in, Father.

EKDAL (*Going inside*): You're not coming with me?

HJALMAR: You know what? I almost think I . . . (*Seeing* GINA *at the kitchen door*) No—I haven't got time. I must get on with my work! Oh I forgot—my contraption! (*He tugs on a string. From the inside a drapery falls downward, the lower part of which is made of old sailcloth. The upper half is a piece of stretched-out fishnet. When it is in this position, the attic floor cannot be seen. He walks to the table.*) Well, now, can I finally be left in peace for a while?

GINA: Is he rummaging around in there again?

HJALMAR (*Sitting down*): Would you like it better if he sneaked out to Madame Eriksen's? Do you want something? You were saying—

GINA: Do you think we could set up the lunch table in here?

HJALMAR: Of course—don't we have any sittings this morning?

GINA: No one until those two lovebirds who want their picture taken together.

HJALMAR: Damn it! Why couldn't they pose some other day?

GINA: Well, my dear Ekdal, I carefully scheduled them for the afternoon—you know you'll be taking your nap then.

HJALMAR: Well, that's all right. Good! Let's eat in here!

GINA: Yes, yes, all right. But there's no rush to set the table yet. You use it a little longer if you want.

HJALMAR: It seems to me that even you could see I'm using the table for all I'm worth!

GINA (*Going into the kitchen*): Good. That way, later on you'll be free.

EKDAL (*After a short pause, peeks through the net at the attic door*): Hjalmar!

HJALMAR: What?

EKDAL: I'm afraid we'll have to move the water barrel after all.

HJALMAR: Well, that's what I said from the start.

(OLD EKDAL *mumbles in agreement and walks away from the doorway.* HJALMAR *works for a while, glances toward the attic, and halfway rises.* HEDVIG *enters from the kitchen.* HJALMAR *sits down quickly.*)

HJALMAR: What do you want?

HEDVIG: I just came in to see you, Father.

HJALMAR (*After a short pause*): Why are you snooping around? Were you sent in here to keep an eye on me?

HEDVIG: Oh no.

HJALMAR: What's your mother doing out there?

HEDVIG: She's busy making a herring salad. (*Walking over to the table*) Is there any little thing I can help you do, Father?

HJALMAR: Oh, no—it's best that I do all this alone. Have no fear, Hedvig, everything will be all right. As long as your father can keep his health, why, then—

HEDVIG: No, Father, don't say such sad things. (*She walks around a bit, stops at the attic door, and looks in.*)

HJALMAR: What's he up to, Hedvig?

HEDVIG: I think there's going to be a new path to the water barrel.

HJALMAR: He'll never manage that by himself. And here I sit—confined—

HEDVIG: Let me have the brush, Father.

HJALMAR: Nonsense—you'll hurt your eyes.

HEDVIG: Oh no I won't. Come, give it to me.

HJALMAR (*Standing up*): Well, I won't be more than a minute or two.

HEDVIG (*Taking the brush*): Oh, pooh! That doesn't matter. There we are. (*Sitting down*) I can begin with this one.

HJALMAR: But don't ruin your eyes. Do you hear me? *I* won't take the responsibility for that—you'll have to take that upon yourself. Remember, now, what I'm telling you.

HEDVIG (*Busy with the photograph*): Yes, yes, I know. I will.

HJALMAR: You're such a clever one, Hedvig. Just a couple of minutes, you understand. (*He sneaks into the attic through one side of the drapery.* HEDVIG *is working. He and* OLD EKDAL *can be heard from the attic, arguing. He comes to the net.*) Oh Hedvig, bring me the pliers. They're lying on the shelf. And the chisel, too. (*He turns toward the inside of the attic.*) Just you wait, Father, and you'll see! Let me show you what I mean.

(HEDVIG *collects the tools from the bookcase and hands them through the net to* HJALMAR.)

HJALMAR: Thank you. Well, it was a good thing I came in here, Hedvig.

(HJALMAR *disappears again. The sound of hammering and chattering begins.* HEDVIG *remains at the net and watches. After a moment there's a knock at the hall door.* HEDVIG *doesn't hear it.* GREGERS *enters and stands in the doorway. He is not wearing an overcoat or a hat. He clears his throat.*)

HEDVIG (*Turns around and walks toward him*): Good morning! Please come in.

GREGERS (*Looking toward the attic*): Thank you. It sounds as if you have workmen in the house.

HEDVIG: No. That's father and grandfather. I'll tell them you're here.

GREGERS (*Sitting on the sofa*): No, no, don't do that. I'd prefer to wait a little while.

HEDVIG (*Starting to clear away the photographs*): Oh, it's so untidy here—

GREGERS: Let it be! Are those photographs supposed to be finished?

HEDVIG: Yes. It's a little bit of work I'm helping father with.

GREGERS: Please don't let me disturb you.

HEDVIG (*Putting the photographs down nearby, sits down to work*): Oh no, you're not.

GREGERS (*Watches her in silence. After a pause*): Did the wild duck sleep well last night?

HEDVIG: Yes, thank you, I'm sure she did.

GREGERS (*Turning toward the attic*): In the daylight it looks quite different from the way it looked by moonlight.

HEDVIG: Yes, it changes so much. In the morning it looks so different from the way it looks in the afternoon. And on a rainy day it's different, too, from a sunny one.

GREGERS: Then you've noticed it, too?

HEDVIG: Yes—you can't help seeing it!

GREGERS: Do you like being in there with the wild duck?

HEDVIG: Oh, yes. Whenever there's an opportunity, I—

GREGERS: But you probably don't have that much free time. You go to school, don't you?

HEDVIG: Not any more. Father's afraid I'll ruin my eyes.

GREGERS: Oh. Does he read your lessons to you?

HEDVIG: He promised he would, but he hasn't found time yet.

GREGERS: Isn't there anyone who helps you?

HEDVIG: Yes. Mr. Molvik does, but he isn't always . . . well, he—

GREGERS: He's drunk?

HEDVIG: Yes, I think so.

GREGERS: Well then, you do have free time for something worthwhile! And I should imagine that in there it's like a world all its own.

HEDVIG: Completely! There are so many strange things in there!

GREGERS: Oh?

HEDVIG: Oh, yes! There's a big closet of books, and many of them have pictures.

GREGERS: Ah, I see.

HEDVIG: And then there's a bureau with drawers and flaps that slide out. And there's a big clock with figures that come out when the hour strikes—but the clock doesn't work any more.

GREGERS: Time has stopped, then—in there with the wild duck.

HEDVIG: Yes. And there's an old artist's case full of paints and things like that—and then all the *old* books, too.

GREGERS: Do you read them?

HEDVIG: Oh, yes—when I can. But most of them are foreign and I can't understand them. But I look at the pictures. There's one very big book called *Harrison's History of London*. Why, it's almost a hundred years old, I think. It has a lot of pictures. On the front there's a picture of Death with an hourglass, and a Maiden. That seems all wrong to me, but then, there are always the other pictures with churches and castles and streets and big ships that sail over all the oceans.

GREGERS: Tell me—where did all those marvelous things come from?

HEDVIG: Oh, an old sea captain lived here once and he brought those things home. They called him the "Flying Dutchman." That's so strange, because he wasn't even Dutch.

GREGERS: Wasn't he?

HEDVIG: No. He was lost at sea, though, and all his things were left behind.

GREGERS: Tell me, now—when you sit in there and look at the pictures, don't you long to get out into the world and see all those things yourself?

HEDVIG: No, I don't. I want to stay here always—and help father and mother.

GREGERS: With the photographs?

HEDVIG: Not only that—the thing I want to learn most of all is how to engrave pictures like those in the foreign book.

GREGERS: Oh, and what does your father think about that?

HEDVIG: I don't think father likes the idea. He's so peculiar about things like that. Do you know what he wants me to learn? Braiding straw! And basket weaving! Well, I don't think I'd like doing that.

GREGERS: Neither do I!

HEDVIG: But father's right about one thing. If I *had* learned, I could have made a new basket for my wild duck.

GREGERS: Yes, you could have. You're the closest one to it, aren't you?

HEDVIG: Yes. She's my wild duck.

GREGERS: Yes, she is.

HEDVIG: I own her. I let father and grandfather borrow her whenever they want to, though.

GREGERS: Really? What do they do with her?

HEDVIG: Oh, they fuss with her and build her things and do things like that.

GREGERS: I see. The wild duck is the most distinguished guest in there, isn't she?

HEDVIG: Oh yes, she certainly is. She's a real wild bird. Life is so pitiful for her—she has no one to love, poor thing.

GREGERS: No family, like the rabbits!

HEDVIG: Yes. The hens have so many friends that they were chicks with, but she's been absolutely separated from her family. And anyhow, wild ducks are so very strange. No one knows anything about her—or where she came from.

GREGERS: And she's been to the very depths of the sea.

HEDVIG (*Looks quickly at him and suppresses a smile*): Why do you say "the depths of the sea"?

GREGERS: What else should I say?

HEDVIG: You could have said "the bottom of the sea."

GREGERS: Can't I just as well say "depths"?

HEDVIG: Yes. It just sounds so strange for someone else to say it, that's all.

GREGERS: Why? Tell me.

HEDVIG: No, I don't want to. It'll sound stupid.

GREGERS: I don't think so. Tell me why you smiled.

HEDVIG: Well, every now and then when I'm alone in there, I think about all the living things around me, and it seems that the whole room and everything in it is "the depths of the sea." Oh, I told you it would sound silly!

GREGERS: No—no—

HEDVIG: But it's only an attic!

GREGERS (*Looking at her carefully*): Are you sure?

HEDVIG (*Bewildered*): What? That it's only an attic?

GREGERS: Yes. Are you absolutely sure it is?

(HEDVIG *remains silent, looking at him open-mouthed.* GINA *enters from the kitchen with the tablecloth.*)

GREGERS (*Standing up*): I've probably arrived too early.

GINA: Well, you have to be someplace! Anyway, it'll all be ready in a few minutes. Clear off the table, Hedvig.

(HEDVIG *clears the table. She and* GINA *set the table during the following.* GREGERS *sits in the armchair and thumbs through an album of photographs.*)

GREGERS: I hear that you can retouch photographs, too, Mrs. Ekdal.

GINA (*Glancing quickly at him*): Yes. Yes—I can do that.

GREGERS: It must come in very handy.

GINA: What do you mean, handy?

GREGERS: Well, I mean since Ekdal has become a photographer—

HEDVIG: Mother can *take* photographs, too!

GINA: Yes—I've had to teach myself that as well.

GREGERS: Then perhaps you really run the studio?

GINA: Well, when Ekdal doesn't have time to do it himself, then—

GREGERS: I can see that his old father takes up a good deal of his time.

GINA: Yes, and anyway, photography is no job for a man like Ekdal—taking photographs of the common rabblers.*

GREGERS: I agree with you there. But now that he's adopted this profession—

GINA: Mr. Werle, you can't possibly suggest that Ekdal is just a run-of-the-mill photographer!

GREGERS: No, of course not, but—

(A *shot is fired in the attic.*)

GREGERS (*Jumping up*): What was that?

---

* This mispronunciation and others (and in one instance a malapropism) found throughout the play are deliberately used by Ibsen to establish Gina's character and background.—Ed.

GINA: Oh—they're shooting again in the attic.

GREGERS: Do they shoot in there?

HEDVIG: They go hunting.

GREGERS (*Goes to the attic door*): What? Are you hunting, Hjalmar?

HJALMAR (*From behind the net*): Oh! You're here? I didn't know—I've been so busy— (*To* HEDVIG) And you didn't tell us. (*He enters the studio.*)

GREGERS: Are you shooting in there?

HJALMAR (*Showing him a double-barreled pistol*): Just with this.

GINA: One of these days the two of you will have an accident with that pifstle.*

HJALMAR (*With irritation*): I believe I've told you before that this weapon is called a pistol!

GINA: I don't see how that helps things.

GREGERS: So you've become a hunter, too, eh, Hjalmar?

HJALMAR: Oh, I just shoot a little rabbit now and then. It's mostly for the old man's sake. You can understand that.

GINA: Men are such a strange lot—always have to have something to diverge* their attention.

HJALMAR: Exactly! As Gina says, we must always have something to divert our attention.

GINA: Well, that's just what I said.

HJALMAR (*To* GREGERS): Actually, the attic is favorably situated. No one can hear when we shoot. (*He puts the pistol back on the shelf.*) Don't touch the pistol, Hedvig. One of the barrels is still loaded. Remember, now.

GREGERS (*Looking through the net*): You have a shotgun too, I notice.

HJALMAR: That's father's old one—it doesn't work any more. There's something wrong with the lock, but we enjoy hunting with it just the same. Sometimes we take it apart and clean it and give it a good oiling with goose grease and then put it together again. Well, it's mostly father who tinkers with these things.

HEDVIG (*Near* GREGERS): Now you can really see the wild duck!

GREGERS: Yes, I was just looking at it. It seems to me that she drags one wing a little.

HJALMAR: Not too surprising—that's where she was shot.

GREGERS: And she limps on one foot a bit, too, doesn't she?

HJALMAR: Perhaps—just a bit.

HEDVIG: That's where the dog bit her. There in the foot.

HJALMAR: She has no other defects or injuries. That's really amazing when you remember she had that buckshot in her and was carried in the jaws of a dog—

GRECERS (*Glancing at* HEDVIG): —And was down in the depths of the sea.

HEDVIG (*Smiling*): Yes.

GINA (*Setting the table*): Oh, that blasted wild duck! You all pamperate* her too much.

HJALMAR: Hmm! Is lunch ready?

GINA: In a minute. Hedvig, come help me now. (*They go into the kitchen.*)

HJALMAR (*In a low voice*): I don't think you should stand there and watch father. He doesn't like it.

(GREGERS *walks away from the door.*)

HJALMAR: And I'd better close up before the others get here. (*Clapping his hands to frighten the birds away*) Shoo! Shoo! Away with you! (*He pulls up the sailcloth and netting and slides the doors together.*) This contraption is my own invention! Quite pleasant to fuss with things like this. And then when they break down, they keep me busy! Besides, they're absolutely necessary, because Gina will *not* allow the rabbits and chickens to come into the studio.

GREGERS: No, of course not. Your wife manages the studio, then?

HJALMAR: I can generally leave the current photographic accounts to her, yes. In that way I can be in the parlor all by myself—thinking over more important things.

GREGERS: And they are—? What kind of things?

HJALMAR: I was wondering why you hadn't asked me that before. —Or perhaps you hadn't heard about my invention?

GREGERS: Your invention? No.

HJALMAR: Really? You haven't? Well, I suppose not—not up there in the forests and wastelands.

GREGERS: So you've invented something!

HJALMAR: Not exactly invented it yet, but I'm working at it. You must know that when I decided to sacrifice myself to a life of photography, it certainly wasn't to take pictures of the common herd that comes walking in here.

GREGERS: That's what your wife just said.

HJALMAR: I swore that since I was sacrificing my strength to this craft, I would elevate it so high that it would be both an art and a science. It was then I decided to make this remarkable invention.

GREGERS: What's it made of? What does it do?

HJALMAR: Oh, please don't ask about details yet. You know it takes time. And don't think it's my vanity that drives me on—I'm certainly not working for my own sake. Far from it! The one thing that stands before me night and day is that I have a mission in life.

GREGERS: What? A mission?

HJALMAR: Can you forget the old man in there with the silvery hair?

GREGERS: Your poor father. What can you ever do for him?

HJALMAR: I must restore his self-esteem by resurrecting the name of Ekdal to the place of honor and dignity that it once deserved.

GREGERS: And that's your life's mission?

HJALMAR: Yes. I shall rescue that shipwrecked old man! He was already overboard when the storm broke, and all during those dreadful investigations he was not himself. That pistol over there, Gregers—the one we use for shooting the rabbits —it has already played its role in the tragedy of the Ekdal family.

GREGERS: How?

HJALMAR: When the sentence was pronounced and he was going to be taken to prison, that pistol was in his hand—

GREGERS: And he—?

HJALMAR: Yes. But he didn't dare. He was a coward. His soul was so decayed by that time—oh, how can you understand? A lieutenant in the army who had the bravery to kill nine bears. A descendant of two lieutenant colonels—his father before him and his grandfather. Do you understand it, Gregers?

GREGERS: Yes, I understand it all very well.

HJALMAR: Well, I don't. The pistol was to play another role in the family history. When he was wearing his prison clothes, sitting behind lock and key—well, that was a dreadful time for me, you can well imagine. I had the shades drawn across both my windows. When I did look out, I saw the sun shining as it always had—and I didn't understand. I saw people on the street laughing and smiling, talking about ordinary things—again I didn't understand. I expected the whole world to hold still as if in an eclipse.

GREGERS: That's how I felt when mother died.

HJALMAR: And it was at that moment that Hjalmar Ekdal turned that pistol against his own chest.

GREGERS: You, too?

HJALMAR: Yes.

GREGERS: But you didn't fire?

HJALMAR: No. At the critical moment, I won a glorious victory over myself. I remained alive! But, believe me, it goes against a man's grain to choose life under such circumstances.

GREGERS: Well, it all depends on how one looks at it.

HJALMAR: Decidedly. And it was all for the best, because now I shall soon make my invention. Dr. Relling believes, as I do, that *then* my father will be able to wear the uniform again. I shall demand that as my only reward.

GREGERS: You mean it's the *uniform* that he—?

HJALMAR: Yes! That's what he desires above everything! You can't imagine how it cuts me to the heart—for his sake. Every time we celebrate a little family affair like our wedding anniversary—or whatever the occasion—the old man enters dressed in his lieutenant's uniform from his happier days.

But if there's a knock at the front door, back he scurries into his room as fast as his old bent legs can carry him. He doesn't dare show himself to visitors, you know. Oh, it's heartbreaking for a son to see these things!

GREGERS: When will your invention be finished?

HJALMAR: Good God, don't ask me to deal with such trivialities as time! An invention is something that even the inventor doesn't completely master. It depends a great deal upon intuition and inspiration, and it's impossible to predict when they'll come along.

GREGERS: Are you making progress?

HJALMAR: Yes, most certainly. We're moving forward. I struggle with it every day. I'm full of it. Every afternoon after I've eaten, I lock myself in the parlor where I can meditate in peace. But they can't hurry me. Relling says not to let them, because if I'm rushed it won't amount to anything.

GREGERS: But don't all your contraptions in the attic take you away from your work and diffuse your energies?

HJALMAR: No. No, just the opposite. You mustn't even say that. You certainly couldn't expect me to spend all my time constantly brooding over the same exhausting problem. I must have something else to fill up the time while I wait to be inspired. Inspiration and intuition only come . . . well, they come when they come!

GREGERS: My dear Hjalmar, I almost think there's something of the wild duck in you!

HJALMAR: Wild duck? How do you mean?

GREGERS: You, too, have plunged down and fastened yourself to the weeds—

HJALMAR: Are you referring to that almost fatal shot that struck father in the wing, and myself along with it?

GREGERS: No, not that particularly. I don't mean you're wounded. You're in a poisonous swamp, Hjalmar. There's a creeping disease in your body, and you've plunged yourself to the bottom to die in the darkness.

HJALMAR: Me? Die in the darkness? Really, Gregers, you must stop talking like that!

GREGERS: But don't worry, Hjalmar. I'll bring you up to the surface again. I discovered last night that I have a mission in life, too.

HJALMAR: That may be, but don't include me! I guarantee you that except for some easily explained melancholy, I'm just as sound as anyone.

GREGERS: Ah, that *too* is the result of a poison.

HJALMAR: My dear Gregers, be kind and stop talking about poisons and diseases. I'm just not used to that kind of conversation. In my home no one speaks to me of morbid things.

GREGERS: I can believe that.

HJALMAR: I don't feel healthy in that kind of atmosphere. There's no poisonous swamp here, as you suggest. In the poor photographer's home the roof is low and the means are meager, I am aware of that. My circumstances may seem insignificant, but I am an inventor—you must remember that, Gregers—and I do support a family. That carries me above my humble surroundings. Ah! Here they come with lunch.

(GINA *and* HEDVIG *bring bottles of beer, an aquavit decanter and glasses, and other luncheon things. At the same time* RELLING *and* MOLVIK *enter from the hall door. They are both without hats or overcoats.* MOLVIK *is dressed in black.*)

GINA (*Putting things on the table*): Well, count on those two to come right on time!

RELLING: Molvik imagined he could smell herring salad, and there was no holding him down. Good morning, Ekdal.

HJALMAR: Gregers, may I introduce you to Mr. Molvik and Dr. — Well, you and Relling already know each other.

GREGERS: Yes, vaguely.

RELLING: Ah—it's young Mr. Werle! Yes, we've been at each other's throats before, haven't we? Up at the Hoydal Works. You've just moved in, eh?

GREGERS: This morning.

RELLING: Molvik and I live downstairs, so you don't have far to go for a doctor or a minister if you should ever need either.

GREGERS: Thank you. It might be necessary. Yesterday there were thirteen of us at the table.

HJALMAR: Now don't start being morbid again.

RELLING: Don't fret about it. It won't hit *you*, by God!

HJALMAR: I hope not, for my family's sake. But let's sit down and eat, drink, and be merry!

GREGERS: Shouldn't we wait for your father?

HJALMAR: No, he'll eat in his room later on. Come, now— please sit down. (*The men sit down and begin to eat and drink.* GINA *and* HEDVIG *go in and out of the kitchen waiting on the table.*)

RELLING: Molvik was rolling on his heels last night, Mrs. Ekdal.

GINA: Oh? Again last night?

RELLING: Didn't you hear him when I brought him home?

GINA: No, I can't say I did.

RELLING: Well, that's a good thing! Because last night, God knows, Molvik—you were ghastly!

GINA: Is this true, Molvik?

MOLVIK: Let us eradicate the events of last night by drawing a line right through them! Such occurrences as last night do not truthfully represent my better nature.

RELLING (*To* GREGERS): It comes over him like an inspiration? Then off I have to go with him—both of us, off on a lark. Mr. Molvik, you see, is daemonic.

GREGERS: Daemonic?

RELLING: Yes, Molvik is daemonic.

GREGERS: Oh?

RELLING: And daemonic natures are not created to walk on their legs straight through life. They must get out on the bumpy side roads every now and then. So you're still up there at those dreadful black Works, eh?

GREGERS: Yes, I've held out until now.

RELLING: Did you ever collect on that claim you were demanding from everyone up there?

GREGERS: Claim? (*Understanding*) Oh, that!

HJALMAR: I didn't know you were collecting on a claim up there, Gregers.

GREGERS: Oh, nonsense.

RELLING: He certainly tried! He went around to all the workers' cottages insisting that he had a right to claim the ideal!

GREGERS: I was very young then.

RELLING: You most assuredly were—dreadfully young. And as long as I was up there you never collected one thing.

GREGERS: No. Nor since then, either.

RELLING: Well then, I hope you're wise enough now to put your price down a little?

GREGERS: Never. Not when I'm dealing with a genuine man.

HJALMAR: Well, that seems rather reasonable to me! Some butter, Gina.

RELLING: And a slice of pork for Molvik.

MOLVIK: Oh, no! No pork!

(*There is a knock on the attic door.*)

HJALMAR: Open the door, Hedvig—father wants to come out. (HEDVIG *opens the sliding doors a little.* OLD EKDAL *enters with a fresh rabbit skin. She closes the door after him.*)

EKDAL: Good morning, gentlemen! What a good day for hunting! I shot a big one!

HJALMAR: And you've already skinned it before I could help you!

EKDAL (*Waving the rabbit skin over the lunch table*): Salted it, too. It's good dark meat, this rabbit meat. So sweet! Tastes like sugar. Have a good lunch, gentlemen! (*He goes into his room.*)

MOLVIK (*Standing up*): Excuse me— I can't— I just have to hurry—quickly—

RELLING: Drink some soda water—ass! (MOLVIK *hurries out through the hall door, his hand to his mouth.*)

RELLING (*To* HJALMAR): Let's drink a cup to the old hunter!

HJALMAR (*Clinking glasses with him*): To the sportsman with one foot in his grave! Yes!

RELLING: To the gray-haired one! (*Drinks*) But tell me—does he have gray hair, or is it white?

HJALMAR: I think it's somewhere in between—there's not much left!

RELLING: Well, one can get through life just as nicely with a wig. You're a very happy man at heart, Ekdal. You have this beautiful mission in life to struggle for—

HJALMAR: And I am struggling, too, believe me.

RELLING: And an able wife who jogs along so calmly in and out on felt slippers, hips swaying, making things nice and comfortable for you.

HJALMAR: Yes. Gina. (*Nodding to her*) You're a good companion on this road of life.

GINA: Oh, don't sit there and eulotize* about me now!

RELLING: And then you also have your Hedvig, too, Ekdal.

HJALMAR (*Moved*): Yes, my child. My child—the most important of all! Hedvig, come here to me. (*Stroking her hair*) What day is it tomorrow? Tell me—tell me.

HEDVIG (*Shaking him*): Oh—don't say anything about that, Father. Don't tell them.

HJALMAR: It's like a knife right through my heart when I think how meager it will be. A small birthday celebration in an attic.

HEDVIG: Oh, but it's going to be just wonderful!

RELLING: Just wait until your father's remarkable invention is introduced to the world, Hedvig!

HJALMAR: Yes, indeed—you will see! Hedvig, I have decided how to secure your future. You'll be comfortable as long as you live. I will demand that you get . . . hmm . . . something or other. That will be the poor inventor's only reward.

HEDVIG (*Whispering, her arms around his neck*): Oh my kind, kind father.

RELLING (*To* GREGERS): Well, how do you like this for a change? Sitting at a table in a happy family circle!

HJALMAR: Yes, these moments at my table—I truly value them more than anything.

GREGERS: I, for one, can't thrive in swamp air.

RELLING: Swamp air?

HJALMAR: Oh, don't start that talk again!

GINA: I'll tell you this much, Mr. Werle, you won't find any swamp air in here. I air out this place every single day!

GREGERS (*Leaving the table*): The smell I refer to can't be aired out!

HJALMAR: Smell?

GINA: Ekdal, what do you think of that!

RELLING: I beg your pardon—it wouldn't be you, by any chance, who brought that smell in here from that black mine, would it?

GREGERS: Oh, it's so like *you* to call what I bring into this house a stench!

RELLING: Listen now, young Mr. Werle, I have a strong suspicion that you're still walking around with that claim of yours—unabridged—in your back pocket.

GREGERS (*Indicating his chest*): I carry it here.

RELLING: Well—whatever damn place you carry it—I warn you, don't impersonate the collector here as long as I'm around!

GREGERS: And if I do?

RELLING: You'll go flying down those stairs head first! And I mean it! (*He goes toward* GREGERS.)

HJALMAR (*Standing up*): Wait now, Relling—

GREGERS: All right, throw me out!

GINA (*Coming between them*): Oh my, my! Now you can't do that here, Mr. Relling! And as for you, Mr. Werle—for someone who made all that mess with the tile stove this morning, you have some nerve to complain about a smell to me!

(*A knock is heard at the hall door.*)

HEDVIG: Mother, someone's knocking.

HJALMAR: That, too! Now I suppose people will start running in and out of here again!

GINA: Just let me see to it. (*She walks over and opens the door. Startled by what she sees, she steps back in surprise.*) Oh! Well!

HAAKON WERLE (*In a fur coat. Steps one step into the room*): I beg your pardon, but I understand my son is living in this house.

GINA: Yes.

HJALMAR (*Going to* WERLE): Please, Mr. Werle, sir, won't you do us the honor and—?

WERLE: Why, thank you. I wish to speak to my son.

GREGERS: Very well, go right ahead. Here I am.

WERLE: I wish to speak to you in your room.

GREGERS: In my room? Very well, then. (*He starts to exit.*)

GINA: No—my God! It just isn't nice enough—

WERLE: Well then, out in the hallway. But I must talk to you man to man, and in private.

HJALMAR: You can do that in here, Mr. Werle. Come into the parlor, Relling. (HJALMAR *and* RELLING *walk* RIGHT *into the parlor.* GINA *takes* HEDVIG *into the kitchen with her.*)

GREGERS (*After a short pause*): Well? This is private.

WERLE: Yes. You passed a few remarks last night insinuating that—well, since you've rented a room here at Ekdal's, I presume you intend to do something against me.

GREGERS: I intend to open Hjalmar Ekdal's eyes! He's going to see things as they really are. That's all.

WERLE: Is that what you meant last night about having something important to do in life?

GREGERS: Yes. You've left me no other choice.

WERLE: Am I the one who has ruined your mind, Gregers?

GREGERS: You've ruined my entire life! And I'm not just talking about all you did to mother. No. I carry around a feeling of guilt that constantly haunts me, and I have *you* to thank for that! This damn guilt won't stop gnawing at me!

WERLE: Oh, it's your conscience that's in weak health, is it?

GREGERS: I should have stood up to you a long time ago, when you laid that trap for Lieutenant Ekdal! I should have warned him. I *must* have suspected what was going on.

WERLE: Then you certainly should have spoken out.

GREGERS: I didn't dare—I was such a coward. I was so wretchedly terrified of you then, and for a long time afterward, too.

WERLE: It sounds as if you've overcome your terror.

GREGERS: By God, I have! Your crimes against old Ekdal and me—and others—can never be absolved, but I can liberate Hjalmar from this perpetual web of lies and deceit and silence that's pulling him down.

WERLE: And you think you'll be doing a good deed?

GREGERS: I pray so.

WERLE: Are you sure that this photographer is the kind of man who will thank you for this proof of your friendship?

GREGERS: Yes. He is just that kind of man.

WERLE: Hmm! We'll see.

GREGERS: Yes, we'll see. Then, too, I must find a cure for my sick conscience, if I'm to continue living.

WERLE: Your conscience will never be healthy. It's been sickly ever since you were a child. You inherited that from your mother, Gregers—that's the only thing she did leave you.

GREGERS (*Smiling scornfully*): Haven't you ever recovered from your big disappointment? Oh, how badly you miscalculated when you thought you'd get rich through her!

WERLE: We are not going to discuss irrelevant matters! Do you still intend to lead Mr. Ekdal upon what you presume to be a path of enlightenment?

GREGERS: Yes. I'm resolved.

WERLE: Then I could have saved myself the walk up here. There's no use, I suppose, in asking you to come home again?

GREGERS: No.

WERLE: And you have no ambitions to go into the firm, either?

GREGERS: No.

WERLE: Very well. As I now stand to be married again, I am dividing the estate between us.

GREGERS (*Quickly*): No! I don't want any part of it!

WERLE: You don't?

GREGERS: No. I wouldn't dare take it—my conscience wouldn't let me.

WERLE (*After a moment*): Will you go back to the Works again?

GREGERS:  No. I consider myself resigned from your service.

WERLE:  What will you do?

GREGERS:  I'll work at my mission in life. Nothing else.

WERLE:  And later on? How will you support yourself?

GREGERS:  I've put aside a bit of my income.

WERLE:  How long will it last?

GREGERS:  It'll be enough for *my* life.

WERLE:  What does that imply?

GREGERS:  I don't want to answer any more questions.

WERLE:  Good-by, then, Gregers. (*Exits*)

GREGERS:  Good-by.

HJALMAR (*Looking in*):  Did he leave?

GREGERS:  Yes.

(HJALMAR *and* RELLING *come out of the parlor.* GINA *and* HEDVIG *come in from the kitchen.*)

RELLING:  Well, that lunch went into the sink!

GREGERS:  Get dressed, Hjalmar. You must take a long walk with me.

HJALMAR:  Yes, I'd be glad to. What did your father want? Was it anything to do with me?

GREGERS:  Just come along. There's something we've got to talk over. I'll go get my coat. (*He leaves by the hall door.*)

GINA:  You shouldn't go out with him, Ekdal.

RELLING:  No, don't. Stay where you are.

HJALMAR (*Taking his hat and overcoat*):  What? He's my child-hood friend and he feels the need to open up his heart to me in private—

RELLING:  Damn it all, man! Don't you realize that poor, mis-guided fellow is mad—crazy mad?

GINA:  You can tell it from the way he talks! His mother had the same kind of sieges* at times.

HJALMAR:  All the more reason for his friend to keep a cautious eye on him. Be sure that dinner's ready when I get home. Good-by for a while. (*He leaves by the hall door.*)

RELLING:  What bad luck that the damn fool didn't fall into one of those mines up there at Hoydal and drop straight down to hell!

GINA: Oh, good heavens! Why do you talk like that?

RELLING (*Mumbling*): I have my reasons.

GINA: Do you think young Mr. Werle is really crazy?

RELLING: No. Unfortunately, he isn't any craizer than most people. But there is some terrible sickness in him.

GINA: What do you think it could be?

RELLING: Well, I'll tell you this much, Mrs. Ekdal—he suffers from an acute fever of self-righteousness!

GINA: Self-righteousness fever?

HEDVIG: Is it a new kind of sickness?

RELLING: My young lady, it's a national disease! But we only see it sporadically. (*Nodding to* GINA) Thank you for lunch. (*He leaves by the hall door.*)

GINA (*Pacing nervously*): Oh—that Gregers Werle! He always was a bad egg!

HEDVIG (*Standing by the table, looks questioningly at* GINA): Everything here seems so strange.

**CURTAIN**

# ACT IV

HJALMAR's *studio. A photographic sitting has just taken place. The camera is still out, and a black cloth hangs over half of it. A tripod, several chairs, and a folding table are also in evidence. There is an afternoon light, but the sun is setting. During the course of the act it begins to get dark.*

AS THE CURTAIN RISES, GINA *stands at the open hall door with a small box and a wet glass plate in her hand. She is talking to someone outside.*

GINA: Very well. Definitely! When I make a promise, I keep it! On Monday, then, the first dozen will be finished. Good-by. Good-by.
(*Someone is heard going down the stairs.* GINA *closes the door. She puts the plate into the small box and places it in the camera.*)
HEDVIG (*Entering from the kitchen*): Did they leave?
GINA (*Tidying up*): Yes, thank God—I finally got rid of them.
HEDVIG: Can you figure out why father isn't home yet?
GINA: Are you sure he's not at Relling's?
HEDVIG: Yes. I ran down the kitchen stairs a while ago and asked.
GINA: His food's getting cold, I suppose?
HEDVIG: Yes. And father is usually so punctual for dinner!
GINA: Oh, he'll be here soon. You'll see.
HEDVIG: I wish he'd hurry. Everything seems so strange today.
GINA (*Calling out*): There he is!
(HJALMAR EKDAL *enters through the hall door.*)

HEDVIG (*Running toward him*): Oh, Father! You don't know how we've waited for you!

GINA (*Glancing at him quickly*): You certainly stayed away a long time.

HJALMAR (*Not looking up*): Yes. I was detained.
(HJALMAR *takes off his overcoat.* GINA *and* HEDVIG *try to help him, but he gestures them away.*)

GINA: Did you have something to eat with Werle?

HJALMAR (*Hanging up his coat*): No.

GINA (*Going toward the kitchen*): Then I'll get your food out.

HJALMAR: No, never mind the food. I won't eat now.

HEDVIG (*Going closer*): Father, aren't you well?

HJALMAR: Well? Oh yes, considering. Werle and I had an exhausting . . . walk.

GINA: You shouldn't have done that, Hjalmar. You're not used to it, you know.

HJALMAR: Hmm. There are many things a man must get used to in this world. (*Wandering about the room*) Was anyone here while I was out?

GINA: Just those two lovebirds.

HJALMAR: No new orders?

GINA: Not today.

HEDVIG: You'll see, there'll be someone tomorrow, Father.

HJALMAR: I hope so. Because tomorrow I intend to begin work without stopping.

HEDVIG: Oh, no! Don't you remember what tomorrow is?

HJALMAR: Oh, that's true. Well, then, day after tomorrow. From now on I'll do everything myself in this studio. I will be completely alone in my work.

GINA: What good will that do, Hjalmar? You'll only be miserable again like you were before. Now, I can certainly go on taking care of the photography part of the studio—so that you can have time to stay with your invention.

HEDVIG: And think of the wild duck, Father, and all the chickens and the rabbits and—

HJALMAR: Don't talk to me again about those things! Starting tomorrow, I'll never set foot in that attic again!

HEDVIG: But Father, you promised me—tomorrow we're having a party!

HJALMAR: Hmm! That's true. Well, then, day after tomorrow. That damn wild duck! I feel like wringing its neck.

HEDVIG (*Springing up*): The wild duck?

GINA: Well! I never heard such talk!

HEDVIG (*Shaking him*): But Father, the wild duck is mine!

HJALMAR: That's just why I won't do it. I haven't the heart to —for your sake, Hedvig. But I feel very deeply that I should. I should not tolerate any creature living under my roof who has passed through those hands!

GINA: Oh, good God! Just because grandfather got it from that old nitwit Petersen!

HJALMAR (*Pacing the floor*): There are certain demands . . . what shall I call them? Claims. Yes—claims to the ideal. There are certain claims that a man cannot neglect without doing damage to his soul.

HEDVIG (*Following him*): But think of the poor wild duck, Father.

HJALMAR (*Stopping his pacing*): Didn't you hear me say I'd spare its life for your sake? I won't touch a hair on her— well, as I said, I'm going to spare it. Now I must deal with greater problems than that. Hedvig, you should go for your walk. It's getting dusky now, and the light won't hurt your eyes.

HEDVIG: But I don't want to go out now, Father!

HJALMAR: You're going! I've been watching you squint in here —in here, against all this bad air. Yes. The air, like everything else under this roof, is bad!

HEDVIG: I'll go down the back stairs and out for a little walk. My hat and cloak . . . where—? Oh, they're in my room. Father, you mustn't hurt the wild duck while I'm out!

HJALMAR: No. No, I won't touch a feather of its little head. (*Pressing her close to him*) You and I, Hedvig—we two! Well, run along now, Hedvig.

(HEDVIG *nods at her parents as she leaves through the kitchen.*)

HJALMAR (*Walking around, not looking up*): Gina.

GINA: Yes?

HJALMAR: Starting tomorrow, or let us say, day after tomorrow, I feel like taking over the household accounts myself.

GINA: Oh—now you want to keep the accounts, too?

HJALMAR: Yes. Well, at least I insist on making a list of the money that comes into this house.

GINA: God save us, that's easy to do!

HJALMAR: I don't think so. It seems to me you make it stretch a surprisingly long way. (*Pausing, looks deeply at her*) How is that done?

GINA: Hedvig and I—we don't need much.

HJALMAR: Is it true that father is more than generously paid for the copying work he does for Mr. Werle?

GINA: Well, I don't know if it's all that generous. How would I know what the prices are on that kind of work, anyway?

HJALMAR: About how much does he get? Tell me.

GINA: Well, he gets different amounts—it always covers his keep, and it gives him a little pocket money.

HJALMAR: You never told me that!

GINA: How could I? You were always so happy believing he got everything from you.

HJALMAR: And all the time it came from Mr. Werle?

GINA: Oh, well, there's more where that came from, there is.

HJALMAR: Light the lamp for me.

GINA (*Lighting it*): And then, we don't even know if it's the boss himself. It could be Graberg, you know.

HJALMAR: Why do you use him as an excuse?

GINA: I don't know. I just thought—

HJALMAR: Hmm!

GINA: Well, I didn't get this copy work for grandfather, remember. It was Berthe Sorby—when she went to work there as the housekeeper.

HJALMAR: I believe your voice is shaking.

GINA (*Putting the shade back on the lamp*): Is it?

HJALMAR: And your hands are shaking, too. Am I mistaken?

GINA (*Grimly*): Come out with it, Ekdal! What's he been telling you about me?

HJALMAR: Is it true? Could it be true that when you served in

Mr. Werle's house there was a . . . relationship between you?

GINA: That is not true—not then, anyway. Oh, Mr. Werle kept after me, all right. And then the Mrs.—she thought there was something going on, so she kicked up such a fuss and furation, she hit me and abused me so—oh, believe me, she did—that I left her service.

HJALMAR: And then? What then?

GINA: I went home. And my own mother— Oh, she wasn't the simple, fair-dealing woman you took her to be, Ekdal! She kept talking about this and that, and . . . well, Werle had just become a widower, and—

HJALMAR: Well, go on.

GINA: Well, I suppose it's best that you know. He didn't give up until he got his way.

HJALMAR (*Pounding his hands together*): And you are the mother of my child! How could you keep a thing like this from me?

GINA: I suppose it was wrong of me. I should have told you a long time ago.

HJALMAR: You should have told me right from the start! Then I would have known what kind of woman you are.

GINA: Would you have married me?

HJALMAR: How can you even imagine that I would?

GINA: Well, you see! That's just why I didn't dare tell you. I'd become so very fond of you, you know—I just couldn't see why I should make myself so utterly miserable.

HJALMAR (*Pacing back and forth*): And that's the mother of my Hedvig! And now to know that everything my eyes see— (*Kicking a chair*) my entire home—I owe it all to my wife's ex-lover! Oh, that lecherous Werle!

GINA: Do you regret the fourteen—fifteen years we've lived together?

HJALMAR (*Stopping in front of her*): Well, you tell me! Haven't you regretted every hour of every day you've lived in the web of lies that you've spun around me like a deceitful spider? Haven't you honestly gone around here suffering and writhing in regret?

GINA: My dear Ekdal, I've had plenty on my mind with the housework, I can tell you.

HJALMAR: Then you've never questioned your past?

GINA: No, by God—I've forgotten all about those old complications!

HJALMAR: Oh, your dull, insensible complacency! It's revolting to me! Just think—not even regret!

GINA: Tell me, Ekdal—what would have become of you if you hadn't married a wife like me?

HJALMAR: Like you?

GINA: Yes. I've always been more practical and more reliable than you. But then, that may be only natural—I'm a couple of years older.

HJALMAR: What might have become of me—!

GINA: You were off on the wrong foot when I first met you— that you can't deny!

HJALMAR: Wrong foot, eh? Oh—you never understood a man in sorrow—a desperate man—especially a man with my fiery temperament.

GINA: Well, that might be, and I'm not saying anything against you. You became a very good husband as soon as you got a house and home of your own. And now that we've made it so cozy and comfortable, so homelike— Why, we were just becoming able, Hedvig and I, to allow ourselves a little extra for food and clothes—

HJALMAR: In this swamp of deceit?

GINA: Oh, that hateful Gregers! Why did I ever allow him to set foot in this house!

HJALMAR: I always thought my home was such a wonderful place to be. Well, that was a delusion! Where will I ever find the strength I need to bring my invention into this world of reality? Perhaps it'll die with me—and your past will be the reason for it.

GINA (*Close to tears*): Oh no, you mustn't say things like that, Ekdal! I've only done, always, what I thought was best for you—all my life.

HJALMAR: Well, then—now I ask you! What will become of that dream the family supporter held so dear? What? Every day when I lay in there on the sofa and brooded over my invention, I suspected that it would devour all my remaining strength. I knew that on the day I held the patent in my hands at last—that day would be the day of my demise. And always—always—my dream ended with you sitting there as the departed inventor's wealthy widow.

GINA (*Drying her tears*): You mustn't speak that way, Ekdal. Good Lord, let the day never come when I sit here as a widow!

HJALMAR: One's the same as the other. It's all finished, anyhow. Everything.

(GREGERS WERLE *opens the hall door cautiously.*)

GREGERS: May I dare come in?

HJALMAR: Yes. Come in.

GREGERS (*Walking over with a radiant, rejuvenated face, holds out his hands to them*): Well, my dear friends! (*He looks alternately from one to the other and whispers to* HJALMAR.) It hasn't happened yet?

HJALMAR (*Loudly*): It has happened.

GREGERS: It has?

HJALMAR: I have just experienced the most bitter hour of my life.

GREGERS: And the most elevating, I hope.

HJALMAR: Well, for the present, we have managed to live through it.

GINA: God forgive you, Mr. Werle.

GREGERS (*Greatly surprised*): I don't understand!

HJALMAR: What?

GREGERS: Your attitudes! After such a great crisis—a crisis upon which you can build a whole new life, a *true* relationship, a marriage built on truth, without any deceits—

HJALMAR: Yes, I know all that very well, Gregers.

GREGERS: I had expected, when I came through that door, to see the glorious light of transformation shining between husband and wife. But all I find is a heavy oppression—solemn, dreary, and dark.

GINA (*Removing the lampshade*): Well, then?

GREGERS: You don't understand, Mrs. Ekdal. No—no, of course not. It'll take a little time for you. But what about you, Hjalmar? You must feel exalted after this great purge.

HJALMAR: Yes, naturally I do! That is—I do, in a way.

GREGERS: There can be nothing in the world comparable to this glorious experience—the joy of forgiving someone who has sinned, and then raising her up to you, in love!

HJALMAR: Do you think a man can drink as bitter a draught as I have with ease?

GREGERS: A common man, no. But a man like you—

HJALMAR: Yes—good God, Gregers—I know! But don't force me—I need time.

GREGERS: You have much of the wild duck in you, Hjalmar!

RELLING (*Entering from the hall door*): Oh God! Is that wild duck still around?

HJALMAR: Yes. Mr. Werle's winged victim.

RELLING: Mr. Werle's? Oh, you're talking about him?

HJALMAR: Yes, about him, and the rest of us too.

RELLING (*Half aloud, to* GREGERS): Oh, go to hell.

HJALMAR: What?

RELLING: I have just expressed an inner wish that this duck would get lost on his way home. If he stays here, he's quite capable of ruining both your lives.

GREGERS: These two lives will not be ruined, Mr. Relling! We don't have to discuss Hjalmar—we both know what he is— but she, too, deep inside, has something sincere and worthy.

GINA (*Almost in tears*): You should have left me alone, to be what I am.

RELLING: Would it be impertinent to ask what you want in this house?

GREGERS: I want to help lay the foundations of a true marriage.

RELLING: In your opinion it's not good enough as it is?

GREGERS: It's as good as any other, I regret to say, but it hasn't yet become a true marriage!

HJALMAR: You've never had a taste for ideals, Relling.

RELLING: Rubbish, my boy! With apologies, Mr. Werle, just how many true marriages have you seen in your life?

GREGERS: I don't think I've seen a single one.

RELLING: Neither have I.

GREGERS: But I've seen innumerable ones of the other kind, and I've watched them degrade and destroy two human beings.

HJALMAR: Yes, that's the dreadful part. A man's entire moral code—his laws of life—give way.

RELLING: Well, I've never been married, so I don't dare judge. But this I do know—children also belong to marriage, and in this case you will leave the child alone!

HJALMAR: Hedvig! Oh, my poor Hedvig!

RELLING: Yes. I beg you, keep Hedvig out of this! You two are grown, and in God's name you're allowed to fuss around and tamper with anything you want if it pleases you. But you must handle Hedvig gently— Be careful, I tell you—you may do her great harm.

HJALMAR: Harm?

RELLING: She might harm herself—and perhaps others, too!

GINA: How do you know about that?

HJALMAR: But there's no immediate danger with her eyes, is there?

RELLING: I'm not talking about her eyes! Please understand! Hedvig is at a delicate age. She might find out all the wrong things.

GINA: Yes! That's so true. She's already started! She's been very naughty lately with the fire in the kitchen. She calls it her "wild fire." Oh, many are the times she could have burned down the house.

RELLING: Well, there you see! I knew it!

GREGERS (To RELLING): How do you explain a thing like that?

RELLING (Quietly): She's changing into . . . well, she's maturing, my boy.

HJALMAR: As long as the child has me—as long as I'm alive and breathing—
(There is a knock on the door.)

GINA: Sh! Ekdal! There's someone outside. (She calls out.) Come in, please.

MRS. SORBY (*Enters, in an overcoat*): Good evening.

GINA (*Walking over to her*): Ah! Is it you, Berthe?

MRS. SORBY: Yes. But maybe I've come at the wrong time?

HJALMAR: A messenger from the house that—

MRS. SORBY (*To* GINA): To be candid, I'd hoped not to find any men here at this time of day. I dropped by to have a little talk with you and to say good-by.

GINA: Oh? You're going away?

MRS. SORBY: Yes, early tomorrow morning—up to Hoydal. Mr. Werle left this afternoon. (*Casually, to* GREGERS) He sends his regards to you, Gregers.

GINA: Imagine that!

HJALMAR: So Mr. Werle left! Are you following him?

MRS. SORBY: Yes. What do you have to say about that, Ekdal?

HJALMAR: Take care!

GREGERS: I should explain to you that my father is marrying Mrs. Sorby.

HJALMAR: Marrying?

GINA: Oh no, Berthe, did it finally happen?

RELLING (*His voice shaking*): Oh, this can't be true!

MRS. SORBY: Yes, my dear Relling, it's true enough.

RELLING: Do you want to get married again?

MRS. SORBY: Yes, that's how it is to be. Werle got a special license, so there'll be no delay. We'll celebrate the wedding quietly up at Hoydal.

GREGERS: Then, as a proper stepson, I must wish you happiness.

MRS. SORBY: Thank you very much—if you mean it. I hope we find happiness, too, both Werle and myself.

RELLING: That's a safe wish! Mr. Werle never gets drunk as far as I know, and I'm comparatively sure that he never beats his wives, as your late lamented horse doctor did.

MRS. SORBY: Ah, now, just let Sorby rest in peace where he is. He had his good side.

RELLING: But Mr. Werle, it seems, has better ones!

MRS. SORBY: At least he hasn't let his best qualities go to waste. The man who does that must suffer the consequences.

RELLING: Tonight I go out drinking with Molvik again!

MRS. SORBY: You shouldn't do that, Relling. Not on my account.

RELLING: There's nothing else for me to do. (*To* HJALMAR) Want to join us?

GINA: No thank you! Ekdal doesn't go out on those kinds of spreezers.*

HJALMAR (*Angry, in a half whisper*): For God's sake, keep quiet!

RELLING: Good-by, Mrs. . . . Werle. (*He leaves by the hall door.*)

GREGERS (*To* MRS. SORBY): I didn't know you and Dr. Relling knew each other so well.

MRS. SORBY: Yes, for many years. At one time I even thought our friendship might grow into something more lasting.

GREGERS: It was a good thing for you it didn't.

MRS. SORBY: How true! I've always been careful not to act impulsively. After all, a woman can't just throw herself away.

GREGERS: Aren't you afraid I'll mention this to my father?

MRS. SORBY: You must be clever enough to know that I've already told him all about it.

GREGERS: Really?

MRS. SORBY: Your father knows every single thing that could possibly—in truth—be said about me. I've told him everything of that nature. It was the first thing I did when he began to take me seriously.

GREGERS: Then you're more candid than most women.

MRS. SORBY: I've always been that way—I believe it's best.

HJALMAR: What do you say about that, Gina?

GINA: Oh, we women are all so different. Some find one way the best, and some the other.

MRS. SORBY: Well, Gina, I think to arrange things as I have is the wisest way, and Mr. Werle hasn't concealed anything from me, either. It's a bond between us that makes us very close and holds us together. Now we can both sit down and talk to each other with the open frankness of children. He's never had the opportunity to do that with anyone before.

Imagine! That vigorous and healthy man seems to have spent his youth—and his best years, too—listening to nothing but reprimanding sermons. And from what I've heard, most of them were undeserved!

GINA: Yes, that's as true as the day is long.

GREGERS: Well! If the ladies are going to discuss that subject, it's best that I leave.

MRS. SORBY: You needn't as far as I'm concerned. I won't say another word. I wanted you to know that I haven't carried any tales or done anything underhanded. I have had a fortunate stroke of luck in my life—in a way—but I must say that I don't take more than I give. I shall never deceive him. I'll be waiting on him and helping him as no one else has, and I'll never fail him in these things when he becomes helpless.

HJALMAR: Helpless?

GREGERS (*To* MRS. SORBY): Don't talk about that here.

MRS. SORBY: There's no use hiding it any longer, as much as we might wish to. He's going blind.

HJALMAR (*Startled*): Blind? That's strange . . . strange. He's going blind, too?

GINA: Many people do.

MRS. SORBY: You can just imagine what it can do to a businessman. Well, I shall try to use my eyes for his eyes as best I can. But now I mustn't stay any longer. I'm so busy these days—so busy. Oh yes, this is what I wanted to tell you, Ekdal. If there's anything that Werle can ever do for you, you've only to get in touch with Mr. Graberg.

GREGERS: Hjalmar Ekdal will gratefully decline that offer!

MRS. SORBY: Oh? Is that so? Well, I see. But it seems that in the past—

GINA: Well, Berthe, Ekdal doesn't have to take anything from Mr. Werle now.

HJALMAR (*Slowly, with emphasis*): Will you tell your husband-to-be—for me—that in the near future I intend to go to his bookkeeper, Graberg—

GREGERS: Do you want to do that?

HJALMAR: I will go to the bookkeeper Graberg and demand a complete account of the money I owe his employer. I shall repay this debt of honor— (*Laughing sarcastically*) Honor. —But enough of that. I will repay everything—the total sum. With five per cent interest!

GINA: But my dear Ekdal, we don't have the money!

HJALMAR: Will you please tell your fiancé that I am working without cease on my invention. Will you tell him that my spiritual strength is being sustained in this exhausting stress by the solitary wish to be free from this painful debt. That is the reason I'm making this invention. The entire profits will go to releasing me from this pecuniary obligation to your future husband.

MRS. SORBY: Something has happened in this house, hasn't it?

HJALMAR: Yes, it has.

MRS. SORBY: Well, good-by. There was something else I wanted to talk to you about, Gina, but it'll have to keep until another time. Good-by.

(HJALMAR *and* GREGERS *bow silently.* GINA *follows* MRS. SORBY *to the door.*)

HJALMAR: Not over the threshold, Gina!

(MRS. SORBY *exits.* GINA *closes the door after her.*)

HJALMAR: Well now, Gregers! Now I have that pressing debt out of the way.

GREGERS: Well, very soon, at least.

HJALMAR: I believe that the stand I took is to be commended.

GREGERS: You *are* the man I always knew you to be!

HJALMAR: On certain occasions it is impossible for a man to ignore his right to claim the ideal. As the supporter of this family I have to twist and turn under the continuous demand. Do believe me, Gregers, it isn't easy for a man without means to decide to pay an old debt which has, I must say, lain forgotten for so long, under the dust! Be that as it may—the man in me demands justice!

GREGERS (*Placing his hands on* HJALMAR's *shoulders*): Dear Hjalmar. Wasn't it a good thing I came here?

HJALMAR (*Slightly irritated*): Yes, of course. But something is upsetting my sense of justice.

GREGERS: What is that?

HJALMAR: It—hmm . . . well, I don't know if I should talk about your father so freely—

GREGERS: You can say anything, as far as I'm concerned.

HJALMAR: All right. I find it very upsetting that it will be your father who will realize a true marriage, and not me!

GREGERS: How can you say that?

HJALMAR: Because that's how it will be! Your father and Mrs. Sorby are building their marriage on mutual candor and complete trust. Everything above board! There's no deceit in their relationship. They've made a declaration of—if I may express myself in this way—a declaration of mutual forgiveness of sins.

GREGERS: Yes.

HJALMAR: That's it—the whole point! You said it yourself. Only by overcoming all these difficulties can the foundation of a true marriage be achieved.

GREGERS: But that's a different situation, Hjalmar. Surely you can't compare yourself or your wife with those two. No, you've misunderstood me on that point.

HJALMAR: I can't rid myself of this feeling. It violates my sense of justice. It's as if God's perfect justice didn't exist.

GINA: Good heavens, Ekdal, you mustn't say things like that!

GREGERS: Let's not get on that subject.

HJALMAR: And it seems as if I were watching the hand of fate regulating everything. He is going blind.

GINA: We can't be sure of that.

HJALMAR: It's unquestionable. Why doubt it? In this very fact we find righteous retribution. He once took a simple-hearted, confiding, young, fellow human being and blinded him.

GREGERS: He has blinded many.

HJALMAR: And now the mysterious one who cannot be persuaded comes and claims Mr. Werle's eyes.

GINA: How can you say something that evil? You frighten me!

HJALMAR: It's very useful, now and then, for one to plunge down into the depths and see the dark side of life!
(HEDVIG, *wearing her hat and cloak, enters happy and breathless through the hall door.*)

GINA: Back already?

HEDVIG: I didn't want to walk any farther—and how lucky! I met someone in the hallway!

HJALMAR: Mrs. Sorby?

HEDVIG (*Breathlessly*): Yes.

HJALMAR (*Pacing*): I hope you've seen her for the last time.
(*There is a silence.* HEDVIG *looks, bewildered, from one to the other. She tries to find out what they're thinking or what it is that's been going on.*)

HEDVIG (*Coaxingly, approaching* HJALMAR): Father.

HJALMAR: What is it, Hedvig?

HEDVIG: Mrs. Sorby had something for me.

HJALMAR: For you?

HEDVIG: Yes. Something for tomorrow!

GINA: Berthe always gives you something for your birthday.

HJALMAR: What is it?

HEDVIG: No, I can't tell you now! Mother will bring it to me in bed early tomorrow morning.

HJALMAR: Oh! More secrets around here. I'm always on the outside.

HEDVIG (*Quickly*): You can see it if you want! It's a *big* letter.
(*She takes a letter out of the pocket of her cloak.*)

HJALMAR: A letter, too?

HEDVIG: No, there's *only* a letter. Maybe the other thing will come tomorrow. But just imagine—a letter! I've never received one before. And look, it says "Miss" on the outside. (*Reading*) "Miss Hedvig Ekdal." Just imagine! That's me!

HJALMAR: Let me see that letter.

HEDVIG (*Handing it to him*): Here it is.

HJALMAR: This is Mr. Werle's writing.

GINA: Are you sure?

HJALMAR: See for yourself.

GINA: Oh! As if I could tell!

HJALMAR: Hedvig, may I open the letter and read it?

HEDVIG: Of course.

GINA: Oh no, not tonight. We're supposed to wait until to-morrow.

HEDVIG (*Softly*): Oh, can't you let him read it? I'm sure it must be something good, and then father will be so happy and everything will be pleasant again.

HJALMAR: May I open it?

HEDVIG: Yes—please do, Father. It's going to be so nice to find out what's in it.

HJALMAR: Good. (*He opens the envelope, takes out the paper, and reads it through. He seems confused.*) What does this mean?

GINA: What does it say?

HEDVIG: Yes, Father, tell us!

HJALMAR: Keep quiet! (*He reads it once more. He becomes pale, and then speaks, controlling himself.*) This letter is a deed of gift, Hedvig.

HEDVIG: No! Really? What am I getting?

HJALMAR: See for yourself.

(HEDVIG *walks over to the lamp and begins to read the letter.*)

HJALMAR (*With half-clenched fists*): The eyes! The eyes—and now the letter!

HEDVIG (*Stops reading*): It looks as if it's for grandfather.

HJALMAR (*Taking the letter away from her*): Gina, can you un-derstand this?

GINA: I don't know a thing. Tell me, what's in it?

HJALMAR: Mr. Werle writes to Hedvig that her old grandfather doesn't have to do copying any more. From now on he'll have one hundred crowns every month waiting for him at the office.

GREGERS: Ah!

HEDVIG: One hundred crowns! Mother—I read that!

GINA: That will be very good for grandfather.

HJALMAR: One hundred crowns as long as he needs it. That means, of course, up to the time he closes his eyes for good.

GINA: Well, then, he's provided for—the poor thing.

HJALMAR: But now it comes! You didn't read this part, did you,
Hedvig? Afterwards, the gift shall be transferred to you.

HEDVIG: To me, all of it?

HJALMAR: He writes that you're guaranteed the same amount
for the rest of your life. Did you hear that, Gina?

GINA: Yes.

HEDVIG (*Shaking him*): Just think! All the money I get! Father!
Father—aren't you happy?

HJALMAR (*Avoiding her*): Happy? (*Pacing the floor*) What per-
spectives unfold before me! Oh, how clearly I see it all!
Hedvig, is it? She's the one he remembers so—so generously!

GINA: Well, it's Hedvig's birthday.

HEDVIG: And you'll get it all, Father, you know that. I'll give all
my money to you and mother!

HJALMAR: Yes, to your mother! That's it!

GREGERS: Hjalmar, this is a trap my father has set for you.

HJALMAR: Another trap?

GREGERS: When he was here this morning he said, "Hjalmar
Ekdal is not the man you think he is."

HJALMAR: Not the man—?

GREGERS: He said, "You'll see—"

HJALMAR: He thought you'd see me being bought off!

HEDVIG: Mother, what's going on? What's happening?

GINA: Go hang up your cloak, dear.

(HEDVIG, *close to tears, exits.*)

GREGERS: Now, Hjalmar, we'll prove who is right—my father or
me.

HJALMAR (*Tears the paper slowly into two pieces and lays them
on the table*): There is my answer.

GREGERS: I expected that.

HJALMAR (*Walks over to* GINA, *who is standing beside the stove,
and speaks in a low voice*): And now, no more lies. If you
two were through with each other when you first became
fond of me—as you said—tell me, why did he want us to
marry?

GINA: Maybe he liked being welcome in your house.

HJALMAR: Just that? Wasn't he afraid of a certain eventuality?

GINA: I don't know what you mean!

HJALMAR: I want to know if . . . if your child has the right to live under my roof.

GINA (*Drawing herself up, eyes flashing*): You ask me that?

HJALMAR: You shall answer me this one thing. Does Hedvig belong to me or not?

GINA (*Looking at him, coldly defiant*): I don't know.

HJALMAR (*Trembling slightly*): You don't know?

GINA: How could I know that? A creature like me—

HJALMAR (*Turning quietly away from her*): Then I don't have anything more to do in this house.

GREGERS: Think this over, Hjalmar!

HJALMAR (*Putting on his overcoat*): There's nothing a man like me has to think over.

GREGERS: Yes, there is. There are hundreds of things to consider. The three of you must stay together, in order to reach the true frame of mind for forgiveness and sacrifice.

HJALMAR: I don't want that. Never—never. My hat— (*Finds his hat*) My home is falling in ruins around me. (*Bursting into tears*) Gregers, I have no child!

HEDVIG (*Who has opened the kitchen door*): What are you saying? Father, Father! (*She goes toward him.*)

GINA: There, now.

HJALMAR: Don't come near me, Hedvig. Go far away! I can't stand to look at you. Oh, those eyes—! Good-by. (*He goes toward the door.*)

HEDVIG (*Clings to him, crying and screaming*): No! No, no, don't! Don't go away from me! Don't leave me!

GINA (*Crying out*): Look at the child, Ekdal! Look at the child!

HJALMAR: I don't want to. I can't. I have to get out—away from this!

(*He tears himself loose from* HEDVIG *and rushes out through the hall door.*)

HEDVIG (*In despair*): He's gone away from us, Mother. He's gone away from us. He'll never come back!

GINA: Don't cry, Hedvig. Father will be back again!

HEDVIG (*Throwing herself on the sofa, sobs*): No, no, he'll never come home to us again!

GREGERS: Mrs. Ekdal, can you believe me when I say I only wanted the best for you?

GINA: Yes, I almost believe that. But all the same, God forgive you!

HEDVIG: Oh—I think I want to die! What have I done to him? Mother, you must get him home again!

GINA (*Putting on her cloak*): Yes, yes. But be quiet, quiet. Don't cry. I'll go out and look for him. Maybe he's gone to Relling's. But you mustn't lie there and cry. Come now—promise me that!

HEDVIG (*Crying convulsively*): I'll stop! I'll stop—if only you'll bring father home.

GREGERS (*To* GINA, *who is trying to leave*): Why don't you let him fight this one out by himself?

GINA: He'll have to do that later. Right now we've got to get the child quieted down. (*She goes out through the hall door.*)

HEDVIG (*Sits and dries her face*): Now tell me—you've got to tell me what all this means. Why doesn't father want me?

GREGERS: You mustn't ask that again. Not until you're grown up!

HEDVIG (*Sobbing pitifully*): I can't go on being this unhappy till I grow up! I think I know what it is—I guess maybe I'm not father's real child.

GREGERS (*Uneasily*): How could that be?

HEDVIG: Well, mother could have found me! And maybe father found out just now. I've read about things like that.

GREGERS: But if that's how it was, well then—

HEDVIG: Well, it seems to me that he could love me just the same—or even more. The wild duck was given to us, and we love her—oh, so very much.

GREGERS (*Changing the conversation*): That's true about the wild duck. Let's talk about her, Hedvig.

HEDVIG: My poor wild duck. Father can't stand to look at her, either. Just imagine, he wants to wring her neck!

GREGERS: Oh no, he won't do that!

HEDVIG: No, he won't. But he said that he'd like to, and I thought it was so nasty of father to say that—because I pray for the wild duck every night. I pray that she may be spared from death and everything evil.

GREGERS: Do you say your prayers often?

HEDVIG: Yes.

GREGERS: Who taught them to you?

HEDVIG: I did. Once when father was so sick and he had to have leeches on his neck, he said that Death was holding his hand.

GREGERS: Yes?

HEDVIG: Well, I prayed for him as I lay in my bed, and since then I do it all the time.

GREGERS: And now you pray for the wild duck?

HEDVIG: Yes. I thought it was best to include her, too, because she was so sickly at the beginning.

GREGERS: Do you say prayers in the morning?

HEDVIG: No.

GREGERS: Why not?

HEDVIG: Because it's light in the morning, and there's nothing to be afraid of.

GREGERS: Oh. And the wild duck that you love so much—your father wants to wring her neck?

HEDVIG: No, he only said it would be best for her if he did. But he spared her life for my sake. And that was nice of father.

GREGERS (A little closer): What if you were to sacrifice the wild duck for his sake?

HEDVIG (Standing up): The wild duck?

GREGERS: Supposing you were to sacrifice your most valuable possession in the whole world for *his* sake?

HEDVIG: Do you think that would help?

GREGERS: Try it, Hedvig.

HEDVIG (Slowly, with eyes shining): Yes, I'll try.

GREGERS: Do you think you have the courage?

HEDVIG: I'll ask grandfather to shoot the wild duck for me.

GREGERS: Yes, do that. But don't tell your mother a word about this, now.

HEDVIG: Why not?

GREGERS: She doesn't understand us.

HEDVIG: My wild duck? Tomorrow morning I'll try.

(GINA *enters through the hall door.*)

HEDVIG (*Going over to her*): Did you find him, Mother?

GINA: He stopped by Relling's.

GREGERS: Are you sure?

GINA: The porter's wife saw them all leave. Molvik's with them.

GREGERS: He needs solitude more than anything else right now —to struggle with himself.

GINA (*Taking off her overcoat*): Well, men are a complicated lot, they are! God knows where Relling has dragged him off to. I checked at Madame Eriksen's, but they weren't there.

GREGERS: He'll come home. I'll get a message to him tomorrow morning and you'll see how fast he'll come home. You can be sure of that, Hedvig. Now sleep well. Good night! (*He leaves by the hall door.*)

HEDVIG (*Throwing herself on the sofa*): Mother! Mother!

GINA (*Patting her on the back consolingly, sighs*): There, there now, there, that's how it goes. Relling was right—yes . . . yes, that's what can happen—crazy men going around with their claims to the, to the . . . well, whatever they call it. There, there. . . .

**CURTAIN**

# ACT V

HJALMAR EKDAL's *studio. A cold, gray morning light streams in. A rim of wet snow lies on the skylight.* GINA *enters wearing an apron, carrying a broom and a dusting pan. She goes toward the parlor. At the same time* HEDVIG *enters hurriedly through the hall door.*

GINA (*Stopping*): Well?

HEDVIG: Yes, Mother. I'm almost sure he's down at Relling's.

GINA: Well, there, you see!

HEDVIG: The porter's wife said she heard him come in with two people last night.

GINA: Well, that's just what I thought.

HEDVIG: But that doesn't help much if he doesn't want to come up here to us.

GINA: Well, at least I can go down there and talk to him.
(OLD EKDAL *appears at the door of his room. He is in his bath-robe and slippers, and he is smoking his pipe.*)

EKDAL: Hjalmar? Isn't Hjalmar at home?

GINA: No. He—he went out.

EKDAL: So early? In such a damnable snowstorm? Well, he's welcome to it! I'll do the morning tour alone. (*He slides open the attic doors.* HEDVIG *helps, then closes the doors behind him.*)

HEDVIG (*In a low voice*): Just imagine when he finds out father wants to leave us!

GINA: Oh nonsense—such talk! He mustn't hear about it. It was such a Godsend yesterday that he wasn't here for all that fuss and furation.*

HEDVIG: Yes, but—

GREGERS (*Enters through the hall door. Interrupting* HEDVIG): Well, have you heard from him?

GINA: He's downstairs at Relling's.

GREGERS: He's been out with those two?

GINA: More than likely.

GREGERS: But he needed to be alone, to seriously collect himself, alone.

GINA: You may be right.

(RELLING *enters by the hall door.*)

HEDVIG (*Goes toward him*): Is father with you?

GINA (*Simultaneously*): Is he there?

RELLING: Yes, he certainly is.

GINA: And you didn't let us know?

RELLING: No. I'm such an ass! But then, I had a classic ass to watch over! Yes, yes, I mean the daemonic one, of course. And in the midst of all that, didn't I fall so sound asleep that—?

GINA: What did Ekdal say?

RELLING: Not a blessed thing!

HEDVIG: He isn't talking at all?

RELLING: Not a blasted word.

GREGERS: Well, I can understand that.

GINA: But what's he doing down there?

RELLING: He's lying on the sofa—snoring!

GINA: Yes—Ekdal's a heavy snorer.

HEDVIG: You mean he's sleeping? How can he sleep?

RELLING: God knows how, but he can!

GREGERS: No wonder! He's been torn apart in this spiritual battle!

GINA: And of course he's not used to being out all night, either.

HEDVIG: Maybe it's good for him to get some sleep, Mother.

GINA: I think so. Now, we'll take care not to wake him up too early. Thank you, Relling. I've got to get on with the housework now and make it nice in here, and then— Come, Hedvig, give me a hand. (GINA *and* HEDVIG *go into the parlor.*)

GREGERS (*To* RELLING): Can you explain this spiritual turmoil in Hjalmar?

RELLING: I'll be damned if I've seen any spiritual turmoil going on in him!

GREGERS: But this is a turning point in his life! Why, his whole life has a new foundation—and to an individual like Hjalmar—

RELLING: Individual? Him? Well, if he ever did lean toward being such a unique thing as an individual, let me assure you that it was thoroughly rooted out of him before he reached puberty. That I can guarantee!

GREGERS: How can you talk like that? You know he was brought up in a home full of love.

RELLING: Ha! You mean by those two unbalanced, hysterical old maiden aunts of his?

GREGERS: Let me tell you—they were women who never forgot their claim to the ideal! I suppose you're going to laugh at me again.

RELLING: I'm in no mood to laugh, but I'm very well informed about those two ladies. I've had to endure plenty of rhetorical vomit from him about his two "spiritual mothers"! And I don't think he has much to be grateful for from them. Ekdal's great misfortune was that in his own circle he was always considered the shining light.

GREGERS: That's exactly what he is, deep inside!

RELLING: I've never seen a flicker of it! His father believed it, but we won't even discuss that. The old Lieutenant always was a blockhead!

GREGERS: Lieutenant Ekdal always had the pure mind of a child —but then, you wouldn't understand that.

RELLING: Quite right! So, back to Hjalmar! When the dear, sweet boy, by some means or other, passed his exams and got into the university, he was immediately acclaimed by his fellow students to be the "great white hope" of a glorious future. He was handsome, and that helped—pink and white —oh, indeed, the answer to any maiden's prayer! And don't you forget his delicate emotional temperament, so easily disturbed, and his enchanting, heart-throbbing voice, and his talent for declaiming other people's poetry and thoughts.

GREGERS (Furious): Are you describing Hjalmar Ekdal?

RELLING: Yes, with your permission. I'm simply giving you an inside view of the idol at whose feet you grovel in the dust.

GREGERS: I hardly think I'm that blind!

RELLING: Not far from it! Remember, you're a sick man, too.

GREGERS: You're right about that.

RELLING: Yes, sir! And you suffer from a complicated case. First, there's the fever of self-righteousness which is burning you up. And then, what's worse, you're in a perpetual delirium of hero worship. You must always have something outside yourself to idolize!

GREGERS: Yes—I'm constantly searching outside myself.

RELLING: With your flights of fancy, you always did make disgraceful mistakes in judgment about everything you saw or heard. And this time you've simply walked into another worker's cottage, again hawking your wares, and as usual you find them all unable to pay their debt.

GREGERS: If this is your opinion of Hjalmar, why are you constantly with him?

RELLING: Good Lord, man, I'm supposed to be some kind of doctor! I administer to the poor sick ones in this house.

GREGERS: So! You think Hjalmar Ekdal is sick, too?

RELLING: Roughly speaking, just about everyone is, poor things!

GREGERS: And what's your remedy for Hjalmar?

RELLING: My customary one. I cultivate his "life lie."

GREGER: "Life lie"? Did I hear you right?

RELLING: Yes. I said "life lie." You see, it's the stimulating principle.

GREGERS: And what is Hjalmar's?

RELLING: No, thank you! I don't give away my professional secrets to quacks! With that information you'd be capable of confusing this case even more. But my method is infallible! I've used it on Molvik—I've made him daemonic. That's the bee I've put in his bonnet!

GREGERS: He's not daemonic?

RELLING: Well, now, what the hell is daemonic? It's only some mumbo jumbo I invented to save his life. If I hadn't prescribed that, the poor, honest swine would have perished years ago in self-contempt and despair. And so we return to the old Lieutenant. Well, he's managed to find the cure for himself.

GREGERS: Has he?

RELLING: Well, you tell me! What's your opinion of a great bear hunter who goes in there—into that dark attic—and shoots rabbits? There isn't a happier sportsman in the world than that old man when he's allowed to putter around in there with all that rubbish! Those four or five Christmas trees he's dried up and saved are just as important to him as the entire great, green forests of Hoydal. Those roosters and chickens are big game in the pine trees, and the rabbits that stumble and hop around on that floor are the mighty bears that he must tackle! Lieutenant Ekdal! The ancient forester!

GREGERS: Oh, the unhappy old man! He's had to narrow down the ideals of his youth, all right.

RELLING: While I think of it, young Mr. Werle, I must ask you not to use that foreign word—ideals—when we have an excellent native word—lies.

GREGERS: You think they're the same?

RELLING: About as closely related as typhus and typhoid!

GREGERS: Dr. Relling, I won't give up until I have wrenched Hjalmar out of your claws!

RELLING: That would be tragic for him. Rob the average man of his life lie and you take away his happiness in one clean stroke! (*To* HEDVIG, *who enters from the parlor*) Well, little mother of the wild duck, I shall go downstairs and see if the lord and master is still lying on my sofa meditating on his remarkable invention! (*He leaves by the hall door.*)

GREGERS (*Moving toward her*): I can see you haven't done it.

HEDVIG: What? Oh, the wild duck— No.

GREGERS: Didn't you have the courage when the time came?

HEDVIG: It wasn't that. When I woke up this morning and thought about it, it all seemed so strange.

GREGERS: Strange?

HEDVIG: Yes. I don't know why, but last night—at that very moment—it seemed so wonderful. But after I slept and thought about it again, it didn't seem any good at all.

GREGERS: Oh, of course—you couldn't have grown up in this house without something being ruined in you.

HEDVIG: Oh, I don't care about all that! If only father would come up here again!

GREGERS: Ah! If only your eyes were open to the things that give life its importance! If you only possessed that joyful, fearless, true spirit of sacrifice, then you'd see how fast he'd come home to you. I still believe in you, Hedvig!

(GREGERS *leaves by the hall door.* HEDVIG *walks up and down for a while, then begins to go toward the kitchen. A knock is heard on the attic door. She goes over and opens it.* OLD EKDAL *enters, grumbling.* HEDVIG *closes the door.*)

EKDAL: It's not very much fun going the morning rounds alone, Hedvig.

HEDVIG: Wouldn't you like to go hunting, Grandfather?

EKDAL: No. It's not hunting weather. Such a dark day, you can hardly see an inch in front of your nose.

HEDVIG: Don't you ever feel like shooting something other than rabbits?

EKDAL: Hmm! Aren't rabbits good enough?

HEDVIG: Yes, but what about the wild duck?

EKDAL: Aha—she's afraid I'll shoot her wild duck! Never in this world, Hedvig! Never, never.

HEDVIG: No, I suppose you couldn't. It must be very difficult to shoot a wild duck.

EKDAL: I couldn't? Oh, is that what you think? Well, I should say I could!

HEDVIG: How would you do it, Grandfather? I don't mean *my* wild duck—but another one, maybe?

EKDAL: Well, first be sure to get the shot in the chest. That's the surest way. And then be careful to shoot *against* the grain of the feathers, you see, not *with* the feathers.

HEDVIG: Do they die then, Grandfather?

EKDAL: God knows they do when you aim right! Well, now, I suppose I'd better get in there and clean up a bit. You know what I mean, eh?

(*He goes into his room.*)

(HEDVIG *waits a moment. She goes to the parlor door, then*

*over to the bookcase. Reaching on her tiptoes, she takes down the double-barreled pistol and looks at it.* GINA *enters from the parlor. She has a dusting cap on.* HEDVIG, *unnoticed, quickly puts the pistol back in its place.*)

GINA: Don't upset your father's things.

HEDVIG (*Walking away from the bookcase*): I just wanted to straighten it up.

GINA: Go out to the kitchen and see if the coffee's hot. I want to take a tray down to him.

(HEDVIG *exits.* GINA *cleans up the studio. After a while the hall door is thrown slowly open.* HJALMAR *looks in. He wears his overcoat but no hat. He is unwashed and his hair is not combed. His eyes are dull and heavy.*)

GINA (*Standing with the broom in her hand*): Oh Ekdal, you've come back after all!

HJALMAR (*Stepping inside, answers in a dull voice*): I've come back only to leave again.

GINA: Yes, yes, I believe that. But my heavens, how you look!

HJALMAR: Look?

GINA: And your nice winter coat. Ah! Well, it's done for.

HEDVIG (*At the kitchen door*): Mother, shall I—(*Seeing* HJAL- MAR, *she screams for joy and runs toward him.*) Oh Father! Father!

HJALMAR (*Turns away, throwing his arm out against her*): Go away! Go away! (*To* GINA) Keep her away from me, I tell you.

GINA (*Softly*): Go into the parlor, Hedvig.

(HEDVIG *goes quietly into the parlor.*)

HJALMAR (*Carelessly pulling on the drawer of the table*): I must have my books with me. Where are my books?

GINA: What books?

HJALMAR: My scientific books, naturally—the technical maga- zines I need for the invention.

GINA (*Searching in the bookcase*): Are these the ones here— with paper covers?

HJALMAR: Yes, of course.

GINA (*Putting a bundle of magazines on the table*): Should I have Hedvig cut the pages open for you?

HJALMAR: No cutting is necessary for me.

GINA (*After a short silence*): So it's going to happen, is it? You're going away from us?

HJALMAR (*Rummaging through the books*): That goes without saying, I think.

GINA: Yes, yes.

HJALMAR: After all, I can't stay here and have my heart stabbed every hour of the day.

GINA: God forgive you that you think so wickedly of me.

HJALMAR: Well, show me otherwise!

GINA: I think you should show me!

HJALMAR: After what you've done? Ha! There are certain rights . . . oh—I'm tempted to call them rightful claims.

GINA (*Interrupting*): What about grandfather? What's to become of him, the poor thing?

HJALMAR: I've always recognized my duty. That helpless old man will come with me. I'll go to town and make arrangements and— Hmm—did anyone find my hat on the stairs?

GINA: No. Have you lost your hat?

HJALMAR: Well, of course I had it on when I came home last night—no question about that—but today I can't find it.

GINA: Lord help us! Where have you been with those rabble-rousers?

HJALMAR: Don't question me about trifles! I'm in no mood to remember details!

GINA (*Going into the kitchen*): Well, so long as you haven't caught a cold, Ekdal.

HJALMAR (*Half-aloud to himself, bitterly, while he empties the table drawer*): You're a scoundrel, Relling! A drunkard and a shameless tempter. Oh! If I could only get someone to do away with you! (*He puts some letters aside. Finding the torn pieces of* HEDVIG's *letter, he studies them and puts them quickly back.*)

GINA (*Enters quickly and sets a tray with coffee and food on the table*): Here's a drop of hot coffee, if you feel like it, and then there's some bread and butter and a nice bit of salt meat.

HJALMAR (*Pushing the tray away*): Salt meat? Never under this roof! It's true I haven't had a mouthful of solid food for almost twenty-four hours, but that doesn't matter. My notes! The autobiography I've started! Where's my diary and all my important papers? (*He opens the parlor door, then draws back.*) She's in there!

GINA: Well, good God, the child has to be someplace!

HJALMAR: Come out of there!( *He makes room for* HEDVIG *to pass. She walks by, frightened. With his hand on the knob, he stands by the door and says to* GINA) In the last moments I spend . . . in what I once called my home, I wish to be spared the sight of intruders. (*He goes into the parlor.*)

HEDVIG (*Rushing toward* GINA, *asks softly*): Does he mean me?

GINA: Stay out in the kitchen, Hedvig. No—you'd better go to your own little room. (*Going into the parlor, speaks to* HJALMAR) Now wait a minute, Ekdal, don't upset all the drawers—I know where everything is!

(HEDVIG *stands motionless for a moment. She is in a state of terror and rejection, biting her lips to stifle her cries. She clenches her hands convulsively.*)

HEDVIG (*Softly*): The wild duck. (*She moves quietly over to the bookcase and takes the pistol from the shelf. She opens one of the sliding doors and slips in.* HJALMAR *and* GINA *are heard arguing in the parlor.*)

HJALMAR (*Enters with some notebooks and loose papers. Puts them on the table*): My suitcase won't be big enough. There are a thousand things I must drag with me.

GINA (*Following after him with the suitcase*): Well, don't take them, then! Just take a shirt and some underthings with you. You can come back for the rest later.

HJALMAR: Oh, these exhausting preparations! (*He takes off his overcoat and throws it on the sofa.*)

GINA: The coffee's getting cold.

HJALMAR: Hmm! (*He drinks a mouthful as if not thinking about it, and then drinks another.*)

GINA (*Dusting the backs of the chairs*): Now Ekdal, the most difficult thing for you will be to find another attic like this —one big enough for all the rabbits.

HJALMAR: What? Am I to drag all the rabbits with me?

GINA: You know grandfather can't be without them.

HJALMAR: Well, he'll certainly have to. I'm having to sacrifice higher things in life than rabbits.

GINA (*Dusting the bookcase*): Shall I put the flute in the bag for you?

HJALMAR: No, no flute for me—but give me the pistol.

GINA: You want to take the pifstle?*

HJALMAR: Yes, my loaded pistol.

GINA (*Looking for it*): It's gone. He must have taken it in with him.

HJALMAR: Is he in the attic?

GINA: Yes.

HJALMAR (*Takes some bread and butter and finishes the cup of coffee*): The lonely old man.

GINA: If we hadn't rented the room, you could move in there.

HJALMAR: And live under the same roof as—? Never!

GINA: Couldn't you stay in the parlor for a day or two? You have everything to yourself in there.

HJALMAR: Never within these walls!

GINA: Well, then, downstairs with Relling and Molvik?

HJALMAR: Don't mention their names! I could lose my appetite just thinking about them. Oh—now I have to walk out in this storm—through the wind and the snow—and go from house to house seeking shelter for my father and me!

GINA: But you have no hat, Ekdal. You've lost your hat.

HJALMAR: Oh, those two debauchers—how rich they are in vices! Well, a hat has to be found! (*Taking another piece of bread and butter*) Some arrangements must be made, because I certainly don't intend to endanger my life in this weather. (*He searches for something on the tray.*)

GINA: What are you looking for?

HJALMAR: The butter.

GINA (*Going to the kitchen*): I'll get more right away.

HJALMAR (*Calling after her*): Don't bother. I can very well eat dry bread.

GINA (*Bringing a plate of butter*): Look—this is freshly churned! (*She pours another cup of coffee for him. He sits on the sofa, spreads more butter on the bread, and eats and drinks for a while in silence.)*

HJALMAR: Could I—without being disturbed by anyone, by anyone whatsoever—could I live in the parlor for a day or two?

GINA: Yes, I'm sure you could.

HJALMAR: I just can't see how I can get all my father's things out of here in such a hurry.

GINA: And you'll have to tell him you don't want to live with us any more—

HJALMAR *(Pushing the coffee cup away)*: Yes, there's that, too. I'll have to lay it wide open to him—the whole sordid story. I must have time to catch my breath and be by myself. I simply can't carry all these burdens in a single day all by myself!

GINA: And in such nasty weather.

HJALMAR *(Moving HEDVIG's torn letter)*: I see that piece of paper is still cluttering up the house.

GINA: Yes. I won't touch it.

HJALMAR: Well, it doesn't concern me, either.

GINA: I'm not going to make use of it.

HJALMAR: But there's no reason for it to get lost, either. In all this moving and confusion it could easily—

GINA: I'll take care of it, Ekdal.

HJALMAR: The deed of gift, first of all, belongs to father. It's his decision whether or not to use it.

GINA: Yes—poor old father.

HJALMAR: For safety's sake—where the glue?

GINA *(Going over to the bookcase)*: Here.

HJALMAR: And the brush?

GINA *(Bringing them to him)*: Here.

HJALMAR *(Picks up the scissors, cuts, and glues)*: Just a strip of paper on the back. It was far from my intention to violate someone else's property, least of all that of a penniless old man—or the other one's, either. There now. Let it lie for a while and when it dries, take it away. I don't ever again want to lay my eyes on that document!

GREGERS (*Entering through the hall door*): What? Are you sitting here, Hjalmar?

HJALMAR (*Standing up quickly*): Oh, I sank down from exhaustion.

GREGERS: By the looks of it, you've eaten breakfast.

HJALMAR: The body also makes claims.

GREGERS: What have you decided to do?

HJALMAR: There's only one road to take, for a man like me. I'm in the process of collecting my most important belongings. And that takes time, as you can well understand.

GINA (*A bit impatiently*): Do I fix the parlor for you, or do I pack your suitcase?

HJALMAR (*After a glance at* GREGERS): Pack—and get it ready!

GINA (*Taking the bag, goes into the parlor*): Yes, yes—then I'll pack the shirt and—the other things. (*She closes the door after her.*)

GREGERS (*After a short pause*): I never dreamed you'd be doing this! Is it necessary for you to leave your house and family?

HJALMAR (*Pacing nervously*): What would you want me to do? I'm not made to be miserable, Gregers. I have to live in surroundings that are cozy and secure.

GREGERS: But that's what this place will be to you, now that you have solid ground to build on. You can begin all over again from the beginning. And remember, you have your invention to live for.

HJALMAR: Oh, don't talk to me about that invention. It seems so far away from me now.

GREGERS: Really?

HJALMAR: Well, good Lord! What is there left to invent? Other people have invented almost everything already. It gets more difficult day by day.

GREGERS: But you've put so much work into it!

HJALMAR: Oh, that debauched Relling got me started—

GREGERS: Relling?

HJALMAR: First, he made me aware of my abilities to invent something remarkable in the science of photography.

GREGERS: Ah, so it was Relling?

HJALMAR: And I've been so truly happy with it. Not so much in the invention itself, but because Hedvig believed in it. Believed in it with a child's complete power and strength. Well, at least I was idiotic enough to think she believed in it.

GREGERS: You can't possibly think Hedvig was deceiving you—Can you?

HJALMAR: It's possible to believe anything now. Hedvig is standing in my way, and now she'll blot out the sun for me the rest of my life.

GRECERS: Little Hedvig! How could she do that?

HJALMAR (*Not answering*): I've loved that child so devotedly. I was totally happy each time I came back to this simple house and she would run to greet me with her sweet, squinting eyes. Oh, trusting fool that I was—I loved her beyond words! I deluded myself that she loved me in return.

GREGERS: You think that was delusion?

HJALMAR: Oh, how will I ever know? I can't force Gina to tell me. Besides, she's totally insensitive to the idealistic side of this problem. I must confess to you, Gregers, my dreadful doubt that perhaps Hedvig never honestly loved me.

GREGERS: If she could prove it to you beyond any doubt, what would you— (*Listening*) What was that? I thought I heard the wild duck cry out.

HJALMAR: It does that when father's in the attic.

GREGERS (*His face full of joy*): Oh! Is he in there? I was saying . . . the proof—you may soon have the proof that your pathetic, misjudged Hedvig loves you.

HJALMAR: What proof could she give? I don't dare believe anything she says or does.

GREGERS: Hedvig doesn't even know the meaning of the word deceit.

HJALMAR: But Gregers, that's just what I fear! Who knows what Gina and Mrs. Sorby are always whispering about, right here where Hedvig could listen? Perhaps that deed of gift didn't come as such a surprise to her. I noticed how she took it at the time.

GREGERS: What's possessed you Hjalmar?

HJALMAR: My eyes have been opened! You'll see! This deed of gift is just the beginning. Mrs. Sorby has always been very generous to the child, and now she's in a position to give her anything. They'll come any time they like and take her away from me.

GREGERS: Hedvig will never leave you!

HJALMAR: Don't be too sure of that! They will only have to show her their full hands. And I've loved her so immeasurably! I wanted to make it my greatest happiness to take her by the hand and lead her through life—as one would lead a child who is afraid of the dark through a large, empty room. Now I'm tortured with the knowledge that the poor photographer in the attic has never honestly meant anything true to her. With cunning, she's managed to be on good footing with him—until the time comes to leave for a better life.

GREGERS: You don't believe that yourself!

HJALMAR: The dreadful thing is, I just don't know what to believe—and I never will find out! But tell me, don't you think what I'm saying is true? (*Laughing shortly*) You rely too much on your claim to the ideal, my good Gregers. The others will come here with full hands and call for the child. "Go away from him—you'll have everything you want in life with us—"

GREGERS (*Quickly*): Do you think that will happen?

HJALMAR: If I asked her, "Hedvig, are you willing to give up your life for me?"— (*Smiling scornfully*) No, thank you! You'd soon hear her answer!

(*A pistol shot is heard from the attic.*)

GREGERS (*Crying out joyfully*): Hjalmar!

HJALMAR: He's hunting again!

GINA (*Entering the room*): Ekdal! Grandfather's in there all by himself, blasting away with that gun!

HJALMAR: I'll look in on him—

GREGERS (*Highly excited*): Wait! Do you know what that was?

HJALMAR: Of course I know what it was.

GREGERS: No you don't—but I do! It was your proof!

HJALMAR: What proof?

GREGERS: The child's sacrifice. She made your father kill her wild duck!

HJALMAR: Kill the wild duck?

GINA: Well, of all things!

HJALMAR: What good will that do?

GREGERS: She wanted to sacrifice her dearest possession for you so that you'd love her again.

HJALMAR (*Tenderly, with emotion*): Oh that child!

GINA: The things she thinks of!

GREGERS: She wants to win back your love. She doesn't want to live without it.

GINA (*Fighting back her tears*): There! You can see for yourself, Ekdal!

HJALMAR: Where is she?

GINA (*Sniffing*): Poor thing—she's out in the kitchen, I think.

HJALMAR (*Opening the kitchen door*): Hedvig! Come here. Come in to me. (*Looking around*) No, she's not there.

GINA: Then she's in her own little room.

HJALMAR (*From offstage*): Not in there either. (*Returning*) She must have gone out.

GINA: Well, you couldn't stand her anywhere in the house!

HJALMAR: Oh, God! If she'd only come home soon, I could tell her! Everything is going to be fine, Gregers. I feel now we can begin our lives all over—from the beginning.

GREGERS (*Quietly*): I knew it. The resurrection would come through the child.

(OLD EKDAL *appears at the doorway of his room, in full uniform, buckling on his sword.*)

HJALMAR (*In amazement*): Father? You—there?

GINA: Were you shooting in your room?

EKDAL (*Indignant, going toward* HJALMAR): So you go hunting alone now, eh, Hjalmar?

HJALMAR: Didn't you shoot—?

EKDAL: What?

GREGERS (*Surprised, calls to* HJALMAR): She's shot the wild duck herself!

HJALMAR: What? (*He rushes over to the attic door, opens it, and calls loudly.*) Hedvig!

GINA: Oh, God, what is it?

HJALMAR (*Going into the attic*): She's—she's—lying on the floor!

GREGERS: Hedvig—on the—! (*He goes into the attic with* HJALMAR.)

GINA (*Speaking at the same time as* GREGERS): Hedvig! (*Inside the attic*) No, no, no, no!

EKDAL: Ho! Ho! So now she's shooting, too!

(HJALMAR, GINA *and* GREGERS *all carry* HEDVIG *into the studio. The pistol is in her hand. Her arm hangs limp.*)

HJALMAR (*Dazedly*): The pistol went off! She's hurt herself! Call for help! Help!

GINA (*Runs out the hall door and calls down*): Relling! Doctor Relling! Get Relling! Come up—quick!

(HJALMAR *and* GREGERS *put* HEDVIG *on the sofa.*)

EKDAL (*Softly*): The forest will get back its own.

HJALMAR (*On his knees beside* HEDVIG): She'll come to now. Yes, yes, she's coming around. Yes—yes.

GINA (*Re-entering*): Where did she hit herself? I can't see anything—

RELLING (*Enters quickly, followed by* MOLVIK, *who is wearing an open shirt without a waistcoat or cravat*): What's going on?

GINA: They say Hedvig shot herself!

HJALMAR: Come here—help!

RELLING (*Pushing the table aside, examines her*): Shot herself?

HJALMAR (*Kneeling, anxiously looks at* RELLING): It isn't serious, is it, Relling? She's hardly bleeding at all. It can't be serious.

RELLING: How did it happen?

HJALMAR: Oh, I don't know.

GINA: She wanted to kill the wild duck.

RELLING: The wild duck?

HJALMAR: The pistol must have gone off.

RELLING: Hmm, I see.

EKDAL: The forest will get back its own. But I'm not afraid. (*He goes into the attic and locks the door.*)

HJALMAR: Relling, why don't you say something?

RELLING: The bullet went into her chest.

HJALMAR: Yes, but she's coming around, isn't she?

RELLING: Can't you see that Hedvig is not alive?

GINA (*Bursting into tears*): Oh, my child! My child!

GREGERS (*Huskily*): In the depths of the sea.

HJALMAR (*Jumping up*): Yes, yes, she must live! Oh for God's sake, Relling, just for a moment—until I can tell her how I always loved her—beyond words.

RELLING: The bullet went through the heart. Internal hemorrhage. She died instantly.

HJALMAR: And I? I pushed her away from me like an animal! And so she crawled into the attic and died out of her love for me. (*Sobbing*) I will never, never atone to her. I can never tell her! (*Clenching his hands and shouting upward*) Oh Thou up there, if Thou art there, why hast Thou done this unto me?

GINA: Hush—hush! Don't talk like that. Maybe we didn't have the right to keep her.

MOLVIK: The child is not dead, she sleepeth.

RELLING: Rot!

HJALMAR (*Becomes silent. He walks to the sofa, with his arms folded, and looks down at* HEDVIG.) There she lies—so still and silent.

RELLING (*Trying to remove the pistol from her hand*): It's so tight. It's so—

GINA: No—don't break her fingers.

HJALMAR: She shall take it with her.

GINA: Yes, yes—let her. But the child mustn't be laid out here. She'll go to her own little room, she will. Here—help me, Ekdal. She will be in her own little room tonight, that she will. Help me, Ekdal.

(HJALMAR *and* GINA *carry her between them.*)

HJALMAR (*While carrying* HEDVIG): Oh Gina, Gina, can you endure this?

GINA: We must help each other now. At least we can share her now, the two of us.

MOLVIK: (*Stretching out his arms, mumbles*): Praised be the Lord! To dust thou shalt return! To dust thou shalt return!

RELLING (*Whispering*): Shut up, you ass! You're drunk!

(HJALMAR *and* GINA *carry the body out through the kitchen door.* RELLING *shuts it after them.* MOLVIK *sneaks out through the hall door.*)

RELLING (*Going over to* GREGERS): No one can ever lie to me about this! This was no accident.

GREGERS (*Who has been in a state of shock, shakes convulsively*): No one can say how this dreadful thing happened.

RELLING: The powder burned her dress. She pressed the pistol very tight against her own breast . . . and fired.

GREGERS: Hedvig didn't die in vain. Did you notice how this sorrow and grief released all that is noble in him?

RELLING: Most people look ennobled when they stand in mourning beside a corpse. How long do you think that grandeur will last?

GREGERS: Why won't it last all his life and grow with the years?

RELLING: Ah! Before a year is over, little Hedvig will be nothing to him but a beautiful new theme for declamation!

GREGERS: How dare you say that about Hjalmar Ekdal?

RELLING: We will talk together before the first grass has withered on her grave. You'll hear your share of his rhetorical vomit about "the child too early torn from the father's breast"! You'll see him wallow in the emotions of self-admiration and self-pity! Just you wait!

GREGERS: If you're right and I'm wrong, then life is not worth living.

RELLING: Oh, life could be almost tolerable, really, if we didn't have these damn debt collectors pushing us ordinary people right out of doors—with their claims to the ideal!

GREGERS (*Staring straight ahead*): If that's true, I'm glad my destiny is what it is.

RELLING: And what, if I may presume to ask, is your destiny?

GREGERS (*As he goes toward the hall door*): To be the thirteenth at table. (*Exits*)

RELLING: Damn it—that's how it is!


CURTAIN

# R. V. FORSLUND

Mr. Forslund is a graduate of Stockholm University and the Swedish Royal Academy. Both in Sweden and the United States, where he now lives, Mr. Forslund has been involved in all phases of theater: writing, directing, acting, and producing. His translations of Ibsen, Strindberg, and Holberg have been performed at the Royal Academy of Dramatic Arts, London; at the reading series of the Donnell Branch of the New York Public Library; at the Actor's Playhouse in New York's Greenwich Village; and at the Vanguard Theater in Detroit.